Viella History, Art and Humanities Collection
4

Giovanni Ricci

Appeal to the Turk

The broken boundaries of the Renaissance

Translated by Richard Chapman

viella

First edition: may 2018
ISBN 978-88-6728-991-2

This book is the revised and enhanced edition of *Appello al Turco. I confini infranti del Rinascimento* (Viella 2011).

viella
libreria editrice
via delle Alpi, 32
I-00198 ROMA
tel. +39 06 84 17 758
fax +39 06 85 35 39 60
www.viella.it

To Nikolas

Contents

1. Introduction: unmentionable acts?

1. There was an era when all, or at least many, committed in secret the unmentionable acts that this book will attempt to bring to light. It was something very serious, at times even tragic, but on occasion involuntarily comical: but as is well known, the tragic and the comic are often intermingled in history.

2. At times exalted, at times condemned, the theory of the 'Clash of Civilisations' stimulated great debate in the passage between the 20th and the 21st centuries. Then, like all things excessively favoured by fashion, the theory rapidly went out of fashion. As historians we do not wish to open up this political case again, infected as it has been by the dregs of ideologies linked to the present. We are only concerned with identifying a pair of reactions coming from countries with Muslim roots but partially secularised and desirous (up to now at least) of good contacts with the West; Turkey and Tunisia.[1] From these two singular observation points the historical simplifications at the basis of the theory of the clash of civilisations have been much criticised; all the more so because analyses that are apparently innocuous, because they deal with epochs long past, have generated predictions for the future, and recommendations for preventive military reactions.

The truth is that the past, if observed in detail and without preconceptions, presents us with a distinct permeability in the dividing line between Christians and Muslims, even if it was undeniably tense. This permeability revealed itself in numerous ways and at the most diverse levels: undeclared alliances between Venice (a bastion of Christianity in the East, according to the propaganda) and the Ottoman Sultan; formal agreements between the (officially most Christian) French monarchy and the Sultan; threats of agreements with the Turk by German Lutheran princes in conflict with the Pope and with the Catholic Holy Roman Emperor; conversions in both directions, even if more often from Christianity to Islam; mediation carried out by the Jews in a more or less equidistant manner; trade, contacts, friendships, love and sexual relationships of every kind, in the shadow of banners that were, in principle, opposed. Crusade rhetoric, knightly desire, the yearning for martyrdom,

1. See Hadhri, *La Méditerranée*; Tschirgi, "The Middle East". For origins, Huntington, *The Clash of Civilizations*.

the dream of converting the infidel: all operated as showy languages of appearance. On occasion they were sincere languages, sometimes not. In any case they were often unrealistic, pronounced by those who were unable to comprehend the complexity of reality. The theologians who, since the Middle Ages, had theorised the illegality of alliances with the Infidel could say what they liked,[2] and it counted for little that in the political-religious struggle a rhetorical *topos* that has been defined as the Turkification of the enemy was all the rage.[3]

3. It is against this background that the appeal to the Turks that we are looking at stands out. With this expression we mean, quite literally, the ease with which Christians turned to the Turks to solve their most hopeless problems, both political and personal. What had been the rule in the internal struggles of the late Byzantine Empire, strangled by the Turks and their tribute well before its fall; what had been the rule among the despots and *voivodes* of the Danube and the Balkans, exposed on the front line as they were, vulnerable and vassals of the Turks;[4] well, all of this was not absent from the Italian Renaissance *signorie* that were much further away and better protected. What is more, the Turks called upon by the Italians were not only the Ottomans with their iron military discipline, but there were even those who called on the corsairs of the Maghreb, the Barbary pirates, by definition irregular forces and devoted only to sacking the coasts. The Barbary populations were also Turks, judged on the basis of the terminology of the time that defined not only the subjects of the Sultan of Istanbul as such, but all the followers of the "Mohamad Sect".[5]This equivalence between Turks and Muslims among Christians conditioned the whole perception of Mediterranean life.

Absorption of the very powerful Turks, enemies by definition, into the mental panorama of Christian Europe was more profound than people liked to admit. Europe as a Christian republic (*Res publica*) was a heartfelt mediaeval relic and not much more, which did not impede agreements of every kind with the Infidel. In this discrepancy between image and reality, we can glimpse an anticipation of the system of secular international alliances that the Peace of Westphalia was to establish in 1648, since the Turks were already significant players at the table of European diplomacy before this date.[6] The accusation typically made against the Jews, that they cultivated unmentionable contacts with the Turks,[7] could easily rebound on many Christians who gave themselves over to the same practice. "And where this did not actually occur, at the very least they always suspected each other of it": as Jacob Burckhardt wrote, showing the universal employment of the accusation among the Italian States.[8] Thus the scandal that the appeal to the

2. See Vismara, *Impium foedus*.
3. See Housley, *Religious warfare in Europe*, pp. 137-152.
4. See Ostrogorsky, *History of the Byzantine State*; Maxim, "I Principati Romeni".
5. *Vocabolario degli Accademici della Crusca*, p. 1736.
6. See Telò, *Relations internationales*, pp. 22-25.
7. See Tollet, "Les Juifs".
8. Burckhardt, *La civiltà del Rinascimento*, p. 91.

Turks represented, operated both as an instrument of deterrence and as a tool of blackmail. But, staying with the Jews, the difference was that Christians inhabited a Christian world, Christian lands, under Christian sovereigns. In contrast, Jews did not live in a Jewish world. There was no reason why they should oppose the Turks who were willing to allow legal status to the 'People of the Book' – the adherents of Abrahamic religions – in return for higher taxes.[9]

4. Presenting a rich series of episodes, our intention is to affirm how wide of the mark every reading of the past is when it merely pays tribute to the official line of the period, itself already based on a number of misunderstandings.[10] Instead there were viewpoints, there were other, undeclared, practices, and there were exchanges and interbreeding of every kind that enveloped the Mediterranean and Balkan areas. Whatever the thing that we might call historical truth really is, it is to be sought more in the lower levels of society than in staterooms, and even if this principle is taken as read, historiographical practice has not always shown itself to be up to the task.

The frame of reference is given by the chronology of political and military history. For practical purposes, two global points of crisis circumscribe our observations: the Fall of Constantinople, the great trauma experienced by Europe in 1453; and the victory at Lepanto, the first (apparent) setback suffered by the Turks in 1571. Perhaps we could even have begun earlier. In 1402, Giangaleazzo Visconti, the first Duke of Milan, earned the epithet of *Italicus Baisettus* due to his friendly relations with the Sultan Bayezid I.[11] But after the Turkish triumph on the Bosphorus, everything intensified. And we certainly could have continued our analysis beyond Lepanto, at least until a further moment of crisis, the Siege of Vienna in 1683,[12] when both Turkish expansion and appeals to the Turks launched by the West reached their conclusion. In so doing, the dossier would have been enriched, but also diluted. Instead, the more limited timeframe that we have chosen[13] reveals greater compactness for two reasons.

In the first place, this period corresponds to the peak of the myth of Ottoman invincibility that everyone considered inevitable for geographical and historical reasons. It was then that the shadow of the Turks hung over Italy to its greatest extent. And not only their shadow. In the first fifty years after the fall of Constantinople, the Turks, whether invited or not, physically set foot in Italy many times, in the south as in the north. Appeals to the Turks then intensified in the first years of the Italian Wars which, from 1494, saw the national monarchies compete on Italian soil for European hegemony. The second reason for this compactness is that the period chosen, 1453-1571, coincides with the rise and fall of the Renaissance. Afterwards, with the arrival of the social control produced

9. Publication forthcoming in the proceedings of the conference, *El estatuto legal de los 'dhimmíes' en el Occidente islámico*, Madrid, March 2011.

10. See Norman, *Islam and the West*.

11. See Garin, *Interpretazioni del Rinascimento*, vol. II, p. 95.

12. See Wheatcroft, *The Enemy at the Gate*.

13. A similar chronological subdivision is in Viallon, *Venise et la Porte ottomane*.

by Tridentine Catholicism[14] it became difficult to make appeals to the Turks as people had done before. Mythologised and contested as it may be, the concept of the Renaissance[15] is enriched by obligatory undertones: the intense relationship with the Turks, with the Muslim world. Since the end of the 20th century, scholars have enhanced the value of an integrated history of the Mediterranean, forming a pattern of knowledge which we can refer to with confidence.[16] It is hardly necessary to add that these new perspectives have been stimulated, on a practical level, by the explosion of the conflicts of the present; and on an academic level, by the success of global history.

Asymmetry in power relations is rarely a good counsellor, for the strong as much as for the weak. In the fifteenth and sixteenth centuries the Christians were the weaker party, aware as they were that none of their sovereigns taken singly was able to compete with the Ottoman Sultan. What historians now refer to as the "Turkish Century" was at its height.[17] This climate generated understandably exasperated reactions in the Christian camp, among which we can identify an upsurge in crusader rhetoric that had weakened during the late Middle Ages. We may well permit ourselves to say that the late or modern crusades can be seen as a phenomenon parallel to the appeal to the Turks or one opposed to it.[18]

5. The period from 1453 al 1571 thus has produced plentiful material from which we can remove ideological ingenuities – or ideological malice, the closest ally of ingenuity. But we need to compile a case file. Almost each of the episodes that we place in the collection is well-known and researched to varying degrees, though often interpreted in an inadequate way. The main significance does not, however, belong to the individual episodes, whatever importance they may have. The main significance can only be grasped when these episodes are put together in sequence, letting them interact in a kind of system. Because contemporaries knew this fact, that the Turkish option was always available; they knew that many had tried it in practice, and many more had weighed up the option in secret. Sooner or later, faced with extreme difficulties, it was an option that could be useful: perhaps only to accuse somebody else of the self-same misdeed. Conflict with the Turk remained predominant in strategic planning, the kind that emerges over the long term. But tactics often pushed for a short-term agreement: a timescale that coincided with the historical lifetime allotted to men.

Precedents even existed in the opposite direction. The Turks also made appeals to the Christians. Perhaps they did so less frequently, but they did so, nonetheless. The frontier between Christians and Muslims was not permeable only

14. See Reinhard, "Disciplinamento sociale".

15. See Ricci, *I giovani, i morti*, pp. 9-11.

16. See Abulafia, "Mediterraneans"; Morin, "Penser la Méditerranée"; Trivellato, "Renaissance Italy"; Pedani, "Note di storiografia".

17. See Loiseau, "De l'Asie centrale à l'Égypte".

18. See the collection "Croisades tardives" published by Presses de l'Université de Toulouse-Le Mirail since 2009.

in one direction. The immensity of the distances to be covered, the slowness of communications and the unpredictable nature of weather conditions did not prevent anyone from making appeals to the hereditary enemy. Yet geography and logistics conditioned every action, notwithstanding continuous attempts to overcome them. No one at the time forgot this; and we shall not forget it either. Ever since Fernand Braudel supplied us with a model that is difficult to improve, interactions between space and time force themselves into the attention of historians.[19] But this attention has not yet returned politics to the technical spaces and times that were its own. The waters of the Mediterranean Basin, often agitated by the will of Nature or Man;[20] the mountains of the Balkans, rendered treacherous by the same forces; these very different and yet complementary environments did not merely constitute passive interstices between Italy, the Maghreb and Istanbul. On the contrary, by their very existence they imposed themselves as theatres capable of modifying the texts of the actors involved.

6. This is the object of study of this work. This object will receive observations that are inevitably partial, coming from a subject that has its own points of view: it is as well to declare this at the outset.

By insisting, as we do, on the semi-clandestine contacts continually established between Christian Europe and the Turks, we do not intend to engender a misapprehension. So let it be clear that we are not neglecting the fear that gripped the majority of Christians at the mere mention of the name of the Turks – and vice-versa. Let it also be clear that we are not forgetting the sense of civilized superiority cultivated by European humanists and communicated to their rulers in the guise of warlike impulses; just as we do not forget the verbal arrogance that accompanied Ottoman militarism, with its bloody outbursts of rage. Lastly, let it be clear that we are not underestimating the acts of violence inflicted and suffered by one and by the other. And if we are not attempting to account for them in a kind of double-entry ledger, it is because the result would be different depending on times and places, and would leave everyone dissatisfied. In short, we are not using an unrealistic pacifism as a substitute for an image of perennial warfare that is just as unreal. There is nothing simple and linear in this story; often diametrically opposed truths are both true and we would be mistaken if we committed ourselves to a single, unequivocal argument.

For these many reasons we are persuaded to pursue a model of relations that takes into account human impulses in their complexity, without debasing their variations with the banal category of 'betrayal'. Here we have it: the word betrayal will not be positioned at the centre of interpretation. And besides, what kind of betrayal are we talking about, when we find the religious and political leaders of Christendom as the prime movers in the appeal to the Turks? And here it should be understood that we are referring to Latin Christianity, because the Orthodox

19. Braudel, *The Mediterranean and the Mediterranean World.*
20. See Slot, *Archipelagus turbatus.*

tradition had already been forced to find pragmatic forms of understanding with the Muslim powers centuries earlier.[21] But how could France "betray" by means of its most continuous line of international policy, which had for three or four centuries built bridges towards the Orient? How could Venice "betray", in always being faithful to its anti-Roman autonomy and always being able to find support in the Turks? And especially, how could the Papacy ever "betray" as the source of all legitimacy in the Catholic system?

7. Actually, the Renaissance Popes did collaborate with the Turks, and they allied themselves with them, to the detriment of other Christian rulers. They did it when political expediency demanded it, or when their theocratic pretensions were under threat. Thus argued Hans Pfeffermann in a book published in Switzerland in 1946, reviewing all the pro-Turkish acts of the Renaissance popes.[22]Original in its inception, even if imperfect in its argumentation, the book seems to have suffered a form of boycott in Catholic lands. Indeed the Vatican Library claims it does not possess the book: we may doubt that the restrictions of the post-war period provide sufficient justification for the absence of this volume. To make up for this, a scandalised review appears in the most authoritative Italian historical journal of the time ("insolent", "offensive", "tendentiousness", "uncharitable derision").[23] With this a trial for *lèse-majesté* rooted in Italian Catholic anthropology is brought to a conclusion.[24]

Returning to betrayal: unless it is only what less important actors than the king of France, the Pope or the Venetian Senate perform. Desperate people, who saw no way of achieving justice for a wrong suffered; exasperated people, who had no other way of giving vent to their anticlericalism, the popular sentiment that permeated throughout Renaissance Italy before Tridentine discipline snuffed it out. A curious fact to point out in passing: both the most curial popes and the rulers most inclined to secular government, and the most rebellious and anticlerical subjects turned to the Turks for help. It is difficult to find an international appeal made by such a heterogeneous mix of subjects. But it is clear that blame for treachery could only be attached to some, to the weak. Then, as always, the definition of treachery was a product of hegemonic discourse; it was spiced up with doses of paranoia, references to conspiracy theories and searches for a scapegoat.[25]

Instead, we are interested in shedding light on the contrast between the hypocritical abhorrence of a certain kind of behaviour and its universal practice. Beyond this, we would aim to dismantle the intellectual ploys that transfer thoughtless impulses towards fanaticism over into social life. Beyond political-military explanations, the tensions stirred by difference tend to release regression

21. See Ducellier, *Chrétiens d'Orient*.

22. See Pfeffermann, *Die Zusammenarbeit*.

23. Picotti, "Review". Less emotional is the criticism by Babinger, "Maometto II", in part. p. 486.

24. See Levi, "Storia d'Italia e antropologia cattolica".

25. See Smith, *Treason in Tudor England*; Flores, *Traditori*.

impregnated with violence in the human psyche.[26] In the subject under analysis here, such uncontrolled mechanisms often show themselves: in the past no less than in the present.

The present is certainly a child of the past, but it remains separate from it. Today deep difficulties of understanding distance a part of the Muslim from the non-Muslim world (the West, most of all, but not exclusively). It is as if agreement were even lacking on the most basic principles of coexistence in the global village. It is as if no one were aware that the word tolerance, before becoming a philosophical ambition of the Enlightenment, was born during the wars of religion of the sixteenth century as a simple synonym for forbearance of the other; and, in its functional dimension, this was already a significant achievement.[27] Present-day misunderstandings between the Muslim and non-Muslim worlds are the fruit of every phase in the past, but only belong fully to the present. In an analogous way, the permeability between the political-religious blocks studied in these pages may have left some legacy, but really only fully belongs to the centuries under examination.

The best mode of acknowledgement to friends and colleagues who have supplied me with materials, ideas, and advice is to be found in the citation of their academic works throughout the book. For the English edition, I am particularly grateful to the translator, Richard Chapman; to Francesca Ortalli and Noemi Rubello, who took on the task of editing the work; and to Cecilia Palombelli of Viella Editrice.

26. See Fornari, *Psicoanalisi della guerra*, pp. 75-80; Sabatini Scalmati, "Riflessioni psicoanalitiche"; Raniolo, "L'eutopia e il fanatismo religioso".

27. See Prosperi, "Il grano e la zizzania".

2. Mehmed II, Christian emperor

1. The example came from high up, from the Pope in person, when in Rome he planned a spectacular violation of borders that were declared inviolable. Geopolitical and religious borders; rhetorical borders; borders that shaped minds. To reach this point required a new age of iron and fire, and this came along with the Turkish advance. The Ottoman State had become the principal Muslim power, substituting the Arab Emirates which had been weakened by the medieval crusades. The title of Sultan obtained by the Ottoman sovereign in 1383 (up to then he had been an emir) confirmed this rise in status.

The Fall of Constantinople in 1453 produced a wave of panic in Europe that we can fully appreciate if we compare it with the enthusiasm of the winners.[1] But the Turk was also interpreted as the executor of divine punishment against Christians: the Byzantine schismatics, antipathy for whom was not spared;[2] and the sinful, quarrelsome Roman Catholics. With this, people imitated the judgement expressed by some of the Fathers of the Church who had seen in the barbarians the vengeful hand of God against the sins of Rome. Attempts of varying degrees of imaginativeness to guarantee a formal kind of survival for the Byzantine world had failed; there had even been a longing to create a territory for the last exponents of the Palaiologoi, the lords of the Despotate of the Morea.[3] Many foresaw that Italy itself would soon be conquered. Christianity would be burned in a new Apocalypse, after which a universal sovereign would arrive, destined to rule until the Day of Judgement. The Sultan Mehmed, the Conqueror, was, in the meantime, the historical precursor, being the heir to all empires and the lord of subjects belonging to all peoples and all religions. The End of Days, the Reign of the Beast, The Seventh Plague, the Coming of the Antichrist: these were the expressions that resounded in the churches and palaces of government.[4]

As soon as he knew of the catastrophe that had befallen the Second Rome, the humanist, Enea Silvio Piccolomini commented: "No power persists in eternity. The Romans were once the lords of the universe; now the empire of the Turks is

1. See Heers, *Chute et mort de Constantinople*, pp. 233-260; Tursun Bey, *La conquista di Costantinopoli*, pp. 61-83; L'Europa dopo la caduta di Costantinopoli.

2. See Agapiou, "Enea Silvio Piccolomini et les Grecs".

3. See Ronchey, *L'enigma di Piero*.

4. See Schnapp, *Prophéties de fin du monde*, pp. 165-224.

beginning".[5] Besides military defence, problems of an intellectual nature asserted themselves. What providential significance was to be attributed to such a shocking chain of events? Had the medieval prophetic tradition found a historical foothold in this new apocalypse?[6]

2. In 1458, only a few years after the Fall of Constantinople, Piccolomini became Pope with the name of Pius II. Stricken by pessimism, he conceived of one of those astonishing manoeuvres for which the Roman Church had become famous when it found itself forced to face a deadly challenge. It was at the end of 1460 or the beginning of 1461 and Mehmed II had just crushed the last flickers of Byzantine resistance: precisely the Despotate of the Morea, and the so-called Empire of Tresibond on the Black Sea. In this climate, the Pope composed an epistle to the Sultan in which he exhorted him to convert, offering him in return the title of Emperor of the Christians and the beginning of an era of peace:

> A tiny matter can transform you into the greatest, the most powerful, the most celebrated of all men that are presently living. You ask me what? It is not difficult to find and you do not need to search for it far and wide, it is to be found everywhere: a drop of water to baptize you, and you to adopt the Christian rites and believe in the Gospel.[7]

For the occasion, the Pope had to take inspiration from some of Mehmed II's peculiarities that had been recounted in stories. Some were certain, some were the fruit of invention. Son of a Christian slave, the Sultan had participated in the Christian liturgy several times; with the fury of conquest spent, he loved to converse with the Patriarch Gennadius Scholarios and with other Orthodox dignitaries; in his library he kept numerous Greek and Latin manuscripts; he indulged in the cult of relics, in devotion to Mary and in love for Western figurative art.[8] And perhaps, in the presence of the powerful sovereign, the myth of the Christian caliph that was deeply rooted in the medieval vision of Islam re-emerged. A few years before Pius II, some learned prelates (Juan de Segovia, Nicholas of Cusa) had supported a peaceful conversion of the Muslims.[9]

With hindsight, all this seems a simple exercise of the intellect, but it should be borne in mind that in the event of a Turkish conquest of Italy, the alternatives for the Pope would have been worse: escape to his possessions in Avignon and then to find himself reduced to being chaplain to the King of France, like in the times of the Avignon captivity? Remain heroically in Rome and find himself reduced to an Ottoman high functionary, like the Patriarch of Constantinople? Better to

5. *La caduta di Costantinopoli*, vol. II, p. 65.

6. See Flori, *L'Islam et la Fin des Temps*, pp. 387-404.

7. In D'Ascia, *Il Corano e la tiara*, pp. 157, 236-237. Viallon-Schoneveld, "L'epistola latina a Maometto II", pp. 165-177 adds little more.

8. See Rogers, "Mehmed the Conqueror", pp. 80-97; Akasoy, "Mehmed II as a Patron of Greek Philosophy".

9. See Schwoebel, *The Shadow of the Crescent*, pp. 223-225.

take remedial action in advance. This also because every incidence of unruliness among the Italian princes brought with it the risk of Turkish involvement. And the Italian princes were very unruly.

3. Even if only to deny it, fear of the arrival of the Turks in Italy runs through an entire epistle addressed to the Great Conqueror. Witness how the Pope rubs salt into the wounds:

> Do not entertain the hope that the internal struggles of Christianity can favour the realisation of your desires: all Christians will unite if ever word should come that you are reaching the heart of Christendom [...] It will be said: "the internal struggles that tear our people apart could give you the chance to land in Italy: one prince will keep you out of his territories, but another will let you in and permit you passage". Certainly. There are numerous, serious and dangerous divisions, enmities and rivalries: if only there were not! But there is none who wants to submit himself to a non-Christian master: all want to die in the right faith [...] And should one then turn to you, he would attract the hatred of the whole of Italy.

And further:

> The Venetian Republic, rich in gold and in political intelligence, devoted to Christ, would let itself be destroyed from top to bottom (at least that is what we think) rather than allow an enemy of the faith to enter Italy.[10]

And here, in mentioning the steadfastness of Venice, the essential meaning is to be found in the rather dubious remark in parentheses: "at least that is what we think". One may ask whether considerations of this nature would dissuade Mehmed from the enterprise; or if they wouldn't attract him to Italy instead. However, an enduring pattern in communications between the Pope and the Ottomans was established: mixing flattery and advances with threats and blackmail. Even when they were dealing with common interests – and this happened often – the lack of a shared religious link lowered the level of mutual trust.

Nourished by the then flourishing wave of prophetism that in its turn identified in the Sultan the universal sovereign, the epistle circulated in various languages. It had been printed eight times by 1482, and was still translated and annotated a century later.[11] The epistle, however, was never sent to Istanbul, while Pope Pius II took up the more ordinary register again: opposition. The Pope did not renounce doctrinal rejection of Islam: "rituals of a vain superstition", he proclaimed in the face of the Sultan. And, in fact, in 1459, he summoned a diet at Mantua of princes from Italy and from beyond the Alps to announce a crusade against the Turks.[12] Preparations were arduous, given the lack of conviction of the Emperor Frederick III of Habsburg and other rulers,

10. See D'Ascia, *Il Corano e la tiara*, pp. 154-156, 235-236.

11. See Helmrath, "Pius II und die Türken", in part. p. 126; Piccolomini, *Epistola al Gran Turco*, pp. 15-22; Margolin, "Réflexion sur le commentaire".

12. See Setton, *The Papacy and the Levant*, vol. II, pp. 231-270; *Il sogno di Pio II*; Baldi, *Pio II e le trasformazioni*.

and given the reluctance of Venice, from whom the main part of the naval fleet was supposed to come. Eventually the machinery of war was set in motion and the old Pope announced, amid general consternation, that he would personally participate in the enterprise, with the Doge of Venice and the Duke of Burgundy. Then the death of Pius II at the port of Ancona in 1464 extricated everyone from the awkward situation: the undertaking was wrecked before it had begun, while princes and generals returned, relieved, to their homes. The epistle to Mehmed II was left in the records. Whether the real addressees were the sovereigns of Europe, reluctant to commit themselves to holy militia, the fact remains that the subject of the imperial offer to the Turk was plausible if its use had been under consideration; it was a theme that could be played politically.

4. The failure of 1464 signalled the end of the medieval model of crusade. This model was characterised by its universalism, its offensive impetus, its millenarianism, its juridical qualification (a Papal bull of announcement, the penitential doctrine of the vow, the promise of indulgences, propagandistic sermons). From then on, instead, it was a case of organising single defensive undertakings on European soil to block the Turkish push towards the west.[13] The geography of the crusades no longer resounded with names such as Jerusalem, Saint John of Acre, Nicopolis, Varna, Constantinople; instead they were to speak of Otranto, Mohács, Vienna, Lepanto. The difference compared with the dream of marching to the Holy Places is hardly a small one. So, at the moment when the last medieval-style crusade failed, the very Pope that had resuscitated it, Pius II, ushered in a new means of relating to the Turks: by appealing to them.

How and where would this coronation of the new Christian emperor have taken place? In Rome, in Saint Peter's? In Constantinople, in the Hagia Sophia? A Hagia Sophia that would not be a mosque any more, obviously, but changed back into being a church; not a Greek Orthodox church anymore, but obviously Latin. All things considered, it was easier to find an agreement with infidels willing to convert than with the hated Byzantines who were guilty of schism. The epistle to the Sultan does not go into these details. But those who had produced the basic idea must have imagined some scenario of operations. The seriousness of the historian's profession does not forbid us from giving play to the imagination when an exceptional event occurs. And this is certainly the case here. So let us ask ourselves again: what Christian name would the Sultan have taken, who in Istanbul, until the day before, had called himself Mehmed, Mohammed?

After Pius II's failure, the idea of a universal sovereign was no longer cultivated in the papal court; it continued, however, to live on in its Ottoman counterpart. Granted, Mehmed II did not become the new Constantine. Nevertheless, in 1481 his obsequies abandoned the sobriety laid down by the Law of the Koran. Rather

13. See Matschke, *Das Kreuz und der Halbmond*; Poumarède, *Pour en finir avec la croisade*, pp. 200-245.

they expanded in both time and space, modelling themselves on the obsequies of Constantine, the emperor who had Christianised Rome and founded Constantinople:[14] a surprising convergence, given the cultural and religious differences. From Christian Europe strange appeals arrived in Istanbul: and Istanbul did not avoid these out of principle, rather she equipped herself symbolically for the role of universal capital that the same adversaries seemed to attribute to her.

14. Necipoğlu Kafadar, "Dynastic Imprints on Cityscape".

3. A military tract as a gift to the Sultan

1. Pius II did not only write sensational epistles, he did not only plan crusades that were destined to fail. He was also deeply involved in the political disputes between the Italian States. In particular, a fierce and mutual hatred linked him to Sigismondo Pandolfo Malatesta, Lord of Rimini, who was formally a vassal of the Pontiff. Sigismund was aiming to widen his dominions in the Romagna-Marche area, which the Church claimed and only barely controlled. Conflict with Pius II was thus inevitable, and this was added to an old resentment harboured by the Pope, Sienese by birth, for a supposed betrayal of the Republic of Siena by Sigismund.

The incarnation of the ideal general, and himself expert in physical exercises, Sigismund also promoted an ambitious cultural politics. In 1455 the humanist most closely linked to his court, Roberto Valturio, completed a manual of military instruction in twelve books, the *De re militari.* The influence of ancient theorists (Frontinus and Vegetius, but also philosophers and every kind of writer) was evident in this compilation. But attempts to adapt the teachings of the classics to changed strategic realties were not lacking; so much so that the text takes its place among the forerunners of so-called military humanism. While on the battlefields the infantryman began to put the knight into the shade, Valturio analysed the effects of firearms on permanent fortifications. This was the first time that a book had done this in such a systematic way, although the author then inclined to the belief that the Ancients knew of explosives, and that the word *tormentum* might even have indicated a bombard in their time.[1]

In addition, the *De re militari* was enriched with visual representations of the secret techniques of military engineers that the more literary tracts had neglected up until then. The author of these diagrams seems to have been the Veronese engraver Matteo de' Pasti, another of the eminent characters of the Malatesta court. Over the years, Sigismund had numerous illuminated copies of the tract made in order to send them the powerful figures of the time: Francesco Sforza, Duke of Milan, Lorenzo de' Medici, ruler of Florence, Federico da Montefeltro, Lord of Urbino, Matthias Corvinus King of Hungary, Louis XI King of Francc. At

1. See Verrier, *Les armes de Minerve*, pp. 107-108, 229, 255; Drévillon, *L'Individu et la Guerre*, pp. 15-46.

least twenty-two handwritten codices remain in European and American libraries. The first printed edition was produced in Verona in 1472; second impressions in Latin and translations into Italian and French followed.[2]

2. In 1461 Matteo de' Pasti prepared a special copy of the tract. It was destined for Mehmed II, the Conqueror, whom Matteo de' Pasti himself was supposed to visit and depict in a portrait in accordance with a request made by the Sultan. Mehmed's love for western figurative art, although in contradiction with the precepts of the Koran, is well known. Later, in 1479, the Conqueror was to ask the Senate of Venice to send him a star painter. The one chosen, to his chagrin, was to be Gentile Bellini, who was to work intensely in Constantinople.[3] In anticipation of that more significant development, it comes as something of a surprise that the Great Lord should remember a local minor potentate like Sigismund. Perhaps a humanist from the Romagna resident in Constantinople, Angelo Vadio, played a role as intermediary in this artistic contact between the Sultan and the captain in rebellion with the Church of Rome.

The fact remains that Matteo de' Pasti set sail for the Orient but was intercepted at Crete by the Venetian governors. In his luggage, besides the military manuscript, there was an accompanying letter in Latin written by Valturio and a map of the Adriatic Sea. The traveller and the documents were sent back to Venice because in Crete it was understood that the story deserved more thorough investigation. It was difficult to have dealings with the orient without the Republic finding out about them, and all the more so as all movements used Venetian galleys and bases. Even the rich Florentine Signoria depended on Venetian organisation when it had to communicate with the Turks. Only in exceptional circumstances did Florence follow the land route via Faenza and Ancona, and then the sea route to Ragusa (now Dubrovnik), the Dalmatian republic from which the inland roads radiated into the Balkans.[4]

When the confiscation in Crete occurred, the international climate was tense. Troops for the crusade called by the Diet of Mantua were being gathered together; Sigismund Malatesta himself had spoken there in favour of the undertaking in fiery tones. Meanwhile, Matteo de' Pasti was investigated in Venice by the Council of the Ten. Acquitted only with reluctance, he was ordered never to go to the Turk again. The confiscated codex was then delivered to Pius II who asked to examine it. The Pope kept it for a long time, so much so as to provoke the protests of Venice, and there is no evidence of any restitution to the Senate.[5] The letter, the map and the gift were thus never delivered from Rimini to Constantinople, as often happened with delicate correspondence that the Christians addressed to the Great Turk.

2. See Settia, *De re militari*, pp. 44-49.
3. See Chong, "Gentile Bellini in Istanbul".
4. See Babinger, "Lorenzo de' Medici e la corte ottomana", p. 316.
5. See Turchini, *Il Tempio malatestiano*, pp. 580-581.

3. Why did Sigismund want to ingratiate himself with the Sultan? Was it purely the vainglory of a soldier before the Conqueror? Certainly, the only early-modern captain named in the *De re militari* next to the ancients was Sigismund: only his figure transgressed Humanistic formalism. Nevertheless, the tract illustrated aspects of European military technology which interested the Turks greatly. No-none had forgotten that the conquest of Constantinople had been assisted by bombards constructed by Christian engineers in the Sultan's pay. And following that epoch-making example, the innovative character of the profession of ballistics had been reinforced. It is true that some of the machines illustrated in the tract were more spectacular than practical; but others were certainly effective and contained the germs of further developments. Then as always, creative imagination and practical design were not too distantly separate.

The two pictures we present here, belonging to the two extremes of the spectacular and the practical, are taken from a Vatican codex deliberately chosen from the range of surviving documents. This codex has some likelihood of being the copy confiscated in Crete and which then reached the hands of Pius II via Venice. In fact, it belonged to a branch of the Piccolomini, the Pope's family, before passing to the Vatican Library. Or, if it is not the very same manuscript that was at the centre of the scandal, it could at least be a direct copy of the original codex examined by Pius II.[6] Whatever the case may be, the figures demand comment. If the dreadful "Arab war-machine for taking cities" challenges all the laws of terrestrial physics, and, with its dragon-like form, seems made only to terrify with its appearance; on the contrary, the designs for bombards capable of flattening walls with stone projectiles leave little room for irony (figs. 1 and 2). The pictures by Matteo de' Pasti could not be considered entirely innocent.

4. So we can also advance other hypotheses. Did Sigismund's gift anticipate an extreme action? For example, an unmentionable alliance with the Sultan, should the Papal vice tighten on the Malatesta dominions? When the arrest of Matteo de' Pasti on Crete became known, the Italian courts spread the news that Sigismund had invited Mehmed II to Italy. From this, a sort of commonplace was started which was either self-perpetuating or was intentionally stirred up. Emanating from the halls of power, the tale of the Malatesta appeal to the Turk reached men of every cultural level. A minor chronicler from Forlì, a certain Giovanni di Pedrino, commented on the confiscation of the map of the Adriatic from the hands of Matteo de' Pasti in this way:

> this man had drawn the whole of Italy with his own hand to take it to the Turk. It is believed that this was on the orders of Lord Sigismund so as to inform the Turk of the geography of Italy, of its mountains and plains, lands and waters [...] for when the Turk wanted to send soldiers to Italy to the detriment of the Pope.[7]

6. R. Valturi, *De re militari*, Vatican Apostolic Library, ms. Reginense lat. 1946, ff. 136*v*, 148*v*. See Frioli, "Per la tradizione manoscritta di Roberto Valturio", pp. 85-87.

7. In Campana, "Una ignota opera di Matteo de' Pasti", p. 107.

The map was supposed to have been accurate and so, as a result, dangerous. "It showed much of the country", the chronicler from Forlì explained further on; a chronicler who was also a painter and so knew what he was talking about. An appeal to the Turk accompanied by cartographical documentation?

To tell the truth, Pius II, in a letter of 1462 to Duke Borso d'Este did name the grave crime ("Sigismund tried to call the impious Turks into Italy"), but the mention is so fleeting as to seem merely the echo of an insulting rhetorical topos.[8] Let us limit ourselves, then, to established facts. The years of the gift to Mehmed are those in which Pius II excommunicated Sigismund as a heretic (1460), later condemning him to three executions in effigy in Rome: in the churchyard of St. Peter's, on the Capitol and in the Campo dei Fiori (1462).[9] Execution in effigy was a punishment inflicted on absent criminals by means of an image resembling them. The text of the sentence against Sigismund (represented by life-size wooden statues which were then burned) is very detailed but does not include the crime which would have been ultimate proof of his indignity, the appeal to the Turks. On the contrary, in the ruling another of Sigismund's crimes is emphasised which is much less serious, even if detrimental to ecclesiastical jurisdiction: that he had despoiled the Basilica of Saint Apollinaire in Classe in Ravenna of marbles to decorate the Malatesta Temple in Rimini.[10] Hence, precisely in light of the overall behaviour of Pius II, Sigismund's intentions when he conceived of the gift to the Sultan still largely remain to be clarified.

5. But the story does not end here. First of all, Sigismund in his turn hanged the Pope in effigy in front of the Cathedral of Rimini, and the gesture says much about the mettle of the Lord of Rimini. Later, however, Sigismund capitulated. Buckling under political-religious pressure and in need of money, he accepted the commission from Venice to fight against the Turks in Morea. The task was to defend the remnants of the Republic's possessions in continental Greece. Federico da Montefeltro, the first candidate contacted by Venice, had refused the commission because it was too difficult and dangerous, but Sigismund was a true professional and a man in straitened circumstances. He stayed in Morea from 1464 to 1466, achieving some success around the Byzantine city of Mistrà, which was by then in the possession of the Turks.[11] But Sigismund's four thousand soldiers were not able to resist for an extended period of time, faced by the preponderant forces of Omar Bey ("Marabeo" in the Italian sources). More significantly than anything else, the crusade promised at Mantua was stranded at Ancona, and no other help could be hoped for from Italy. And, in addition, fevers raged in the

8. See Soranzo, "Una missione di Sigismondo Pandolfo Malatesta"; Soranzo, *Pio II e la politica italiana*, p. 272; Roberts, "The Lost Map of Matteo de' Pasti".

9. See Edgerton, *Pictures and Punishment*, pp. 68-72.

10. See Ricci, "Ravenna spogliata", pp. 544-546.

11. See Falcioni, "Malatesta, Sigismondo Pandolfo", pp. 112-113.

small army and the Morea enterprise was abandoned. Sigismund returned to Italy with a trophy that confirmed his image as a patron of the arts, the remains of Georgius Gemistus Plethon, taken from Mistrà and transferred to the Temple at Rimini.[12] Rather than bringing the Turks to Italy, Sigismund brought the body of the last Byzantine Neo-Platonist to safety from the Turks.

Exactly like the detested Pius II, Malatesta oscillated between the appeal to the Turks and war against the Turks. Ultimately choosing war, he forced the new Pope Paul II to forgive him. On his return from Morea, Sigismund was invested with the Order of the Golden Rose and received the title of apostolic vicar of Rimini. But he continued to remain at the forefront of things, as we shall see a little later, and supported the pro Turkish plot hatched in 1468 by the Roman Platonist intellectuals. The perennial changeability of the Turkish card, in an Italy divided between terror of the Turk, hopes for his arrival and the wait to ally oneself with the winner, whoever that might be. As a record, once more, something remains in an Italian library: the war codex destined for Mehmed II, the enemy of Christianity who had risked becoming its legitimate emperor. And even if the Malatesta codex never arrived in the Sultan's hands, the library in the Topkapı Palace nevertheless possesses an example of the first Veronese printing of the tract, dated 1472.[13] Evidently the subject continued to interest the court in Istanbul, even if it was no longer brought up-to-date or kept in secret.

12. See Ricci, *Il Tempio malatestiano*, pp. 291-295; Runciman, *Mistra*, pp. 116-117; Bertozzi, "George Gemistos Plethon".

13. See Weiss, "The Adventures of a First Edition", pp. 297-304.

4. The Roman Academy plot

1. At Rimini it had become a high-stakes game. Meanwhile, Pius II's eastern policy had left its legacy in Rome itself. However the famous epistle to the Sultan might be interpreted, the Turks had been accredited as potential interlocutors of the highest Christian authority. The first to pay the price for this was Pius II's successor, Paul II, incumbent of a pontificate torn by wars, intrigues and divisions. Tensions reached their peak in 1468 with a curious – and mysterious – plot hatched against the Pope by the intellectuals belonging to the Roman Academy. Discovered before they could act, the members of the Academy were imprisoned in the Castel Sant'Angelo. The most famous of the prisoners were Bartolomeo Platina and Pomponio Leto. However, the academician Callimacus (alias Filippo Buonaccorsi from San Gimignano), who was also the prime suspect, managed to escape.

In the confused scene of the Roman plot something seems clear. And this is that suspicion of agreements with the Sultan was not publicized by those investigating the academicians. While on future occasions we shall see the accusation of intelligence with the Turk brandished vociferously, as a weapon of extreme de-legitimisation, here it was preferred to keep silent on the matter. The subject was judged to be too acute, all the more because the actions of the academicians did not seem to be isolated, but, on the contrary, they seemed to fit neatly with other evidence. Three years earlier, in 1465, the humanist George of Trebizond had been sent to Constantinople at Paul II's expense to "explore and understand the condition of the peoples and the country of the Turk". Thus reported Agostino de Rubeis, Milanese ambassador to the Roman Court, on 3rd November 1466. It seems as if the Pope, in an extreme leap of medieval proselytism, intended to give the conversion-of-the-Sultan card one more try; however, the corollary to Pius II's recognition of the Sultan as emperor of the Christians does not turn out to be the case on this occasion.

2. The harshness of Paul II's reaction to the academicians is surprising if we consider the minor threat the defendants posed as individuals, and the generic nature of the accusations brought against them (although they were for serious crimes: sodomy, offences to the clergy, heresy). It seems, however, that there was something else: an intrigue with Sultan Mehmed II and other schemes to provoke a schism or a council, both of which were very unpopular with Rome. The ambassadors of the Italian States exchanged alarmed dispatches on the subject, without anyone managing to disentangle the affair.[1] This was also because the cultural context as a whole did not aid comprehension. The majority of the Italian humanists had by that time assumed a hostile attitude towards Ottoman power. The desire to understand, when it was not actual benevolence, shown by medieval scholars towards the religion of Islam was now only a memory. By this time, the despotic barbarity of the Turk was always emphasised, while the conflicts of the period were interpreted as the last stage of the collision between Europe and Asia that had its archetype in the Greco-Persian wars. The redefinition of the Turks in terms of ancient history had done nothing for their reputation.[2]

And instead these Roman intellectuals seemed to follow other paths: they felt no repugnance for the Turk. The later behaviour of Callimachus confirmed all suspicions. After various vicissitudes, he found refuge in Constantinople, where he manoeuvred in vain to have the Genoese island of Chios fall into the hands of the Turk. He then passed to the Polish court, where he pursued a policy of harmony with the Turks that was unpalatable to the Papacy. Paul II's attempts to take Callimachus back into his power, even after the release of the other academicians from imprisonment, were fruitless. The motives for Callimachus' tireless conspiracies remain uncertain. A craving for money, and thus susceptibility to corruption seems an inadequate explanation. It was said that his accomplices were the King of France, Louis XI, the King of Naples, Ferdinand of Aragon, and the inevitable Sigismund Malatesta. Meanwhile, Ferdinand of Aragon, who had entered into conflict with Paul II, maintained that he could ally himself with the Turk whenever wished. And this Pope, in contrast to some of his predecessors (and successors), had not developed any strategy at all in the event of the Turk sweeping through Italy. The Neapolitan sovereign waved his threat again during the 1485-1486 war against Pope Innocent VIII, and everybody said that Venice would help him by bringing Turkish troops with her.[3] However, these were nothing but words.

3. George of Trebizond's official mission to Constantinople had been a failure: the Sultan had not even allowed him an audience. Returning to Rome halfway through 1466, after a few months George had been imprisoned in the Castel

1. See Medioli Masotti, "L'Accademia Romana"; also Di Bernardo, *Un vescovo umanista*, pp. 209-215; Gardi, "Congiure contro i papi", pp. 36-38.

2. See Bisaha, *Creating East and West*, pp. 43-87; Meserve, *Empires of Islam*, pp. 65-116.

3. See Meli, "Firenze di fronte al mondo islamico", p. 256; Caselli, "Spie italiane", pp. 787-798.

Sant'Angelo on the orders of the Pope. It seems as if, brazenly, he had started calling the Sultan "emperor of the Romans and of the world," in other words, universal sovereign; something which the ambassador de Rubeis also attests to. And to think that he was a Byzantine, Trapezuntius; his family had its origins in the defunct empire of Trezibond, which had been the last fragment of Byzantine land to fall into Turkish hands in 1461. In principle, then, Trapezuntius should not have been well disposed towards the Turks … Instead things took a different turn, and we will better understand the reasons for this when we speak of the oscillations of Orthodox Christians, trapped as they were between the Pope and the Sultan. Like many other survivors from the Byzantine elite, Trapezuntius ventured into a reflection on history within which the ascent of the Turks took on a providential significance. After an event as striking as the Fall of Constantinople, nothing could be excluded, including world conquest on the part of the Sultan.

Besides paying homage to Mehmed II with this resounding title – as if that wasn't enough – it appears that Trapezuntius sent compromising letters to Istanbul. In these, "he informed the Turk of everything that was happening here, and how discontented the various peoples were, encouraging him to hurry his arrival in Italy." Even from prison, de Rubeis noted, Trapezuntius "continued to praise the Turk immensely and is convinced he should be the Lord of the world". In the absence of the conversion of the Sultan, these things could be said no longer; although many people still thought them, they had become treachery. The case was handled quickly and discreetly. "Having been warned about him, the Pope had him imprisoned in a palace in secret, not wanting the case to be reopened": thus de Rubeis concluded his dispatch.[4] This anticipated the policy of silence that was then to be confirmed with the plot of the academicians three years later.

The exchange of glances between the first Rome, Christian and no longer imperial, and the second Rome, imperial and no longer Christian, continued intensely. We know the way world history developed, but those living at that time were not aware of this. The sensation was widespread that the struggles between the two Romes were still open; in the meanwhile, better the people were kept in the dark. Even so, the hand of power on whoever ventured into those treacherous areas was merciful. In his youth, Paul II (Pietro Barbo, the Venetian) had been a disciple of George of Trezibond. Then, as Pope, he had sent him on a diplomatic mission to the court of the Sultan. And now, in order to release his old teacher, he only required a retraction based on the distinction between external actions and the feeling of the heart. This type of distinction was to be exploited by the Inquisition in the following era to settle thorny cases in which there was a desire to show clemency. Indeed, we can see the declaration signed by Trapezuntius: "I deny that this person is king and emperor of the Romans, although I have written it". But this was not enough, it was necessary to correct the interpretation of the conquest of Constantinople by Mehmed II:

4. De Rubeis' despatch is published by Mercati, "Le due lettere di Giorgio da Trebisonda", pp. 68-69. For the whole event see Monfasani, *George of Trebizond*, pp. 179-194.

> I deny as a sinful thing what I have said, and that is to say that he occupied the see of Constantinople by divine will […] I have not seen other virtues in him besides military virtues and above all a rapidity of action, thanks to which he took the city of Constantinople. I retract all declarations of this type, those that I remember and those I do not remember.[5]

The Great Turk is unnamed: "he" (*ille* in the original Latin); but the guilt is confirmed by the person directly involved. Trapezuntius had indeed gone around saying that the Sultan was "king and emperor of the Romans" and master of Constantinople "by divine will".

5. *Ibid.*, p. 359.

5. Venice the "scoundrel"

1. After so many words and so much waiting, after provocations and deceptions against all sides, Mehmed II threw himself into the conquest of Italy for real. In the August of 1480 a Turkish army coming from Albania landed in Apulia, at Otranto. A great distance from there, the chronicler from the Romagna, Giuliano Fantaguzzi, immediately upon receiving the news of the event, reported a singular interpretation. This interpretation was supposed to have been conceived by a hermit who lived on the hill of Garampo, situated just above the town of Cesena:

> The prophecy of the hermit came true. He had predicted that the Turks would arrive in Italy, when vows made to the Virgin of Loreto were allowed to be changed into money. Indeed, in that year Pope Sixtus had commuted them, going against what is right.[1]

In short, if Pope Sixtus IV released the vows made to the Virgin of Loreto in exchange for money, Providence enrolled the Turks to punish the impious gesture. Here is an expression of popular anticlericalism; and here a new way of calling the Turks to Italy is revealed: to sin so gravely as to force God to react through them.

A hundred years later a local historiographer from Otranto, Michele Laggetto, recalled the drama experienced by his city in more political terms. So he identified the complicity from which the Turks had benefitted: "the Signoria of Venice allowed them to come with freedom and safety". The matter certainly displeased God, Laggetto went on, since "these scoundrels of senators and bad Christians who had encouraged it came to an unhappy end", while the Republic lost "the Aegean, the Greek Archipelago, Negroponte, Morea, and Cyprus, to the advantage of the Turks".[2] In short, the Venetian retreat from the Levant was interpreted as divine punishment for the supposed betrayal. The mythical hagiography that grew up on the memories of Otranto gave confirmation of Venetian guilt after the event. One way or another, God was always involved in the deeds of the Turks.

Michele Laggetto was not the only one to harbour suspicions about Venice. After signing a peace agreement with the Turk in 1479 that cost her the loss of

1. Fantaguzzi, *Caos*, p. 31.

2. In Antonaci, *Otranto*, p. 52. On the dubious authenticity of the source, see Houben, "La conquista turca di Otranto", pp. 8-14.

Negroponte (Euboea), Venice had gone to war with Ferdinand of Aragon, king of Naples. Despatches had circulated among the capitals of Italy like the one that follows, sent from Rome to Ferrara on 19th August 1480, immediately after the Turkish landing at Otranto:

> It is considered a certainty that the arrival of the Turks in the realm was brought about by the Venetians [...]. They never sleep, they are always plotting, we have to be watchful; they want to get revenge in any way on anyone who is not to their liking, it is as sure as the Gospel, the Venetians are capable of anything.[3]

Here there are truly no doubts about Venice's culpability: "It is considered a certainty...". But the issue was so delicate that the author of the despatch, the Duke of Ferrara's ambassador to the Papal court, wrote in code out of caution.

Be that as it may, Venice was at the centre of suspicions before Otranto. In 1476, the noblewoman Bianca d'Este visited the Arsenal in Venice with the Hungarian ambassador, and she took advantage of the occasion to say what she thought. "Excellent equipment", she commented, but it was of no use in helping Hungary "to defend our faith from the Turks". If the Italian powers would like to cooperate, the Venetians replied pointedly, we are always ready to do so. But the lady silenced them with these words: "You did the same with Constantinople, which you chose not to help and which fell into the hands of the Turks".[4] No doubt this opinion expressed by Bianca d'Este was a simplistic judgement: it was unlikely that anyone could have altered the destiny of Constantinople.

2. With the war of Otranto concluded, the Senate of Venice gave orders to its consul in Apulia to congratulate the king of Naples for regaining the city. It pointed out, however, that the congratulations were to be communicated verbally and the letter with the instructions burned, so that the Turks would not find out about it. Another major player in Italian politics, Lorenzo de' Medici, faced with the setback suffered by the king of Naples at the hands of the Turks, assessed the situation in exactly the same way as Venice. Shamelessly, Lorenzo the Magnificent reached the point of commissioning a medal to celebrate Mehmed II's feat at Otranto.[5] Official enemies, the Turks? Perhaps: but enemies of whom, exactly? Enemies of the Kingdom of Naples certainly, at that moment; but enemies of Venice and Florence as well?

As far as the guilt of Venice is concerned, it is difficult to go beyond identification of a motive. Espionage operations, plots, vendettas and the like are carried out without making a paper record, or at least being sure to destroy the proof: the darker side of the political coin does not appreciate the light.[6] And calling the Turks into Italy was officially the highest disgrace, although there were many

3. In Foucard, "Fonti di storia napoletana", p. 142.

4. Caleffini, *Croniche. 1471-1494*, p. 162. See Ricci, "Profezie e forchette per Mattia Corvino", pp. 179-180.

5. See Babinger, *Mehmed the Conqueror*, pp. 386-387; Hankins, "Renaissance Crusaders", pp. 125-126.

6. In general see *L'envers du décor*.

who could imagine doing it. On the other hand, Mehmed did not need invitations to decide to make the step, convinced as he was having a right to Italy for various reasons: he was master of the second Rome; he was the direct heir of the imperial rank that had been extinguished with the last Palaeologus; he was the indirect heir of ancient Troy, from which the Italians themselves, through Aeneas, were mythically descended.[7] It is easier to think that on the occasion of Otranto, Venice had accepted or endured the Turkish card, rather than played it intentionally. Perhaps she confined herself to allowing her spies, hidden everywhere, to turn a blind eye when the Turkish invaders gathered in the Albanian bay of Valona: and Valona is not many miles away from the Venetian stronghold of Corfu.[8]

3. It was easy to criticise Venice, given the unscrupulousness of the policies the Republic pursued. But no-one took into account the fact that Venice was also victim of peculiar operations hatched by other Christian powers. We shall speak of these again later. In these cases, indeed, there was a tendency to strike at Venice at its points of greatest vulnerability, its possessions in the Levant surrounded by the Turks. It was another matter, almost unimaginable in its boldness, to find the Turks in the lands nearest to the capital. Instead, following the Turkish advance in the Balkans, it was exactly this that was to occur.

In the last thirty years of the fifteenth century, incursions of irregular Turkish contingents struck at Friuli and eastern Veneto. The invaders arrived from Ottoman Bosnia, attracted by a desire for booty and without any plan of conquest.[9] However, on the occasion of the raid in 1477, the rumour ran that Emperor Frederick III of Habsburg secretly favoured the aggressors, on an understanding with Leonard, Count of Gorizia. The motive for such plotting, just as dangerous for those that were whipping it up, might have been to strike at the Republic in a sector where Austro-Venetian competition was at its most intense.[10] True or false as it might have been, the rumour shows that the appeal to the Turks belonged to the range of what was possible, even to the extent of involving the Holy Roman Emperor. No-one enjoyed the presumption of innocence in the face of the opportunity to form alliances beyond the limits of Christianity.

The panic left by the Turkish raids did not disappear easily. In 1542 the Bolognese notary Andrea Mamellini recorded what he had learned "by letter written by foreigners worthy of faith". In Lombardy and in Friuli an invasion of locusts had broken out. There were apocalyptic scenes:

> They eat ferociously and wherever they go it looks like a fire that is burning the fields. They go in hordes that seem like clouds, lay eggs and hide them underground [...]. It is said that in Africa they have appeared and driven countless peoples from their cities.

7. See Ricci, *Ossessione turca*, pp. 107-110.

8. See Andenna, "Un tragico punto di svolta", pp. 266-268; Orlando, "Venezia e la conquista turca"; *Lettere degli ambasciatori estensi*, pp. 5-9; in addition, Costantini, "Le isole ionie".

9. See Pedani, "I Turchi e il Friuli".

10. See Cusin, *Il confine orientale d'Italia*, p. 448.

The harm produced by the locusts was shared by many, but the conclusion was completely Friulian: "they screech so much that they are terrifying: in Friuli people armed themselves, convinced the Turks were coming down from the mountains".[11] There were those that invited them, but for others the Turks were as destructive as locusts, and just as free to go wherever they liked. It makes quite an impression, this confusion between Turks and locusts experienced by Venetian Friuli…

11. See Montanari, "Momenti di cronaca", p. 176.

6. Recruiting the Turks is useless

1. The honour of the Christian recovery of Otranto fell to the Duke of Calabria. Son of Ferdinand I of Aragon, the King of Naples, Alfonso was the brother of Eleonora, wife to the Duke of Ferrara, Ercole I d'Este. At that moment all the Aragonese were dedicated to making the most of the victory at Otranto for the creation of their dynastic myth; and it was of little importance that the sudden death of Mehmed II the Conqueror had made their task in Otranto much easier.[1] With the Otranto enterprise completed, the victorious Alfonso was called to the aid of Ferrara, which in the meantime had gone to war with Venice. The equilibrium established in 1454 with the Peace of Lodi held for as long as it held. In the event, the immediate issue was possession of the Polesine di Rovigo. What was at stake strategically, however, was the ability of Venice to impose its dominance over the whole of northern Italy. The fall of Ferrara would certify the new power relationship:[2] for this reason the adversaries resorted to every means, licit or illicit.

The Duke of Calabria brought five hundred Turkish fighters with him to Ferrara. He had captured them at Otranto and had enlisted them in his troops rather than consigning them to the Aragonese galleys. Never before in Italy had so many Turkish soldiers that were not invaders been seen. Venice, in its turn, drawing on the resources of its colonial dominions, lined up the wild Albanian *Stradioti*. Not all of them were Christian, or they were only vaguely so, and for this reason the use of the Turks seemed a suitable way to oppose one evil with another. The very fact that the Albanians of Venice and the Turks of Ferrara were running loose on the banks of the Po confirms the level of Italian exposure to the Orient. But a week after the arrival of Alfonso in Ferrara on 20th January 1483, the irreparable event occurred: "on this night three hundred Turks escaped, of those who had come from Otranto", noted a local chronicler. In two waves the Turks crossed the lines and presented themselves at the Venetian camp. They also took the trouble to try to justify themselves to the people of Ferrara: "this they did, according to the message they sent, to set sail and go home, for the love of their sons, relatives and their homeland". A pity, and to think that "they had good

1. See Barreto, *La majesté en images*, pp. 170-176.

2. See Fuscaldo, *La guerra di Ferrara*, pp. 25-27; Cessi, "Per la storia della guerra di Ferrara".

money from the Duke".[3] After the peace agreed in 1479, Venice searched for the friendship of the Sublime Porte to guarantee itself against its Italian enemies; and furthermore, from Venice one set sail for the East. The desertion of the Turks fitted both political and logistical considerations.

2. We know that the Duke of Calabria was not kind to his Turkish soldiers, at least according to the malevolent Venetians. After the desertion, treatment of those who had remained worsened. Four deserters were retaken and "cut to pieces", writes another chronicler; a fifth fugitive was hanged. Not trusting them anymore, Alfonso had all the Turks disarmed and sent them to Pisa, "in galleys to purge them of their sins". Not even the hero of Otranto was able to tame these infidel warriors; there was nothing else to do but chain them to their natural destiny, the oars. In fact, their behaviour as wretched plunderers had left much to be desired from the first moment. It seems that they demolished empty houses near to their quarters, "to burn the wood and take the ironwork for themselves".[4] This is information that requires interpretation: stealing locks and iron bars from windows is hardly praiseworthy, but if they burned the wooden shutters it means that they did not have wood for fires and they were in the cold of the Po valley in January.

Unfortunately, the hurried escape of some Turks, and the equally quick deportation of the others, supply us with a fragment of an incomplete history. And we add only two small certainties: the appeal to the Turks did not come without risks, even if it was a leader like Alfonso di Calabria who attempted it; and even the Turkish rank and file knew that they could count on Venice, their official adversary in the Levant, in one way or another. As far as the inhabitants of Ferrara were concerned, despite the harsh pressure of the Venetian vice, perhaps they breathed a sigh of relief at the departure of their impromptu Turkish allies.

3. Zambotti, *Diario ferrarese*, pp. 132-133 (the deserters are one hundred and fifty in *Diario ferrarese dall'anno 1409 sino al 1502*, p. 107). See Piva, *La guerra di Ferrara del 1482*, pp. 10-12; Ricci, *Ossessione turca*, pp. 35-37.

4. Caleffini, *Croniche. 1471-1494*, pp. 493-496.

7. Towards the dying Granada as well

1. Seen from the centre of the Mediterranean, from Italy, Islam was not only situated in the Orient, in the Balkans and the Levant; and it was not only present to the south, in North Africa. Until 1492 a political Islam also existed in the West, in the Iberian Peninsula. During the course of the fifteenth century, the Nasrid Emirate of Granada did nothing other than weaken, but it was still in existence. Venice, the most international of the Italian powers, could not leave it out of consideration. Thus the episode we are about to recount came about. An event that was typically Mediterranean, in the sense that in it certain specific and lasting characteristics of the life of the Inner Sea were revealed: the repercussions across the whole of the Mediterranean basin of single, and even remote events; the intermingling of privateer warfare and official wars; discrepancies between formal language and *realpolitik* compromises. The appeal to the Turk presents itself to us here in a new variation: a great Christian power, Venice, offers help to a Muslim power in difficulty, Granada, so that the latter keeps another great Christian power, Spain, occupied for as long as possible. To be precise, Spain was then made up of Castilian and Aragonese forces, that were joined but also distinct. The motive, however, was clear: weaken the Iberians and keep them a long way from Italy.

It all began on the coasts of Andalusia and Valencia. If Spanish sources offer the initial data,[1] the crux of the whole affair is to be found in the geopolitics of Italy. With the Angevins expelled, in 1443 the Kingdom of Naples had passed to Alfonso V of Aragon (Alfonso I, the Magnanimous, in Italy). A deep enmity set the two states endowed with the greatest resources and ambitions against one another: the Kingdom of Naples and the Republic of Venice. These two never failed to strike at one another wherever they could. The successor to Alfonso the Magnanimous in 1458 was his natural, legitimised son, Ferdinand I, who was also a cousin of the sovereign of Aragon (and coregent of Castile), Ferdinand II. The Mediterranean empire of the Aragonese crown reached its greatest extent at this moment. On the death of Alfonso I, the Borgia Pope Callixtus III contested the son Ferdinand's right to the throne, irritated at the insufficient crusading spirit shown by Alfonso during his life. Originally from Valencia like Ferdinand, the Pope objected making use of a report of local provenance: Ferdinando was apparently not Alfonso I's son, but

1. See López de Coca Castañer, "Las galeras venecianas", pp. 135-136.

the son of one of his Moorish slaves. The death of Callixtus III and the arrival of the Piccolomini Pope Pius II brought the dynastic issue to a close in 1459.[2] The fact remains that in Valencia the presence of Muslims left on Christian soil (the *mudéjar*) was so significant[3] as to translate itself into insinuations about the purity of the blood (*limpieza de sangre*) of the King of Naples himself.

2. And so, on the Spanish coast… In the autumn of 1484 a small Venetian fleet, violating the blockade ordered by Isabella of Castile and Ferdinand of Aragon, brought supplies to the Moors at the port of Almería.[4] The Granada War had recommenced two years earlier, Almería was to fall into Christian hands in 1489, and with this the Nasrid Emirate was to lose its last point of access to the sea, given that Málaga had already fallen in 1487.[5] The Almería episode emerges from a letter that Ferdinand II sent from Seville to Ferdinand I at Naples, on 29th December, 1484. After expressing concern that the Turk might prepare a "powerful armada" to attack Italy or Sicily, Ferdinand passed to Spanish affairs. His naval squadron criss-crossed the waters on the Andalusian coast to block any external contact by the Moors. Even so, continued the king, "some days ago five Venetian galleys landed at Almería, a city that belongs to Granada, where they traded and unloaded supplies and other goods, with which the Moors have been helped and strengthened". As soon as it got wind of this, the Castilian-Aragonese fleet attempted to intercept the Venetians. It was night, the sea was stormy, but, "according to letters that reach us from Valencia", the flagship "rammed a galley, while the others escaped".[6] In conclusion, with circumstances on their side, four galleys managed to slip away, while one was left in Valencia, in the hands of the commander-in-chief, Count Álvaro de Mendoza.

Now let us turn our attention to Naples. On 2nd February 1485 Ferdinand I "showed a letter" from Ferdinand II to the curious ambassadors from Milan, Florence[7] and Ferrara. The letter concerned was precisely the one sent from Seville. The contents were immediately reported by the Ferrara ambassador, Battista Bendedei, to his master, Duke Ercole I d'Este. The summary was very detailed, almost a translation of the letter from Ferdinand II,[8] a fact which induces us to honour the memory of the ambassador.

It is astounding that Venice should organise a military action like this in the western Mediterranean, where it did not possess ports or a safe logistical network. Less politically ambitious, Genoa had already given up on trading with the people

2. See Ryder, "Ferdinando I (Ferrante) d'Aragona", p. 177; Álvarez Palenzuela, "Alfonso V, rey de Nápoles"; Galasso, *Storia del regno di Napoli*, vol. I, pp. 626-632.

3. See Hinojosa Montalvo, "Las relaciones entre Valencia y Granada".

4. See Ricci, "'Estaba amancebada con el Turco'"

5. See. Salvador Miguel, "La conquista de Málaga".

6. *Documentos*, vol. II, pp. 171-172. On this topic Ferdinand also wrote to his sister, Joanna, Queen of Naples (*ibid.*, pp. 172-173).

7. See González Arévalo, "La guerra di Granada".

8. See Caselli, "Spie italiane", pp. 810-811.

of Granada. From the thirteenth century, Genoa had been the Emirate's principal economic partner, as the recent commercial treaty of 1479 had confirmed.[9] But at the beginning of 1484, the Genoese Doge, Paolo Campofregoso, personally decided that intervention was necessary. Through the governor (*Baile General*) of the Kingdom of Valencia, the Duke transmitted a formal prohibition to a Genoese captain who intended to take "oil, butter and other things" from Tunisia to Andalusia. Doing so, the Doge said, risked producing "great harm to the goods and persons of all the Genoese who visited places subject to the king of Castile [actually a queen]"; it had to be clear, instead, that Genoa was on the Castilians' side "in the intention to overthrow those infidels". "You will be obliged to obey" intimated the Doge of Genoa to the captain, threatening to fine him, to destroy his house, and even to condemn him to death.[10]

If Genoa reasoned like this, and did so in such a way that everyone knew about it, there must have been some significant reason to induce the prudent Republic of Saint Mark to violate the blockade. The temptation to take Genoa's place in trade with Granada does not seem an adequate explanation in an international climate that was so tense, and with the Granada trade reduced by this time to a minimum, compared to the splendour of the beginning of the century.[11] Rather, the roots of the venture were to be found in Italy; or to be more accurate, they were to be found in relations between the Italian powers and the relations of these powers with the official enemy, the Turk.

3. In Italy the interests of the various states came into conflict with the global interests of Christianity more easily than elsewhere due to the presence of the Papal State, which was both a regional political power and a global spiritual power.[12] In addition, in Italy Islam was applying pressure from all frontiers, both terrestrial and maritime. Transforming the danger into an opportunity, the Italian rulers were accustomed to allying themselves with the Muslims, with varying degrees of secrecy, so as to harm their own Christian adversaries. And in this way the Turk had become the ghost at the table of Italian politics; a guest who on occasion invited himself impetuously to the feast, as he had done at Otranto. Bundling facts and rumours together, everyone pointed the finger at Venice, the queen of multiple games of duplicity, but it certainly cannot be said that the Aragonese were Christians without blemish. Things are more complicated. We have already mentioned that Alfonso I's caution towards the crusade lost him the favour of his fellow countryman, Pope Calixtus III; the king's behaviour was not even altered by a spirited oration that the learned Greek Niccolò Saguntino dedicated to him.[13] During the years that immediately

9. See Heers, *Gênes au XVe siècle*, pp. 321-337; López de Coca Castañer, *El Reino de Granada*, vol. II, pp. 9-11, 131-152; Fábregas, "Redes. El espacio de actuación internacional del comercio nazarí"

10. See Ruzafa García, "Los mudéjares valencianos", pp. 403, 409-410.

11. See González Arévalo, "Italian Renaissance Diplomacy and Commerce".

12. See Prodi, *Il sovrano pontefice*; Schilling, "The two Papal Souls".

13. See Sagundinus, *Ad serenissimum principem*.

followed, we shall see that three Aragonese sovereigns of Naples, Ferdinand II, Alfonso II and Federico I, played the Turkish card on more than one occasion. In short, the Aragonese, transplanted into Italy, acted by this time just like the other Italian princes; they intrigued with the Turk; or they accused others of doing so; or they threatened to do so; or they even pretended to do so.

In the light of these circumstances, the Venetian ships' venture into Andalusian waters becomes clear. The war initiated by Venice against Ferrara had ended in 1484 with the Peace of Bagnolo. Formally the victor, Venice had snatched Polesine from Ferrara. Nevertheless, the Estense Dukdom, although pegged back, had survived with Aragonese help, and Venice's greater ambitions had been denied. Peace having returned, relations between the Italian States started to develop. Milan and Florence, fearing Turkish attacks on Italy, desired to reinstall good relations with Venice. There remained the problem of the interdict pronounced by Sixtus IV against Venice in reply to yet another Venetian threat to appeal to the Turks. Even if he shared their fear of the Turks, King Ferdinand I opposed the idea of Pope Innocent VIII releasing Venice from the interdict for the duration of 1484.

If the King of Naples did not forget past hostilities, the Republic of Saint Mark had a still better memory. Helping the Moors of Granada to resist meant, for Venice, keeping Ferdinand II busy in Spain, preventing him from intervening in Italy at his relative, Ferdinand I's side; and it also meant reminding everyone that no form of Mediterranean politics could leave Venetian involvement out of the equation; or it could perhaps mean gaining the benevolence of the Sultan Bayezid II, in a moment when the peace of 1479 between Venice and the Ottomans was failing.[14] In this game, the fact of those on one side or the other happening to belong to Christianity or Islam was of no influence. At most, it added a touch of faux scandal to the one who allowed himself to get caught in the act.

4. This occurred when the Venetian galley was captured on the coast of Valencia. Beyond the evident rifts, in the integrated and osmotic Mediterranean there was only one political game.[15] At the beginning of 1485, the people of Granada presented a desperate plea for help to Istanbul, and perhaps it was the failure of the Venetian galleys that pushed them into it. They had already made a fruitless attempt in the Orient in 1477, and they were to make another in 1486-7. In 1485, however, they offered Bayezid II sovereignty over Granada. Faced with the hesitation of the Sultan to commit himself in a theatre that was so far away, they suggested he attack the Kingdom of Naples, thus alleviating the situation in Andalusia. "To disturb and distract the King of Castile from the war in Granada, it would be useful if the Great Turk were to attack his Majesty King Ferdinand of Naples, who is brother-in-law to the King of Castile": this is what a Neapolitan spy, sent to Constantinople and Adrianople, reported in the spring of 1485.[16]

14. See Cristea, "La pace tesa".
15. See Valérian, "La Méditerranée".
16. See Caselli, "Spie italiane", pp. 783, 785, 813-815.

But with the army decimated by an attack of plague, the Ottomans could not give succour to their western coreligionists. The idea of an attack on Italy was also shelved, if for no other reason than the fear that someone could use the prince Cem against Bayezid; the half-brother who was a rival of the Sultan and was at once a guest and prisoner in France. The complicated story of Cem will be told later on. Instead of endorsing the idea of the people of Granada, Ottoman resources were channelled into the war of 1485-1491 against the Mamelukes of Egypt.[17] Granada had counted heavily on them as well, but the war between the two eastern empires now crushed the hopes of the Moors of Andalusia.[18] If this was the scenario of intra-Muslim relations, at that moment the city that displayed St. Mark the Evangelist on its vessels intervened in favour of the infidels of Granada. Ferdinand II, in his letter of 29th December 1484 to Ferdinand I, stigmatised the gesture: “the Venetians know nothing about what the service of God consists of, on the contrary they reinforce the enemies of the Catholic faith, and what is more, while we are at war with them”.[19]

The ambassador Battista Bendedei echoed the king in his despatch sent from Naples to Ferrara. Never soft on Venice, the diplomat opined: “the good Venetians will be upset that their ships give help to the infidels and work against his Majesty Ferdinand II”.[20] In this it is not clear whether the disappointment refers to Venetian subjects fearful of God (“good”), or whether we have here an ironic comment against the Venetian governors who were everything but fearful. In connection with these events, there was a process of constructing the ideological apparatus that would make the War of Granada, in itself militarily minor, a founding step towards Spanish, Christian, and European identity.[21] But Venice continued to refuse to take part in this great undertaking.

5. It remains to be understood exactly which galleys they were that took part in the action at Almería. The Venetian chronicler, Marin Sanudo, usually well-informed, maintains that they belonged to state line of navigation, the so-called *muda* of the Barbary: “on 24th December 1484, the Barbary galley was taken by the Spanish armada; it had carried supplies to Granada where the Kings of Spain were at war […] The others managed to escape. This news was known on the day of 14th January”.[22] Flourishing in those years, the Barbary *muda* sailed the western Mediterranean as far as Morocco, then she went up the Iberian coasts to make a long stopover at the trading centre of Valencia. Before the War of Granada broke out in 1482, stops were also made in the ports of Málaga and Almería belonging to

17. See Har-El, *Struggle for Domination*, pp. 133-162.
18. See López de Coca Castañer, “Mamelucos, otomanos”, pp. 229-242.
19. In *Documentos*, p. 172.
20. See Caselli, “Spie italiane”, p. 811.
21. See Prosperi, *Il seme dell'intolleranza*.
22. Sanudo, *Le vite dei dogi*, vol. II, p. 481

Granada.[23] In 1484, the convoy was made up of five galleys, it set sail from Venice in July and reached the Andalusian coast at the end of autumn. The archives of the Senate of Venice indicate to us the names of the owners of the galleys: Francesco Navagero, Francesco Bragadin, Pietro Contarini, Alvise Bondumier, Carlo Valier. It was the galley of the last of these that was captured off Valencia, while the captain of the *muda* was Cristoforo Moro.[24]

Meanwhile a Venetian galley remained blocked at Valencia, but the solution was near at hand. A letter from Ferdinando II to the *Baile General* of Valencia, dated 8th January 1485, ordered the release of the "Venetians from the galley who have stayed in the city". Their departure came about on board the vessel of a Basque captain who was in Valencia, "without any delay or difficulty", including "the goods and things that they had loaded at Cadiz and that would be taken to Genoa".[25] With the rage that had agitated him on 29th December having cooled, Ferdinand II was more than merciful, even having the Venetians' goods transported to Italy (but, out of spite, to the rival port of Genoa). Perhaps Ferdinand judged, (or pretended to judge) that the owners of the galleys had acted off their own bat, out of a thirst for profit. Whoever is under siege, like the Moors were, pays well for "supplies and other provisions", to use the king's words, and the Venetian owners were private contractors. But is also true that the routes and the stopovers of the *mude* were regulated in advance and variations were not permitted to the winners of the annual auction.

6. After unmasking Venice in Andalusia, the Aragonese Crown initiated a cycle of good relations with the Republic. Accommodation was indispensable, seeing as a war between Naples and the Papal States was looming, while King Ferdinand was struggling with the feudal rebellion known as the Plot of the Barons.[26] In the spring of 1485, Ferdinand II made an official gesture towards Venice. Here is the report, again by Marin Sanudo:

> An ambassador of the King of Spain arrived, to induce the Republic to side with King Ferdinand of Naples against the Barons. He also apologised on behalf of his king, who was not to blame for the Barbary galley, belonging to Valier, that had been taken.[27]

The positions seem to be reversed: now it is the King of Aragon, worried about his relative in Naples, who apologises to the Republic for the incident at Valencia. However, he kept the galley, so that people would understand what his real thoughts on the matter were; and Venice did not complain, adhering, on

23. See Guiral–Hadziiossif, *Valence port méditerranéen*, pp. 299-301; Doumerc, "Il dominio del mare", pp. 134-142; Doumerc, *Venise et l'émirat hafside*, pp. 81-101.

24. *Ibid.*, pp. 52, 235.

25. In *Documentos*, pp. 179-180.

26. See Galasso, *Storia del regno di Napoli*, vol. I, pp. 690-714; Visceglia, "Napoli e la politica internazionale del papato"; Igual, "Diplomacia y comercio entre Venecia y los reinos hispánicos".

27. Sanudo, *Le vite dei dogi*, vol. II, p. 518.

her part, to a tacit game of roles. On yet another occasion, distant parts of the Mediterranean influenced each other reciprocally. The vulnerable Barbary and Flanders fleets (*mude*) paraded along the Iberian coasts. In the August of 1485, the Flanders convoy was attacked by French corsairs near the Portuguese cape of São Vicente (Cape Verde), and the King of France justified himself by invoking Sixtus IV's interdict that prohibited Venetian trade (an interdict that had actually already been revoked).[28] In the face of so many dangers prudence advised Venice not to meddle in the destiny of Granada any more. And this presaged Venice's imminent retreat from the seas of the western Mediterranean.

Nevertheless, Venice continued to nourish a grain of nostalgia for those infidels who had been their objective allies. In 1526, thirty-four years after the fall of the Nasrid Emirate, a Venetian diplomat in Spain, Giovanni Negro, was in Granada. He wrote of the place that "the Moors work, and do not do as is done in the rest of Spain, where all consider themselves *hidalgos*, that is to say, gentlemen and they do not want to work". Then concluding: "And so with this their pride they die of hunger and go around pilfering food here and there. Oh, what pride and infinite vanity there is in this Spain!".[29] In rendering honour to the defeated and discouraged people of Granada, the anti-Spanish sentiment of the Venetian élites was reaffirmed. But in the meantime significant Venetian politics, including appeals to the Turks, by now looked only in the direction of the Orient.

28. See Doumerc, *Venise et l'émirat hafside*, pp. 52, 101-103; López de Coca Castañer, "Las galeras venecianas", p. 124.

29. Sanudo, *I Diarii*, vol. XLI, coll. 749-750. See Richer-Rossi, "Les Espagnols vus par les Vénitiens".

8. Boccolino da Osimo's illusion

1. Up to this point, the stories we have recounted have been stories about the upper echelons; stories already known to contemporaries, although immersed in the fog of the secrets of power. Similarly, someone lower in the hierarchy wanted to follow the same lesson. This time, scandal with a Turkish flavour was set in the March of Ancona under the weak pontificate of Innocent VIII, when the territorial disruption of the Papal dominions became more acute. After Rimini and Otranto, the Adriatic coast returned to centre stage. This sea was commonly referred to as the "Gulf of Venice", but the Republic, although still dominant, had difficulty in exercising total control as it had in the past. Seen by the Turks, on the other hand, the Adriatic was attractive because, without departing from Ottoman possessions, it formed a wedge between the Christian territories which reached as far as the northernmost point of the Mediterranean. Here the borders of Italy were porous and critical, the mosaic of peoples and languages complex; here, at a much later date, tumultuous sequences of events were to be witnessed, episodes of ethnic cleansing, migrations; here the same historical and geographical culture would finally enter into the service of nascent nationalism.[1] Before all this, at the beginning of the Early Modern Age, the east of Italy found itself more exposed to the Turkish threat – but also to the temptation the Turks represented. This was the new development of the moment, which many life stories set in this land-water border area confirm.[2]

In 1486, after serving the Dukes of Burgundy and Milan, and after playing a part in the Aragonese reconquest of Otranto and the war between Ferrara and Venice, a captain from the Marches named Boccolino Guzzoni set himself up as the Lord of Osimo. From a military point of view, in addition to his personal curriculum, his power was based on a company of one hundred Morlach soldiers who had followed him from Otranto. As if there were any need, remnants of soldiers gathered together in this war against the Turks continued to liven up the Italian military landscape. The Morlachs were Christians from the internal parts of Dalmatia, speaking a neo-Latin Istro-Romanian language.[3] Forced by

1. See Farinelli, "Storia e geografia dell'Adriatico"; Hyder Patterson, "Sull'orlo della ragione"; Baskar, "L'anthropologie méditerranéenne"; Cattaruzza, *L'Italia e il confine orientale*.

2. See Anselmi, *Storie di Adriatico*; Anselmi, *Ultime storie di Adriatico*.

3. Pop and Bărdașăn, "Elemente moștenite"; *Italy and Europe's Eastern Border.*

the geopolitical situation to survive in the interstices between greater powers, they did not like to align themselves openly as long as they were in their original lands. But once they moved to Italy, Boccolino's Morlachs were revealed to be more reliable than the Turks that Alfonso of Calabria had engaged in the same theatre of war.

Soon Boccolino was besieged in Osimo by the Pontifical forces commanded by Cardinal Domenico Della Rovere and by the Milanese Captain Gian Giacomo Trivulzio. At this moment the self-styled lord sent two men to Constantinople to appeal to the Sultan Bayezid II. The first was his cousin, Pietro Balignani, the second a certain Leone Pifero from Castroleone, a hilltown in the hinterland of Senigallia, today known as Castelleone di Suasa. Others in Boccolino's situation would perhaps threaten the calling of a council, summoning up a spectre from the past that was detested in Rome, but the council card was well beyond our hero's means.

2. Instead, the Turkish card was judged to be within his capabilities, but even in this case there was a touch of presumption. The Neapolitan barons who in 1485-1486 offered themselves as vassals of the Turk just so that they could free themselves from Ferdinand I of Aragon, their king, were something of a completely different order. At Osimo, on the other hand, everything was done in the family, or virtually.

A renegade from the Marches, resident in Constantinople, a certain Cristoforo Castracane, known as "Magrino", received the party from Osimo. This is how the local sources tell the tale,[4] but some doubts weigh on this person's exact name and on the story about him. A Roman chronicle of those years mentions a Cristoforo Castagna known as "Macrino". He was the feudal lord of Castroleone (from where the emissary Leone Pifero also originated) and he had taken refuge in Constantinople "out of desperation" after being deprived of his land by a high prelate. Bayezid II smothered Castagna with presents and flattery; he even promised him rule over Negroponte, the Venetian island in the Aegean that had recently passed over to Turkish domination. Meanwhile, however, Bayezid supplied Castagna with "a little ampule of poison" with which he was supposed to kill Prince Cem, the brother and rival of the Sultan, who at that time was still in France.[5]

We shall tell the complicated story of Cem a little later. The story of "Macrino", on the other hand, is soon told: in 1490 he was discovered in Venice having just disembarked from the Levant. He was extradited to Rome and there horribly dismembered. The Roman chronicle makes no mention of the fact that he was a turncoat. On the other hand, sources from Ferrara define the unhappy

4. See Cecconi, *Vita e fatti di Boccolino*, p. 75.

5. Infessura, *Diario della città di Roma*, pp. 253-255. See Gardi, "Congiure contro i papi", p. 38 (where other variants of the name appear: Cristoforo "Magrino" di Castrano and Marino Castracan).

victim, tortured at Rome for attempted poisoning, merely as "Magrino". He had been a groom for Duke Borso d'Este and he had got himself captured in Venice because he had been showing off with a splendid Turkish horse that he could never have afforded.[6] Despite these differences in the documentary evidence, the basic fact remains: the existence of a character referred to in very similar ways, who had taken refuge at Constantinople for reasons of personal bitterness against the Roman Curia.

The destiny of "Magrino", whoever he was, would be completed by 1490. First, he was still in Constantinople and presented the emissaries from Osimo, bringing them before Bayezid. The Sultan examined the offer to "place his foot in Osimo as his father had done in Otranto". His father, none other than Mehmed II, had miscalculated, the emissaries judged: Osimo, not Otranto is positioned "in a convenient place for the conquest of the whole of Italy". Indeed, Osimo is at the centre of gravity with respect to Rome, Florence and Venice, three of the main nodes of Italian life at the time. In addition, Osimo, even if it is an inland town, is still "near the sea, and for this reason easy to resupply with provisions and people".[7]

Contacts initiated in Constantinople continued in Venice. This time the Sultan chose a trusted man as his representative, a certain Alessio, previously a groom to the Neapolitan noble family of Sanseverino. There is nothing to make us think that these great feudal lords were party to the scheme. As in other phases of these negotiations, everything happened at a low level: indeed, the groom Alessio had been Boccolino's companion in arms in the War of Ferrara. From Osimo, on the other hand, a gentleman named Bartolomeo Ricci was sent to Venice to negotiate.

It was impossible for all this coming and going to escape the watchful eye of the Republic, which indeed decided to inform Innocent VIII and the other Italian rulers. The various characters involved were all arrested in various places on the orders of the Pope. At this point Boccolino was forced to stop delaying. He prepared the outline of a bold agreement and he sent it to the Sultan with his nephew, Angelo Guzzoni. In February 1487 Guzzoni was intercepted at Lecce when he was about to reach Otranto, where he was supposed to embark for Valona in Albania. This remained the obligatory passage for anyone wanting to avoid the Dalmatian route, which was safer as far as navigation was concerned, but was completely controlled by Venetian settlements and galleys. Venice could not easily accept this clumsy act of interference in matters which she considered her own business. Transferred to Rome in chains, Guzzoni met a bitter end: he was dismembered by four horses in Piazza Navona. Dismemberments were not shunned in this affair, confirming to us that the stakes were very high.

3. Thanks to the misfortune of Angelo Guzzoni, we know the documents he was carrying with him. Before his departure for the Levant, Boccolino had delivered

6. See Ricci, *Ossessione turca*, p. 34.
7. In Cecconi, *Vita e fatti di Boccolino*, p. 75.

detailed written instructions to him – and this act of putting things in writing is indicative of the level of ingenuousness of the patron. Guzzoni was supposed to make the Sultan understand “the desire that we have to be slaves and servants of his majesty”, and “how divided and in disagreement Italy is, and how discontented the peoples subject to the tyranny of factions (*parti*) are”.

This is how the local tradition of Osimo cautiously reports things. But a chronicler from the town of Forlì, Andrea Bernardi, known as *Novacula*, interprets the document, which had reached him as a copy, in a different and more threatening way: “how discontented the peoples subject to the tyranny of the priests (*preti*) are”. Notice: priests, not factions.[8] And so ecclesiastical tyranny was introduced, if the interpretation of Boccolino’s words offered by Novacula is correct; and even if this is not a correct interpretation, the fact that it became established is worth noting, whoever the original author of the error might be. It is well known that the process of misunderstanding in the transmission of manuscripts often begins with a reading induced by reason of mental economy;[9] and it is known that the oversights of copyists can often be defined as cases of *lapsus*. In the context we are describing, it could have been more economical to think of ‘priests’ (“preti”) than of ‘factions’ (“parti”) when faced with an ambiguous or poorly written text. But perhaps, to interpret the interpretation given by the chronicler from Forlì, there is no need to trouble applied-psychoanalytical philology. Because, to the eyes of many, in the Italy of that time, tyranny and priests ended up being the same thing: where the one was to be found, due to an automatic mental reflex the others appeared, and vice versa. “The whole of this land awaits, and has no other refuge or hope than Your Majesty” Boccolino replied, and here there are no doubts of interpretation. A few years earlier, we should remember, the learned George of Trebizond recalled in his turn “how discontented the various people were”.

The conquest was not going to be difficult, this was how Boccolino suggested it to the Sultan, and perhaps it was even inevitable because of the “intrigue that the Pope has with Your Majesty’s brother through the Grand Master of Rhodes”. Here Cem is mentioned (or Zizim, also known as “Gigimo” in Italy), Bayezid II’s younger half-brother who had been defeated in the race for the throne. Cem is a key character in the transactions between East and West in those years. For now we shall only say that, in his desire to get away from Bayezid he had found refuge with the Knights of Rhodes in 1482. The Grand Master of the Order, Pierre d’Aubusson, had sold him to France, where Cem had found himself in the peculiar position of being a guest-hostage before being handed over to the Pope. Cem’s situation was ambiguous because he was indeed a tool of manoeuvre against the Sultan, but at the same time Innocent VIII and Bayezid dealt with the prince with implicit and substantive agreement. The Sultan paid 40,000 Venetian ducats a year for the upkeep of his brother, as long as he remained a prisoner and did not return to the East.[10] For several years the sum made up a regular item of income

8. Bernardi (Novacula), *Cronache forlivesi*, p. 165.

9. See Timpanaro, *Il lapsus freudiano*, pp. 9-38, 135-141.

10. See Inalcik, “A Case Study”. Effective but fictionalised: Sablier, *Le prisonnier de Bourganeuf*; Freely, *Jem Sultan*.

on the Papal balance sheet. "The Papacy as a pensioner of the Sublime Porte": this is how this political phase has been summarized.[11]

Besides the Pope and the Turkish Sultan, other people took an interest in Cem, hoping to gain some advantage from him. In practice, all of those who considered Bayezid an enemy, or who feared his power, did so. In the year 1486, the King of Hungary, Matthias Corvinus, was actively involved in this affair, connecting it to the attempt to form an alliance with France, for the coming crusade. But the King of Naples, Ferdinand I of Aragon, and the Mameluke Sultan of Egypt, Qa'it Bey, were also on their guard. At the time, the latter was in open war with the Sultan Bayezid.[12] Cem's mother, Çiçek Hatun, an exile in Egypt, never ceased scheming to restore her son to the throne; so much so that in 1488 she even asked the Doge of Venice, Agostino Barbarigo, for assistance.[13] Perhaps Boccolino was not aware of this secret information, anxious as he was to receive material assistance at once: "great and small artillery; salt and sugar, bread for a month to the soldiers that come here [...] artillerymen, some engineers; shields, spears, swords and saddles and iron, and most of all money". The supplies requested are banal but indispensable. However, we take note of the request also made for "some engineers", or rather specialists in the subjects illustrated in the tract that Sigismund Malatesta had sent to Istanbul some years earlier.

Boccolino's instructions to his nephew close with the geographical-strategic details. The disembarking of men and materials should occur "on the beach of Recanati"; the "Monte de Ancona", which is to say the promontory of Conero that interrupts the Adriatic coastline, which would serve as a reference point. Disembarking would not cause problems because, on the arrival of the first contingent, the people of Osimo would raise "the glorious and undefeated emblems" of the Sultan. This assurance of the good reception that awaited the Turks may seem excessive, almost wishful, by Boccolino in defence of his own interests. Nevertheless, other testimonies show how the inhabitants of the central-northern Adriatic envisaged a landing by the Turks at that time; in particular in the cities of Ancona and Ravenna, motivated by a proud anti-papal civic feeling, openly hoped for one.[14]

4. The text of the agreement envisaged by Boccolino was attached to the instructions delivered to Angelo Guzzoni. This is the only case known to us of a treaty of commitment unilaterally proposed to the Turk from Italian territory. In fact, as we will see later, the letter that Ludovico il Moro was to send to Constantinople in 1499 merely foresees a tributary relationship on the financial level. The singular nature of the document from the Marches forces us to observe both the explicit and the implicit contents with care. On the explicit side there

11. Pfeffermann, *Die Zusammenarbeit*, pp. 82-92.
12. See Har-El, *Struggle for Domination*.
13. See *Le carte del sultano*, pp. 42-43.
14. See Babinger, "Maometto il Conquistatore e l'Italia", p. 486.

are, first of all, the first sixteen articles of general application. “To be allowed to live under our Catholic faith and rites,” and that clergymen and churches be respected; that the treasure belonging to the Sanctuary of the Madonna di Loreto “is not looted now or ever,” in return for payment of one third of its income; that the traditional “freedoms and liberties” of Osimo be maintained; that a vast territory of land be subjected to Osimo, the centre of “the empire of Italy” of the Sultan; that “just as today we say the March of Ancona, as a sign of the honour of our city in future it will be known as the March of Osimo”.

Then a delicate subject comes up. Instead of the usual tributes to the Sultan in “money, men, boys and girls”, every year, “as a sign of vassalage a horse worth two hundred ducats and a pair of dogs” will be offered. This is the latent content. The fate of the Christian peoples of the Balkans, subject annually to the institution of the “blood tax” (*devşirme*)[15] concerned Boccolino. In the West it was much spoken about and it was one of the negative components of the image of the Turks. Boccolino thus attempted to ward off this fate by offering princely tributes on a symbolic level but without great material or moral costs: animals rather than humans. This clause in the treaty indicates that the meeting between the two cultures was not without problems and suspicions. At the end of the document, eight articles were added concerning subjects of personal interest to Boccolino and his relatives: privileges, gifts, fiefdoms.[16] Everything was rigidly regulated, and this by the lesser party.

In his presumptuousness, our *condottierio* was unaware of the fact that the ambassadors of the powers of Europe prostrated themselves before the Sultan in the seraglio of Topkapı; and they did this if they were indeed fortunate, if they had been admitted inside the Sublime Porte. Boccolino did not know that gestures of submission and respect for physical and hierarchical distances were an essential part of the ceremonial instituted by Mehmed II in 1481, mixing Byzantine and Turkish-Mongolian influences.[17] High politics demands possession of some culture and up-to-date information and Boccolino had neither one nor the other.

5. The arrest of his nephew in Lecce as he was on his way to Constantinople closed every escape route for Boccolino. Papal determination to resolve the crisis was reinforced by some attacks by Muslim corsairs on the coast of the Marches; whether these were chance apparitions, exploratory raids or the first signs of invasion no one knew, but it was better not to take the risk. After yearning to find refuge in Turkey, or to commit suicide, or even to set his city alight, in the summer of 1487 Boccolino accepted an honourable peace with Innocent VIII. Thanks to the mediations of Lorenzo the Magnificent, he left Osimo safe and sound and with 1,000 ducats in his pocket. He stayed comfortably in Florence but then moved to Milan in 1493. There, if we accept the testimony of a Florentine chronicler, he

15. See Menage, “Some Notes on the Devshirme”.

16. In Cecconi, *Vita e fatti di Boccolino*, pp. 77-81. Previously, with variations, Martorelli, *Memorie historiche*, pp. 368-374; Guzzini, *Boccolino Guzzoni*, pp. 32-34, 53-57.

17. See Necipoğlu, *Architecture, Ceremonial and Power*, pp. 15-22, 96-110.

would be "hanged by the neck" by Ludovico il Moro with the accusation of being a hired assassin of the King of Naples.[18]

A tragic finale to a story that is at times farcical, starting with the names of some of the protagonists: Boccolino, first of all, and then Pifero, and finally "Magrino". An air of improvisation enveloped these attempts at high politics that were sketched out by the Italian lordlings of the time. Highly professional as it was, the Ottoman chancellery could not fail to take note of the affair, and then consign it to the archives. This is the instinctive comment of a present-day observer, who is aware of Boccolino's fate and of other manipulators like him. But at that time, with the game not yet concluded, was everything quite as superficial as it appears to us? Indeed, Andrea Bernardi, the chronicler from Forlì that we are already familiar with, in his anticlerical spirit outlines a different appraisal of the actions of Boccolino:

> There was never seen in our days a man blessed with greater spirit and capacity, having had the courage to lead the infidels into Italy to conquer it. [...] These are things worthy of Charlemagne or the Paladin Roland.[19]

Boccolino compared to Charlemagne and Roland: surprising, this glorification, in an era when Renaissance epic literature was flourishing. Had Charlemagne and Roland not fought against the Moors, whom everyone considered the forerunners of the Turks? And after the growth of Ottoman power, had Charlemagne not been reinvented as a crusader hero?[20] Boccolino, in contrast, wanted to do the exact opposite of the mythical emperor and the paladin: invite the Turks/Moors into Italy. Yes, it is surprising indeed, this glorification... However, we can compare it with a different judgement by another chronicler from the Romagna, Giuliano Fantaguzzi. According to him, writing in the heat of the moment, as soon as he heard of the hanging, "Boccolino from Osimo was taken and imprisoned in Milan, he who wanted to bring the Turk into Italy".[21] As clear as day. But the subject has the air of triteness expressed in stereotyped language: "bring the Turk into Italy".

6. The *damnatio memoriae* of Boccolino Guzzoni had begun in May 1492, that is to say, before his death, with a violent Papal bull by Innocent VIII: "sunk in the abyss of evil, he did not fear to intrigue with the perfidious and most powerful Turk to the ruin of the Christian religion and faith, not only sending him messages, but repeatedly sending various envoys".[22] In truth, the documents tell us that Boccolino made a distinction between territorial possession and religious belonging, and that he was not considering renouncing his faith at all. On the contrary, he was concerned about the nearby sanctuary of Loreto to the extent of attributing to himself a sort of right of patronage. The sanctuary had grown up

18. Parenti, *Storia fiorentina*, vol. I, pp. 60, 80.
19. Bernardi (Novacula), *Cronache forlivesi*, pp. 167-168.
20. See Matarrese, *Parole e forme*, pp. 35-52; Bisaha, *Creating East and West*, pp. 30-42.
21. Fantaguzzi, *Caos*, p. 44.
22. In Cecconi, *Vita e fatti di Boccolino*, pp. 179-187.

around the House of the Madonna, which had supposedly flown there from the Holy Land to escape the infidels. So Boccolino watched over a place of worship that from its original foundation myth had opposed Islam.[23] But the distinction established by Boccolino between territory and religion, not unknown in Istanbul, was rejected on principle in Rome.

Half a century later, the Bolognese Dominican Leandro Alberti would attribute a "bestial" spirit to Boccolino.[24] Bloodthirsty he had certainly been, even if no more so than many other characters of the time, including clerics. Besides this, Boccolino had merely put into practice what others imagined. But he did not know how one was supposed to behave when dealing with the Great Lord; he only had cousins, nephews or other lesser figures available to him as emissaries to Istanbul, and the Sultan responded to this with grooms sent to Venice; he was incapable of escaping from Venetian surveillance both on land and sea; strengthened by the precedent of Otranto, which had cost the Turks dear, he overestimated the value of his own offer; being untrained in international politics, he confused local municipal minutiae with the grand manoeuvres that took shape around the figure of Cem. And so, thanks to a mix of inexperience and inevitability, this written appeal to the Turk failed.

23. See Scaraffia, *Loreto*, pp. 25-26.
24. Alberti, *Descrittione di tutta Italia*, p. 283*v*.

9. The Borgia Pope writes to Bayezid II

1. Someone much more important than a Boccolino da Osimo was required to construct an operation like the appeal to the Turks. And for the Turks to be persuaded, or almost persuaded, to come, a situation of disorder in Italy was required. Both conditions – a suitable promoter and a suitable context – came about shortly afterwards.

The successor to Innocent VIII, who had cursed Boccolino, was the Spanish Pope, Alexander VI. When he was still a cardinal, Rodrigo Borgia had equipped a galley at his own expense to contribute to Pius II's crusade; he had also gone to the port of Ancona, from where the fleet was supposed to set sail in 1464. But then, elected pope with the name of Alexander VI, the Borgia changed his behaviour, under the pressure of circumstances. In fact, the first half of his pontificate was run through with strenuous attempts to establish cooperation with the Turks.

In 1494, when the clouds heralding the descent of Charles VIII of France into Italy were already gathering, the Spanish Pope, prey to despondency, looked to the Orient. And to say that the immediate objective of the king of France was precisely the crown of Naples that he wished to snatch from Alfonso II of Aragon because he claimed the Angevin inheritance; but a second objective, which was roundly asserted, was to make the southern Italian kingdom the base from which to launch a crusade against the Turks. This crusade was to be decisive at last, given the greater proximity of the bases of departure to the theatres of war. Faced with such an argument, the pope could not object in public. So he entrusted four cardinals with the task of urging King Charles to set off against the Turks, imitating his namesake Charlemagne;[1] once again, the emperor of the medieval epics was superimposed over the characters of the present.

The celebratory atmosphere produced by the fall of the emirate of Granada in 1492 inspired official language at that time. After seven centuries, there were no longer any Arab states to occupy the Christian forces in the West. The eastern crusade, the real crusade towards the Holy Places, could begin again; all the more so as neither the Ottomans nor the Mamelukes had shown themselves able to come to the aid of their coreligionists in Andalusia.

1. See Gilli, "Alexandre VI et la France"; Le Thiec, "Le roi, le pape et l'ôtage".

Meanwhile, letters of completely different tenor left Rome for Istanbul. An initial letter from the Pope to Bayezid II is of 12th May 1494. In it, Alexander VI, declaring himself protector of the Aragonese dynasty, personally (*intime*) entrusted the destiny of the kingdom of Naples to the Sultan. But, most of all, the Pope seemed to place the Papal State itself under the tutelage of the Sultan. Here is the memorable phrase – certainly not the only memorable one in this story:

> we entrust the kingdom of Naples to your power, and we exhort you to take its territories and its men under your protection, just as our State and our lands and those of the Roman Church; we exhort you to look with identical benevolence on the interests of that kingdom as on ours.[2]

Perhaps this was only a dry-run, before advancing more concrete requests. Very soon these came. A month and a half after this first letter, on 28th June 1494, the Pope sent the Sultan a Genoese messenger who knew Turkish and boasted of links with the court in Istanbul. His name was Giorgio Bucciardo. Bucciardo belonged to a Venetian family resident for generations on the Bosphorous, that had later become Genoese through marriage. By the same means, the Bucciardo family had become related to the family of the princes of Cybo.[3] Giorgio Bucciardo had already collaborated with the eastern policy of Pope Innocent VIII (he also being Genoese, and also a Cybo in his original name). He had been an interpreter of Turkish in Italy, and in 1492 he had been sent to Constantinople to communicate to the Sultan that if he had attacked a Christian country, the Prince Cem would have been used against him. But the mission entrusted to him now by Alexander VI was the most important of Bucciardo's career, so much so that the Pope asked him to go, negotiate and return in the shortest time possible. Later we shall give the explanation as to how we possess detailed documentation regarding such a secret affair.

2. In the general agitation produced by the wait for Charles VIII, Alexander VI was not the only one to think of the Turks. Speaking to a Venetian diplomat, Ludovico il Moro confessed: "If I were in King Alfonso II of Aragon's place, I would not only call on the Turks, but the devil as well".[4] Venice itself feared that the confusion brought by the king would have resulted in the Turks coming to Italy on someone's invitation. In these circumstances, the citizens of Pisa proclaimed that rather than being brought back under the yoke of Florence, according to an intention attributed to Charles VIII, they would give themselves to the Turk or they would all have themselves killed.[5] Here we do not know if this was merely a rhetorical topos, or

2. In Thuasne, *Djem Sultan, fils de Mohammed II*, pp. 325 326. There is a complete edition of the correspondence between the Sultan and the Pope: Heidenheimer, "Die Korrespondenz Sultan Bajazet's II"; this part on pp. 518 519.

3. See Zapperi, "Bucciardo, Giorgio"; Lercari, "Il parentado genovese di Caterina Cybo", pp. 136 144. There is no mention of the family in Fleet, *European and Islamic Trade*.

4. See Vianello, "Testimonianze venete su Milano", p. 418.

5. See Luzzati, *Una guerra di popolo*, pp. 31 37; Pellegrini, *Le guerre d'Italia*, p. 51.

if instead the reciprocal aversion between the two cities was truly showing itself: better the Turks than the Florentines? The civic feeing of Italian tradition (all the more as it was Tuscan) did not give ground in the face of any challenge.

But obviously, the figure most threatened by Charles VIII was the King of Naples, Alfonso II, the one they wanted to deprive of the throne. Alfonso was none other than Prince Alfonso of Calabria, the very same ruler who had regained Otranto in 1481, to then enrol the Turkish prisoners in the War of Ferrara against Venice. If there was one person who had committed himself militarily against the Turks it was precisely him. The initiator of the Ferrara tradition of epic poetry, Matteo Maria Boiardo, had celebrated him for this in his lines: "since Italy is defended from the Turks, only by his valour and his courage" ("poiché Italia è difesa da' Turchi / solo dalla sua prodezza e il suo valore").[6] And so the defender of Italy; holder of a kingdom which, in Apulia, was living under the threat of Turkish Albania. Even Alfonso, with his back to the wall, launched a couple of requests to Bayezid for help against France. To this end he used the nobleman, Camillo Pandone, from the family of the Counts of Venafro, as messenger.

On 17th November 1494 – the same day as Charles VIII's entry into Florence – Pandone returned to Naples with three Turkish ambassadors. These were received "with great honour" with trumpeters, flautists and other sounds". This is told by the Neapolitan chronicle written by a goldsmith by the name of Giovanni (or perhaps Leonardo) Ferraiolo. The text revealed that the king planned "to get the Turk to come to the kingdom, because he was desperate and had been abandoned by everyone and understood that he could trust no one". Public appearances of the king at the side of the Turks, who were the only allies remaining to him and were thus covered in "honours and gifts" , were to follow. A month later, the agreement of a "serene peace" between Naples and Constantinople was announced and – the chronicler repeats – "this His Majesty did out of great desperation". A right of free circulation for their respective subjects was established, which in that era was an absolute rarity:

> Let any person wanting to go to Turkey or to come from Turkey to Naples, be free to do so [...] because His Majesty preferred to place his realm under the power of the Turks rather than in the hands of others.

In reply the Sultan offered Alfonso "money and horsemen to the tune of twelve or fifteen thousand" (if true, an enormous number). A certain remaining suspicion was taken into account: "and if His Majesty did not desire the said men for fear that they might deceive him, the Sultan would send horses and money". Within the scope of the negotiations it seems that the King also received the Sultan's promise to attack the Genoese island of Chios to avenge the assistance given by Genoa to Charles VIII.

At the last moment, however, the Ottoman-Aragonese agreement failed. This was due to both the hesitations of the Sultan who had not forgotten the failure of his father's expedition to Otranto, and to his excessive demands. In exchange for the intervention he asked to have the cities of Otranto, Brindisi and Taranto "in his

6. Boiardo, *L'inamoramento de Orlando*, vol. II, p. 1495 (II XXVII 56bis).

power" with the argument that the men sent by him needed places "to dig in". The chronicler Ferraiolo reports the words of the king, faced with Bayezid's request: "The Lord does not want me to be the one who destroys this kingdom by placing it in the hands of the Turks, I believed I was doing the right thing, and instead I would have done wrong".[7] A belated awareness of his mistake, but the king was right. No Neapolitan ruler could ever have conceded the precious Apulian bridgeheads from which access to the Adriatic and movements between Italy and the Balkan peninsula were controlled. Two pen-line drawings that decorate the codex of Ferraiolo's chronicle nevertheless remain to testify to the exchanges between Naples and Constantinople. Drawn around 1498, they show the arrival of the Turkish ambassadors and a mounted procession by King Alfonso in their company (fig. 3). The snub-nosed profile attributed to the two guests appears to be an unsuccessful attempt to reproduce their exotic features, which the turbans and moustaches (only worn by them)[8] underline.

3. So, with Pisan fantasies and desperate Aragonese attempts eliminated, the only serious action was Alexander VI's. The sources connected to the first part of the mission entrusted to Giorgio Bucciardo (his appointment and departure) are reliable, but then things become confused. In November 1494, Bucciardo returned to Italy from Istanbul with a military messenger from the Sultan (technically, a *çavuş*). This man was called Kasım and it was not the first time – and nor was it to be the last – that he came to Italy on a mission: one way or another he had developed an equal and opposite professional skill to Bucciardo. The two sidekicks, Giorgio and Kasım, disembarked in Venice, as people usually did, and then headed for Rome, making use of a sea route as far as Ancona. The port in the Marches was, in those days, a crucial hub for manoeuvres with the Levant. It was here that Pius II's unfulfilled wishes for a crusade, and the more recent plots by Boccolino da Osimo, intersected. And anyway the whole of the Adriatic coast was subject to greater pressures, threats and flattery originating from the Ottoman Orient.

If truth be told, the Christians were hardly joking either on this coast with such a gentle profile. A short way from Ancona, Giorgio and Kasım were attacked by brigands serving Giovanni Della Rovere, the lord of Senigallia. He kept his eye on everything that moved along the coastline, not least because an attack by corsairs on his city a short time before had cost the capture of eighty inhabitants. Recently, Giovanni's brother, the cardinal Giuliano Della Rovere (the future Pope Julius II) had broken violently with Alexander VI and, as a precaution, he had taken refuge in France. The antipapal, anti-Turkish, and pro-French ambush on the two messengers was also the expression of a personal and clan resentment: the Della Rovere against

7. Ferraiolo, *Cronaca*, pp. 38 39, which updates the text published in *Una cronaca napoletana figurata*, pp. 108 112. See Labande-Mailfert, *Charles VIII et son milieu*, pp. 327 328.

8. See Le Gall, *Un idéal masculin?*

the Borgia. The two dimensions, one political and the other anthropological, centring on the idea of vendetta, were fused in an exemplary way, as often happened in the Italy of the Renaissance.[9]

Having fallen into Giovanni Della Rovere's trap, the two travellers, the Turk and the Italian, found themselves in desperate straits. Kasım was robbed of the 40,000 ducats sent by Bayezid for his brother Cem's upkeep. In the commotion he managed to save his skin by taking refuge, first of all, in a nearby castle and then within the walls of Ancona, where the Pope was in control. Later he embarked for Venice, escaping another ambush on the sea organised by the indefatigable lord of Senigallia. From Venice Kasım reached Mantua. There the Marquis Francesco II Gonzaga received him warmly. The last stage of Kasım's journey before returning home was Venice again, where the Republic attempted to calm his indignation for the affront he had suffered. The itinerary of Kasım's escape, from Ancona to Mantua to Venice, traces a geography of the filo-Turkish positions existing on Italian soil at that moment. We have spoken of Venice in these terms, and we shall do so again; we will also have to dedicate some attention to the Gonzaga.

The other traveller attacked near Ancona, Giorgio Bucciardo, was robbed of something no less precious than money: a series of documents. The documents concerned were the instructions given by the Pope to Bucciardo himself when he had left for Istanbul, and five letters with the Sultan's replies to the Pope. Venice protested furiously because she saw herself excluded from the management of an eastern affair, and feared retaliation by the Turk, all the more because the lord of Senigallia was in the pay of the Republic. The Sultan demanded (or pretended to demand) that Venice punish the Della Rovere by sending ten armed galleys to devastate Senigallia. Even if this was not done, a certain unity of purpose between the two opposing powers in the Levant, Venice and the Ottomans, finds confirmation at this stage in events and in the Italian theatre. In his turn, Alexander VI issued an excommunication against the culprit of the ambush, accusing him of violation of papal correspondence and stealing money.

While these various reactions were playing out, the instructions and the five letters were taken to Florence. There the notary Filippo Patriarchi took delivery of them, and published them, after having them translated. One of the Sultan's letters was in Latin, while four were in Greek or in Turkish, and it was the learned Byzantine, Giovanni Lascaris, who dedicated himself to the task of translation. The contents of the transaction between Rome and Constantinople were revealed, complete with legal certification and an oath (obtained under torture) by the poor Bucciardo.[10] The scandal, in Italy and beyond, was great, but short-lived. It could only help, however, to strengthen the determination of Charles VIII for the Italian expedition and the crusade. The path of negotiation between Alexander VI and Bayezid II had been blocked. Having conceded in those same days the title of Catholic Kings to the conquerors of Granada, Ferdinand II of Aragon and Isabella of Castile, the Pope could not openly

9. See Muir, *Mad Blood Stirring*.

10. The complete story can be read in Heidenheimer, "Die Korrespondenz Sultan Bajazets II", pp. 520 535.

oppose the Most Christian King of France, Charles VIII, who was moving against Istanbul. This was the end of the sleights of hand in an international intrigue with all the traits of a novel. Or rather, no, a final hidden aspect remains, and it is this: the original specimen of all these papers disappears from view immediately. But did an original really exist?

4. Issued from Florence in Italian translation, the red-hot documentation was transcribed by numerous local chroniclers.[11] But we owe the most complete report to the Venetian noble gentleman Marin Sanudo. Less than a year after the events, in 1495, Sanudo felt the need to write a long history of Charles VIII's expedition, identified by him as being an irreversible turning point in Italian history. Machiavelli and Guicciardini, who were to write on the topic, could do nothing other than confirm with better arguments the interpretation made by Sanudo.[12] Sanudo recounts things that are not always well-founded, and, in addition, the nineteenth century edition of his work on Charles VIII's descent into Italy does not satisfy present-day criteria; but the wealth of information is substantial, worthy of the author of the monumental *Diari*.

Let us begin then with the instructions given by the Pope to Giorgio Bucciardo with a view to the mission to Bayezid.[13] Principally, he was supposed to ask the Sultan for advance payment of the annual fee laid down for the detention of Cem in Rome: the famous 40,000 ducats, which the parties never ceased to haggle over. Once this money had been received and the "receipt issued in the usual way", the Pope would be able to "provide", in other words, organise his own defence against Charles VIII. Again, an international agreement hinged on Cem. The King of France, "with the greatest land and sea forces", was supposed to be aiming to snatch the hostage from the Pope's hands, who had been keeping him under careful watch since 1489. Once Cem had passed into the power of Charles VIII, "they say they will send him with an army to Turkey". Perhaps via Valona, other sources suggest, completing in reverse the route of Mehmed II's forces when they had targeted Ottranto: and the Turks knew how easy that journey was. Once he had arrived in Turkey, Cem would provoke an insurrection and would be installed as a puppet sovereign. In confirming the French plan in front of the Sultan, the Pope made a gesture that integrated the Ottoman empire into the political game of Christian Europe as a full member.

In September 1494, while the diplomatic fervour was at its height, a legal document drafted in Rome seemed to confirm the Pope's intuitions and the suspicions of the Sultan. Andreas Palaiologos, heir to the Byzantine Empire by the lateral line of the Despotate of Mystras, ceded all his rights to Charles VIII. Continually short of money, the young Palaiologos was to insist on adorning himself with the title "Emperor of Constantinople" (not of Rome, we should

11. Among others, Zambotti, *Diario ferrarese*, pp. 239 242.
12. See Zancarini, "Machiavelli e Guicciardini".
13. In Sanudo, *La spedizione di Carlo VIII*, pp. 42 45.

note); he would sell his rights a second time, to the sovereigns of Spain, but all this was yet to occur.[14]

Cem or no Cem, Alexander VI observed, "if the French were the victors" the objective was clear: Constantinople. In order to convince Bayezid, the Pope named another of his sworn enemies willing to pay out "great treasure" just to get hold of Cem: the "great sultan" of Egypt, the Mameluke sovereign, Qa'it Bey. In his own interests, it was desirable that Bayezid deployed every influence to persuade Venice to side with them against "our French enemies". The expressions of "good and true friendship" for the Sultan present in the instructions to Bucciardo should not deceive us, however. Here we are talking about two powers that are negotiating cynically, and blackmailing each other in turn. So as to leave no doubts, the Pope warned the Sultan that he would be forced to use Cem ("we will make a hard decision") if "Your Majesty decided to persecute Christians and molest them" in Hungary and Croatia.

5. Now we come to Bayezid's letters to Alexander VI. The first announced the dispatch of the 40,000 ducats requested; the second allowed Bucciardo to leave; the third supplied credentials for the ambassador Kasım. The fourth letter, the most curious of them, will be examined later. But the most important document is the fifth letter from the Sultan to the Pope, dated 12th September 1494.

Just to begin, the answer to blackmail is blackmail. If the Pope handed Cem over to the French, "it would be a serious thing much against our will and it will cause great harm to Your Honour, and all your Christians will pay for it heavily". Things having been made abundantly clear, the Sultan put forward the proposal that was supposed to resolve every difficulty: kill Cem. In any case, – this is the argument – Cem is mortal like all of us and has to die sooner or later:

> Together with Giorgio [Bucciardo] we have thought as follows, to calm and to advance Your Power and give satisfaction to me: it would be good that Cem our brother, who in any case is subject to death and risks being snatched from Your Highness, might be hastened to death, which would be for him a new life and would represent benefit and peace for Your Power and for us great satisfaction.

The freedom to choose the technical details of how to offer Cem peace eternal are left to the Pope:

> We ask Your Highness to do us the favour of seeing that Cem be raised from the trials of this world in the way that Your Highness considers best; transferred to the next world, his soul will find peace.

We know that Bayezid had been struggling for some time to obtain this outcome. Fear of Charles VIII (certainly excessive) must have induced him to stake everything on this. This was also because panic had apparently spread among the Turkish coastal population, at least according to Marin Sanudo: "the Turks of the shores, through fear of the French army, had come inland and had closed themselves

14. See Denis, *Charles VIII et les Italiens*, pp. 62-65, 132-133.

inside the fortresses, abandoning houses and barns". In other words, the internal Turkish front showed signs of caving in. This explains the urgency of Bayezid's manoeuvre and his generosity towards Alexander VI. If the Pope had cooperated, in exchange for the brother's body sent "to any place on our coasts", Bayezid would have been generous. He would have paid 300,000 ducats: a very high sum, seven or eight times higher than Cem's annual pension in life. An advance payment, on trust, "before it is delivered" (the corpse, it is to be understood); it would be enough that they guaranteed notification that the thing had been done. With this money the Pope "might have some lands bought for his sons".

The nepotism of the Borgia was perfectly familiar to the Sultan, who took advantage of this to reach his goal; the infidel knew the corruption that was predominant in the Roman Curia and exploited it to his own benefit. The use of Turkish money to organise the defence against Charles VIII is not even mentioned any more. Freed from his brother's bogey, it seems as if the Sultan did not fear the French invasion as before. And besides, the Sultan thought that the Pope himself, deep down, was more concerned with offering a state to his sons than guaranteeing the destinies of the Apostolic See or of the Aragonese rulers of Naples. Protection of the Christians in the Ottoman Empire was also dealt with rapidly: "in our country we shall not cause any obstacle or harm to Christians, of whatever condition they be, neither on land nor by sea". The letter concludes with a religious oath pronounced by the Sultan twice to add greater solemnity. All of this was done "in the presence of the above-mentioned Giorgio Bucciardo", elevated to the level of witness for the Christian side. This is the first formula of the oath: "for the true God, whom we adore, and above our true Gospels"; and this is the second: "for the true God who created the world and every single thing and in whom we believe and we adore".[15]

6. These invocations to God in the mouth of one who had just asked the Vicar of Christ to kill his brother leave us speechless; invocations not to his own God, but, it seems, to a God in common "in whom we believe". On the other hand, the formula "above our true Gospels" is not very clear. It is the Sultan who is speaking, not Bucciardo. To reassure the Pope, did he perform an oath on the Gospels as well? We may doubt this. Or: did the Italian translation produced in Florence call the sacred text of Islam, the Koran, "our true Gospels"? Again we may doubt this. We can do no other than leave the question open, except to note that the formula used seems to respect the sacramental character of the political oath.[16]

Whatever the case may be, religious aspects that are binding for everyone were accentuated to make the agreement work; a sort of ecumenism is placed as a guarantee of a planned assassination. This did not cancel out the reciprocal threats

15. In Sanudo, *La spedizione di Carlo VIII*, pp. 46-47, 158. See Gallotta, Bova, "Documenti dell'Archivio di Stato di Venezia"; Pedani, *In nome del Gran Signore*, pp. 112-114; Preto, *I servizi segreti di Venezia*, p. 33.

16. See Prodi, *Il sacramento del potere*, p. 22.

between the rulers of Rome and Constantinople. At the same time, however, the documentation sequestered at Senigallia reveals the climate of familiarity existing between the two courts. Here we refer to the fourth letter from the Sultan to the Pope. Seeing as he was in contact with the Pope, Bayezid tried to put in a good word for a person who was close to his heart. He asked for the concession of a cardinal's hat to Nicola Bucciardo, archbishop of Arles and Georgio Bucciardo's relative. The Sultan underlined that "already from the time of the previous high Pontiff, Innocent VIII, and up until today", the prelate "has worked for peace and friendship serving both parties faithfully" [17] A very strong sentence, seeing that a bishop should only serve one single party; a sentence that was capable, in the West, of bringing discredit on the Bucciardo family members, the precious intermediaries between Rome and Istanbul. Giorgio Bucciardo must have taken advantage of his position to obtain the intervention of the Sultan; or perhaps he was being rewarded for having had the idea of killing Cem (we remember Bayezid's words: "together with Giorgio Bucciardo we have thought…").

The archbishop Nicola Bucciardo could also speak Turkish, and he had also been involved in Cem's fortunes previously. In 1489 he had gone to Civitavecchia to welcome the Sultan's brother on his arrival from France and he had interpreted for him. At the disembarkation at Civitavecchia the omnipresent messenger, Kasım, was there on the Sultan's behalf. Despite (or perhaps because of) Bayezid's support, Nicola Bucciardo never received the purple.[18] But it is not an everyday occurrence to see a Sultan take an interest in the individual career of a prelate. The hunt for lucrative ecclesiastical benefices had become ferocious in those years, as they gradually became rarer.[19] Not everyone was called Ippolito d'Este, like the son of Ercole I, Duke of Ferrara, who in 1486, at the age of seven, had become primate of Hungary and in 1493, at fourteen, had received the purple.[20] So the idea came to the Bucciardo clan to rout the competition. One could easily say that if Nicola Bucciardo had been promoted to the cardinalate, the patronage of the Sultan would have loomed over the Sacred College: a situation vaguely similar to the one the Greek Church had slipped into. In any case, we will need to refer to the manoeuvres between East and West again, hatched as they were, for different masters, in the house of the Bucciardo family.

These Bucciardo, whatever they might do, seemed to confirm the commonplace according to which the Genoese connived with the Turks. Had they not always provided the Mameluk army, the enemy of the crusaders, with fighting slaves? At the time of the Crusade of Varna in 1444, had they not ferried the Turks across the Bosphorus for money? Did they not systematically sell artillery and confidential information to the Turks? Had they not, from their colony of

17. See Heidenheimer, "Die Korrespondenz Sultan Bajazet's II", p. 525.

18. See Albanès, *Gallia christiana novissima*, vol. III, coll. 881-884; Zapperi, "Bucciardo, Nicola".

19. See Prosperi, "*Dominus beneficorum*: il conferimento dei benefici ecclesiastici"; Meyer, "Spätmittelalterliches Benefizialrecht".

20. See Ricci, "Cardinaux de famille".

Galata, followed the conquest of Constantinople with benevolent neutrality?[21] Yes, the slanderous accusation that many in Italy threw at each other also hung over Genoa and her citizens.

7. The authenticity of the most embarrassing letter of those intercepted by Giovanni Della Rovere, the one in which killing Cem is discussed, has remained in doubt.[22] The resort to Christian era dating, emphasised by some, is not of itself a proof of a fake. It could have to do with an adaptation employed by the translator to make the whole thing more easily understood or persuasive; the same can be said of the numerous stylistic incongruities. We should not look for respect for present-day criteria from a translation of the fifteenth century. This is a case where the exclusive philological trail takes us off course. And besides, we are well aware that between the totally genuine and the complete fake there is an infinite range of gradual variations.[23] But the letter corresponds too well to what the friends of France wanted to read and make public to discredit Alexander VI. And so a falsification carried out by the French party has also been envisaged. All the more because the original is lacking and we have only Giorgio Bucciardo's deposition, obtained under torture, and the Florentine legal translation. The question remains unresolved.

Precious indicators of general authenticity (and so not of the authenticity of the individual words), however, come from three Ottoman chancellery documents. They are the single, partial confirmation of this documentation on the sender's side, in the absence of systematic archives in Istanbul at that time. One document contains the report destined for the Sultan of the arrival of Giorgio Bucciardo in Istanbul. A second includes the summary in Turkish of the letter in Latin from the Pope, dated 28th June 1494 and delivered by Bucciardo: this summary does not contradict in any way the Italian translation circulated after the attack at Senigallia. A third document is the copy of the original letter in Turkish with which Bayezid asks for promotion to the cardinalate of the archbishop Nicola Bucciardo, to reward him for services rendered from the time of Innocent VIII.[24] The fact that this last is a lesser aspect of the Senigallia correspondence does not reduce its importance for the collection of papers as a whole. On the contrary, the detail could serve as a useful clue towards a more significant proof.[25] The remaining reasoning of those who reject these documents is based on moralism

21. See Bitossi, "Genova e i turchi", pp. 91-97; Pellegrini, *Le crociate dopo le crociate*, pp. 166, 261; Airaldi, "Oltre le frontiere".

22. See Pastor, *The History of the Popes*, vol. V, pp. 428-429; Picotti, "Alessandro VI", 197-200. Pfeffermann, gives a superficial reading of the affair, *Die Zusammenarbeit*, pp. 95-110.

23. See Eco, "Tipologia della falsificazione"; Caro Baroja, *Las falsificaciones de la historia*; Canfora, *La storia falsa*; *Épistolaire politique II*.

24. Topkapı Sarayi Müzesi, Arşiv, E 12294, E 7219, E 5456 (the latter reproduced in Ertaylan, *Sultan Cem*, p. 231). I thank Nicolas Vatin who generously supplied me with these documents.

25. See Ginzburg, *Clues, myths*.

(a sentiment that should be unknown to the historian) and on the not-altogether-convincing argument of *cui bono*, seeing as everything corresponds rather too well with the plan to harm Alexander VI.

Circulation of fake letters of the Sultan accompanied Charles VIII's Italian expedition. For example, a letter was printed in which Bayezid offered the French court his own daughter, "who has the same age as the Dauphin" as a bride. King Charles would in this way have had ("in restitution") Constantinople, all the lands of the Moors, Negroponte and the Holy Land, he would have received "the tribute of 100,000 ducats paid by Venice to the Sublime Porte", accumulating "so much money" as to be able to conquer "not only Lombardy but all the Christian countries".[26] They were the fables of French propaganda. But the fury of the Pope was authentic when he learned of the ambush at Senigallia, and Venice's disappointment was also authentic: there was something to hide in those papers. All the more because the papal bull of excommunication made no effort to declare them false, preferring instead to rail against the gesture of taking them and stealing the money.

8. The mysterious death of poor Cem followed. It occurred in February 1495 at Naples, under the conditions of partial freedom that Charles VIII had permitted him after he had taken him from the Pope with a perfectly formal agreement. With the skirmishes and hostile manoeuvres over, Rome and France had come to terms. The black legend of the Borgia, already flourishing at that time,[27] caused the rumour to spread that Cem had been poisoned on the orders of Alexander VI. He would not have wanted the Ottoman Prince, who was by this time beyond his control, to become the tool of the hated king of France. The attentive observer, Marin Sanudo first of all declared: "the thing was not credible, because it would have been to his disadvantage", to Alexander VI, we understand, and it is not clear why, unless it is to imagine that the Pope hoped to reacquire the hostage. Then Sanudo reports that "the French said that the Pope had had him poisoned, because *post mortem* signs of poison were found on his body". And he concludes, without taking sides: "let it be as people want it to be".[28] Faced with the doubts of Marin Sanudo, let us not attempt to reach a conclusion either.

At the end of the tale it is enough for us to know (and about this there are no doubts) that the Vicar of Christ asked the Sultan, the incarnation of the Antichrist, for help to stop the Most Christian King. The circumstances were certainly exceptional: it does not often happen that the brother of a sultan is a guest-hostage of the Pope while the king of France is all set to conquer Naples and leave for a crusade. On the basis of a documentary record that was less abundant than that available today, Ferdinand Gregorovius had reached the same conclusion. And this is that the veracity of Bucciardo's mission is "undoubted"

26. *La proposition faicte au pape*. See Del Balzo, *L'Italia nella letteratura francese*, vol. I, pp. 48-49; Le Thiec, "Le roi, le pape et l'ôtage", p. 75.
27. See Pastore, *Veleno*, pp. 17-18, 27.
28. Sanuto, *La spedizione di Carlo VIII*, pp. 244-245.

and that "the style of the letter of the Sultan, in which he proposes the murder of Cem to the pope, and promises him 300,000 ducats in return, does not appear genuine, but the contents are not surprising".[29] As far as Charles VIII's plans for crusade are concerned, these were soon forgotten: "and no more was there talk of setting out against the Turks, as he had always said at the beginning of this enterprise". Again, this is the voice of Marin Sanudo, who also reports the exclamation of the King when he, in Naples, came to know that Venice had joined the anti-French alliance agreed in March 1495 by the Italian states: "*por ma foi* [...] I would like the Turks to come to Italy!". To punish Venice, we understand, and perhaps other Italians as well, who by opposing the crusading king, effectively consigned themselves to the Turkish danger. Charles VIII had enjoyed the initial support of some Italian princes like Ludovico Sforza, Duke of Milan and Ercole I d'Este, Duke of Ferrara; he had cured crowds of scrofula sufferers in Rome and Naples, showing the miraculous healing power of French royalty; he had caused an unexpected liquefaction of the miraculous blood of Saint Januarius, making explicit homage to Neapolitan popular devotion.[30] But there was nothing to be done, the inhabitants of the peninsula had not allowed themselves to be convinced, and now they deserved their fate.

In the meantime, Apulia started to explode and many inhabitants asked to pass under the protection of Venice: "and if the Republic did not want to accept them, they would call on the Turks because they certainly did not want the French any more [...] who were lazy, dirty and dissolute people,".[31] The sense of superiority that Italy cultivated with regard to foreigners did not give an inch in the face of military inferiority. But, above all, for many Italians (the Apulians in this case) the Turks were preferable to the French; in the same way as for the Pisans the Turks were preferable to the Florentines. And to think that precisely at that time in Apulia the cult of the bones of the Eight-hundred Martyrs, who the Turks had killed, or were said to have killed fifteen years earlier, began to flourish.[32]

Everyone, finding themselves in difficulty, made appeals to the Turks; or at least, threatened to do so; or pretended to do so; or accused others of doing so.

29. Gregorovius, *History of the City of Rome*, vol. VII/1, pp. 365-366.

30. See Blanchard, "Political and Cultural Implications"; Bloch, *Les rois thaumaturges*, p. 242; Le Fur, *Charles VIII*, p. 353; Contamine, "Découverte et conquête"; Rubello, "*Una bella et caritativa cosa*. Épisodes de thaumaturgie royale".

31. Sanuto, *La spedizione di Carlo VIII*, pp. 266-267, 295, 344.

32. See Spedicato, "Il riscatto della cristianità offesa".

10. "The Turk seems necessary"

1. With the crisis of 1494-1495 over, there was a reversal in the position of Alexander VI. King Charles VIII, the enemy of the Turks, had withdrawn from Italy and now the French threat to Rome and Naples had disappeared. And it was the Pope himself, who up to this point had been sympathetic to the Turks, who was to promulgate the crusade. For him it was almost a return to his origins, if we remember that as Cardinal Roderigo Borgia he had contributed to financing Pius II's crusade. The religious occasion coincided with the Jubilee of 1500; military opportunity was given by a resumption of aggressive activity by Bayezid II in the Levant. The death of Cem had freed the Sultan from blackmail, as Marin Sanudo had already predicted in 1495: "not fearing for his brother anymore, he will turn against the Christians, that God would never want […] because his brother was a sufficient reason for the Turkish lord to be cautious".[1] The embalmed body of Cem had been consigned to a Turkish fleet that had arrived at the port of San Cataldo, near Lecce, in 1499. But long negotiations were required with the Pope and the King of Naples, who had both attempted to obtain money and even holy relics in return.[2] As soon as the Sultan had proof that Cem did not exist anymore, he had gone on the offensive against the Venetian possessions in Morea. The Republic, in order to defend itself, had been forced to accept an ideologically oriented alliance: something that it never liked. Various Christian sovereigns promised to join up and then, as per tradition, the alliance revealed itself to be merely a facade. But Louis XII of France committed himself genuinely to the crusade, desirous to reaffirm his credentials as Most Christian King against the Spanish monarchs who had just been promoted Catholic Kings. Always interested in developments in the northern Aegean, her traditional area of influence, the Republic of Genoa agreed to the alliance, while Venice promised much and kept little of these promises.[3] In spite of the support offered by the Knights of Rhodes, the enterprise petered out in 1501 with a defeat of

1. Sanudo, *La spedizione di Carlo VIII*, pp. 243-244.

2. See Vatin, "Macabre trafic".

3. See Heath, *Crusading Commonplaces*, p. 76; Vatin, "Le siège de Mytilène"; Dumont, "Entre France, Italie et Levant"; Airaldi, "Oltre le frontiere".

the French army on the Aegean island of Mytilene. A cutting judgement by Rabelais added the epitaph: "quand on alla à Metelin en la male heure".[4] It was one of the last times the king of France hurled himself against the Turks. Afterwards, a different and diametrically opposed story would begin: we shall see this later on.

The Mytilene Crusade was preceded by circulation of a prophecy written by a humanist from Udine, Girolamo Amaseo. The prophecy was published in Venice by Aldo Manuzio in 1499, with a dedication to the French ambassador to the Republic, Accurse Maynier. The prophecy foretold that France and Venice would conquer the Ottoman Orient and Asia ("En Veneti immixti Gallis navalibus instant/ praesidiis, turcasque fugant toto aequore naves") while Ferdinand II of Aragon, hero of the Spanish *Reconquista*, would complete the Christian victory in Africa. Later, in 1507, the prophecy was offered to Louis XII who at that time was in Milan.[5] Besides Amaseo's need to receive some kind of prebend, the prophecy gave expression to the hope to effect a rapprochement between the sovereigns of Spain and France whom the pro-Turkish policy of Alexander VI had pushed apart. It was a hope that was destined to be left unsatisfied.

2. As for the Papacy, the Borgia Pope confirmed that the Turkish card was always reversible: appeal to the Turks or make war on them? In fact, when the bad news from Mytilene arrived, Alexander VI despaired. This is recounted by the Florentine functionary and scholar, Agostino Vespucci, in a letter sent from Rome on 16th July 1501 to his friend Niccolò Machiavelli:

> The Pope does none other than think about this news of the Turks that has by now spread everywhere; and he groans and he says: "Heu que me tellus, que me aequora possunt accipere?". He doubles the palace guards day and night.

The Latin quotation (a little imprecise) comes from the *Aeneid*. It makes a reference to the moans given out by the fake Greek deserter Sinon when he was trying to convince the Trojans to take Ulysses' horse into the city. The solemn lines ridiculed the fear that the Turk might take advantage of the French defeat to land in Italy, forcing the Pope to roam as a fugitive by land and sea. False like Sinon, Alexander VI; and like Sinon guilty of wanting to introduce the enemy, the Turks, into the city, into the Holy City of Rome, even. Nevertheless, continues Agostino Vespucci, despite his anguish, the Pope never ceases to steal and rage together with "his illicit flock", while every evening "twenty-five women and more are brought to the palace [...] made into a brothel of every kind of filth"; and further in this vein with great tales of procurers and "whores". The inevitable conclusion: "The Turk seems necessary, since the Christians do not make any effort to remove this rottenness of human consorting".[6] And here was the *contrapasso* (fitting punishment): Alexander VI, he who had exposed himself most of all in the appeal to the Turk, now trembled at the thought of his

4. Rabelais, "Pantagruel", pp. 246-250, 262-267; see Glidden, "Ces paillards 'turcqs'".
5. [Amasaei], *Vaticinium quo praedicitur*, s.p. See Tognetti, "Amaseo, Girolamo".
6. Virgil, *Aeneid* 2 (II 69-70); Machiavelli, *Opere*, p. 34.

arrival. Meanwhile, those shocked at Borgia corruption only placed their hopes in the arrival of the Turk. This last was a rhetorical argument, perhaps: but doesn't rhetoric also contain a germ of reality?

"How are things going?" This was the question that went around Constantinople in the face of the convulsions of Italian politics. This politics was less and less decipherable after Charles VIII of France's invasion. "Italian affairs were at one moment rain and the next sun", a Venetian diplomat accredited to the Court of the Sultan prudently replied.[7]

7. Sanudo, *La spedizione di Carlo VIII*, p. 374.

11. The geopolitics of Ludovico il Moro

1. Venice was not only the unscrupulous accomplice of the Sultan, when this was rendered necessary; the Republic could also be the victim of Turkish-inspired manoeuvres hatched by other Christian powers. Following the suspicions against the Habsburgs and against the Count of Gorizia in connection with the Turkish raids in Friuli in 1477, here we have new material: not made up of suspicions, as previously, but of convincing documents. With the invasion of Charles VIII of France in 1494, Italy was transformed into a battlefield on which the national monarchies measured up their respective weights on a European scale. In this climate, danger hung over all the Italian States, and everyone sought help wherever it was to be found. The urgency was such that no one split hairs over ethics (which is not very surprising), or even over real, long-term benefit.

In 1498-1499 it was the turn of Ludovico il Moro to see if, in reality, "Italian affairs were at one moment rain and the next sun". Sforza was pushed into a tight corner by Louis XII of France. The king came into Italy claiming the right to possession of the Duchy of Milan through the female line, possession that the Sforza had usurped after the extinction of the Visconti family line in 1450. Talk of crusade, vaguer than that by his predecessor, Charles VIII, accompanied Louis XII's dynastic ambition: Constantinople, Jerusalem, who knew?[1] Venice supported France, wanting to have revenge on Ludovico, who had favoured Florence in the question of the possession of Pisa. The Republic, in addition, feared that Sforza would aim at recovering the eastern provinces of Lombardy that it had taken from the Visconti in the past. At least in order to keep the nearest enemy, Venice, at bay, Sforza thought up every possibility on the Italian chessboard. In the end, nothing remained to him but the weapon of desperation, agreement with the Turk. We should remember that Ludovico had anticipated this thinking at the time of Charles VIII's invasion, putting himself in Alfonso of Aragon's shoes: "I would not only call on the Turks, but the devil as well".

A chance event in his personal life seemed to favour Sforza: he had been left the widower of Beatrice d'Este, daughter of the Duke of Ferrara, Ercole I. And so he could propose to Bayezid II to take one of his daughters in marriage in exchange for Turkish military assistance. The Sultan was irritated because of events in Cyprus, where in 1489 Venice had managed to gain the crown of Caterina

1. Le Thiec, "De Milan à Constantinople".

Cornaro, widow of the last king of the Lusignan dynasty; for this reason, after the death of Cem, Bayezid pressed Venetian possessions in the Levant. Things would have been easier for him if the Republic had also been committed on the Italian front: this was the reasoning in Milan. Besides, inserting his blood into the Sforza dynasty could in future reveal itself as a good deal for Bayezid. The warm welcome recently accorded to the Turkish ambassadors in Milan constituted an adequate point of departure.

2. Once again, the solution to problems generated by masculine ambitions was to be searched for by means of the female route. Anthropology teaches that in traditional societies fundamental relations are mediated by the exchange of women; matrimonial reciprocity is not established between men and women, but between men, using women.[2] In the case in question, the nuptial transaction presented itself as of particular boldness from every point of view. However, it received the approval of Sforza's younger brother, the worldly cardinal Ascanio Sforza. At least, he said in the April of 1499, it would be possible to "keep a brake on the Venetians and oppose all their plans". And to the prelates who deplored the understanding between Milan and Istanbul, Ascanio replied by comparing it to the alliance between Venice and France; with the mitigating factor that the former had defensive goals, while the latter disrupted the peace when the jubilee of 1500 had already been announced.[3] Thus an old dream of the Sforza dynasty was resuscitated. Previously, in 1467, Galeazzo Maria Sforza had threatened to ally himself with the Turks to punish Venice, who was hurling Bartolomeo Colleoni's mercenaries against him;[4] this time, in 1499, Giovanni Sforza, Ludovico's cousin and lord of Pesaro, who guaranteed the Turks a harbour for landing in his city, also took part in the manoeuvre.

But it was all in vain. Used as he was to receiving these frantic letters, Bayezid must have judged it superfluous to expose himself in Italy so as to prevail in the Levant. Between 1499 and 1500, the Sultan took possession of the Venetian strongholds of Modone and Corone. They were known as the 'Eyes of the Republic' because they were situated on the point of connection between the Ionian and the Aegean seas, to the south of the Peloponnese, from where the routes for Crete, Cyprus, Alexandria and Constantinople radiated outwards. Lepanto also fell, the sentry of the Gulf of Corinth, the small Dardanelles, as they were then called; and Durazzo in Albania fell as well. Following these defeats, Venetian domination in present-day Greece was reduced to the fortified towns of Nafplio and Monemvasia, without the crusade called by Alexander VI managing to invert

2. Lévi-Strauss, *Les structures élémentaires*, pp. 155-168. Case studies in *Regine e sovrane*.

3. See Pellegrini, *Ascanio Maria Sforza*, pp. 684, 738-739, 780. The diplomatic narrative history is supplied by Soranzo, "L'arma della disperazione". In addition: Catalano, "La crisi politica e sociale", p. 499; Benzoni, "Ludovico Sforza", p. 440.

4. See Vaglienti, "Galeazzo Maria Sforza". pp. 400-401.

the tendency.[5] The letters of sympathy sent to the Senate by various sovereigns did not succeed in hiding the hypocrisy. An emissary of the Este family in Venice even had to deny a rumour according to which there had been celebrations in Ferrara with the pealing of bells for the beating suffered by the Republic.[6] Was it more the power of Venice rather than Turkish power that worried the Italian States? Italian civic pride and regionalism refused to lie down.

The same matters were being pondered over by another protagonist of the moment: the King of Naples, Frederick I of Aragon. He was threatened, like Sforza, by Louis XII's descent into Italy, again caused by French pretensions towards the Kingdom of the South and to the consequent crusade. In the July of 1499, chatting with the cardinal Ascanio Sforza, a Neapolitan ambassador declared bluntly: "We prefer the Turks to the French, because the Turks leave us in our homes, provided that we pay them a tribute; but the French do not do the same".[7] Besides waving the Turkish card one more time, the affirmation weighs up the advantages and disadvantages of submission to the Sultan: it is a real-time encapsulation of the much-debated notion of "Ottoman tolerance".[8] But then, Louis XII did not come down as far as Naples, Bayezid did not land in Italy, and Ottoman tolerance was not really tested in the peninsula.

Nevertheless, there had indeed been some contact between Naples and Istanbul. Alexander VI Borgia accused Frederick I of this, and, based on this pretext, he signed up to the Treaty of Granada between Spain and France which dispossessed the Aragonese king. In fact, on 1st February 1500 a Turkish diplomatic mission arrived in Naples with great pomp, but nothing was to come of it. On the contrary, if we listen to the words of the chronicler and witness, Giovan Paolo Certa, certain "men of authority" thought that it was all an act put on by the king: "only as a stratagem, he had people appear in Turkish style clothing, pretending that they were ambassadors, to give people to understand that he had not been completely abandoned and left on his own".[9] At this point, Turkish intervention in this situation was plausible… As for Alexander VI, who was so shocked by the idea, we know that he was far from being innocent in the matter.

3. All this activity did not prevent the Duke of Milan losing his throne following the Franco-Venetian offensive of the summer of 1499.[10] So Sforza crossed Lake Como and then, via the Valtelline and the Stelvio Pass, found refuge at Innsbruck under the protection of Maximilian I of Habsburg. The emperor was

5. See Sallmann, *Géopolitique du XVIe siècle*, pp. 70, 73; Fernández Lanza, "1500'de Türklerin Modon'u Kuşatmasi".

6. See Kissling, "Francesco II Gonzaga", p. 60.

7. See Pellegrini, *Ascanio Maria Sforza*, p. 741.

8. See Veinstein, "Retour sur la question"; Bear, Makdisi and Shryock, "Tolerance and Conversion"; *The Legal Status of ḏimmī-s*.

9. Certa, *Delle cose del Regno di Napoli*, pp. 15-16. See Galasso, *Il Regno di Napoli*, p. 151.

10. See Meschini, *La Francia nel ducato di Milano*, pp. 41-62.

occupied opposing the Swiss and so had not been able to help him, although he was in conflict with Venice for possession of the Patriarchate of Aquileia. Sforza realised at once that the promises made to him in Innsbruck about regaining his lands were just talk. And so he started to play his own game, in secret, in a way that was unlikely to meet with the approval of the Habsburg. "He started to manoeuvre in such a way that the Emperor of the Turks came to Italy against his enemies": thus reports a Milanese scholar and contemporary of the events, the notary Bernardino Corio. Now we shall follow his narration of events, as he shows himself to be very well informed on this point. Already a public official under Galeazzo and Gian Galeazzo Sforza, Corio was paid as a historiographer by Ludovico il Moro until his fall. His history was published in 1503.[11] He never disowned his master, as many others did. Thus Corio cannot be accused of using the subject of the appeal to the Turks to defame Sforza.

So Sforza went down from Innsbruck into South Tyrol, to Brixen, so as to be able to keep an eye on Italian affairs better. From there, on 9th November, he sent two of his trustees to the Orient, Martino Casali and Ambrogio Bucciardo (later named "Bugiardo" (liar) by an infuriated Venetian Senate). Here another Bucciardo enters the stage, another representative of the family that in those years filtered the most delicate relations between Italy and Constantinople. Just like the two we have already met (Giorgio and Nicola), Ambrogio was also able to speak Turkish and boasted high-level contacts with the Levant. It was not the first time that this Bucciardo had been on a mission to Constantinople. It appears that in 1496 the Duke of Ferrara, Ercole I, had sent him there with the task of inciting the Turks against Venice, who always threatened his possessions. However, we do not have any information about this further appeal to the Turks.

4. With the mysterious Ferrara phase over, Ambrogio Bucciardo entered the service of the Sforza. From that moment his comings and goings with the Levant became frenetic.[12] Ludovico il Moro sent him to Constantinople in 1497, and again in 1498. In the critical year for the Sforza territory, 1499, Ambrogio went to Constantinople as many as three times, each time in the attempt to involve the Sultan against Venice. Three journeys as long as these in such a short time were a real exploit. After leaving an Italian port, two weeks' sailing were needed to reach some landing place in southern Dalmatia, and another good two weeks to cross the Balkan interior to reach Constantinople. All in all, almost a month and a half for the trip out and the same for the return, not counting the stay, the wait for an audience and the unexpected obstacles caused by the conditions of the sea and the roads, attacks by pirates and plunderers, and the exactions of local authorities.[13] It happened that galleys went down, that emissaries perished, that letters got lost; and it was even deemed lucky when

11. Meschini, *Uno storico umanista alla corte sforzesca*, pp. 110-125.
12. See Zapperi, "Bucciardo, Ambrogio".
13. See Cardini, *In Terrasanta*, pp. 297-349; Dursteler, "Power and Information".

letters reached their destination “wet”, as occurred in Venice in 1499 with the news about the obsequies dedicated to Cem by Bayezid in Turkey.[14]

Geography, understood here as the time needed to overcome distance, was an independent variable that repeatedly struck at political activity. Relative blindness or the systematic delay in information affected everyone: indeed it was a system. However, it did not affect everyone with the same seriousness. Whoever, being weak, was on the defensive, suffered more from this than those who planned offensive or aggressive actions; and so in a general way, with notable exceptions, the Christians felt the effects more than the Turks. “Your present journey consists to a large extent in speed:” this is what Alexander VI underlined to Giorgio Bucciardo, ready to depart for Istanbul in 1494; “you will thus be urged both to go to the Turk and to return at once”.[15] Beyond an emissary’s ability to hurry, the space-time conditions remained. As Cardinal Giulio de’ Medici (the future Pope Clement VII) wrote in 1517, “the Turk will have taken some Christian ports before we receive the news that he has made a move”.[16] The anxiety was precisely in this: even though the threat was constant and ever-present, there was little that could be done to prevent it.

But let us return to Ambrogio Bucciardo and his intense diplomatic activity. Half-Venetian and half-Genoese, and so a sailor in his blood, in 1499 he succeeded in the enterprise of his several journeys. The third and final trip he made corresponds exactly to the desperate mission entrusted to him by the Duke of Milan.

5. As was the practice with Italian diplomacy,[17] Sforza’s two emissaries, Ambrogio Bucciardo and Martino Casali, were provided with instructions of which the historiographer Bernardino Corio quotes the “draft ”.[18] The Sultan was to be informed of the most recent attempts to make contact with him. These attempts had failed because the messengers had been “dogged three times by vessels of Venice”, so much so that now it had been decided to set sail from the secure port of Pesaro, controlled by Giovanni Sforza. The game of cops and robbers never ceased on the expanses of sea overseen by Venice.

It would then be necessary to explain to the Sultan how the loss of the state had come about, Sforza told his representatives, “and if not all in one go, then on several occasions”. Here the awareness shines through that in Topkapı Palace the ceremonial rule of brief speech, if not silence, held sway. No one could hope to receive long audiences or to deal with the affairs that pressed them in detail. So it was precisely the opposite of the culture of conversation that dominated the Italian and European courts.[19] At Topkapı the dragomans themselves, the Sultan’s

14. Sanudo, *La spedizione di Carlo VIII*, p. 350.
15. *Ibid.*, p. 45.
16. See *I manoscritti Torrigiani*, p. 205.
17. See Senatore, “I diplomatici e gli ambasciatori”, pp. 267-298.
18. Corio, *Storia di Milano 1499*, pp. 1629-1635.
19. See Visceglia, *Riti di corte e simboli della regalità*, pp. 148-150; Quondam, *La conversazione*.

interpreters, had the right to summarise the already brief words permitted to the foreign visitor. They were thus interpreters in the deepest sense of the word, cultural mediators more than simple translators, and theirs was a profession that was esteemed, and often hereditary.[20]

With the introductions complete, the instructions given by Sforza go into a detailed geopolitical analysis that the envoys were to attempt to present to the Sultan. The French, "naturally inclined to put Italy under the yoke", are convinced by this time that, should this attack go well, "then every other plan may easily be successful for them": the crusade, we should understand, or the conquest of the imperial crown of the Orient. The Venetians "have no less ambition nor courage than the King of France", as all their actions show. Rivals to the French in terms of pride, the Venetians now content themselves with joint ownership over Italy, but they are convinced that, "their signoria being immortal, on some occasion of the death of a French king or some other propitious chance event, they will be left the lords of the whole of Italy". The myth of Venice, expressed by institutional continuity never interrupted by crises of succession,[21] would, in short, support a project of hegemony in the long run.

Pope Alexander VI, "of a malignant nature that you know", joined the enterprise against Milan because he only thinks "of obtaining states for his sons in Italy". The Sforza does not equivocate in identifying nepotism as the main interest of the Borgia Pope. This merciless diagnosis was delivered by a Christian prince to the most powerful among the infidel sovereigns; who, far from being unaware of the concern of the Pope, had already made the most of it in 1494, when he had offered 300,000 ducats to the Pope for the murder of Cem. Like everyone else, Sforza had read the publication of the Sultan's letter that contained the proposal to assassinate Cem. Perhaps for this reason, he did not waste any time in discussing possible ideological objections on Alexander VI's part to appealing to the Turks. After the reciprocal advances of 1494 between Rome and Istanbul, it is clear that it was only a question of agreeing a price with the Pope for his consent.

The Duke of Milan lastly comes to the most recent developments. The Franco-Venetian offensive against Lombardy prevented him from sending a Genoese fleet to the Adriatic (Genoa was at that time subject to Milan). It was to have involved "six large ships with other smaller craft [...] in coordination with the Turkish fleet". In the absence of this naval enterprise and other acts of resistance, Louis XII had taken Milan on 6 September 1499. From there the King of France hastened "to make himself truly the lord of Italy". To block the French advance, there was nothing else to be done than press "robustly" on the Venetian front. This was how it would be done:

> We beg your highness the Sultan to blockade Venice by sea with a substantial fleet as soon as possible, but also to press her by land in Italy with huge forces. And these should be regular forces and not just raids, as has been done recently, because this would not be enough, but instead it is necessary to wage real war for three months.

20. See Rothman, "Interpreting Dragomans".
21. See *Venezia da Stato a Mito*.

6. What we have just read is the decisive passage. The Turk is called to war in Italy; real conflict, regular contingents, and not merely incursions. In fact, less than two months previously the most serious of the Turkish incursions that afflicted Friuli in those years had broken out. On 28th September 1499 ten thousand armed men had concentrated near Gorizia, supplied with ferocious attack dogs. They were sent by the *Sanjak-bey* (governor) of Bosnia, Iskender, a Genoese renegade who had forged a brilliant career. The date chosen for the mission, at the end of the summer and so of the season propitious for war, shows that the horsemen wanted to be quick, to raid and not to conquer. They were the land equivalent of the corsairs that infested the coasts, but in the meanwhile they kept Venice in a state of fear. After circumventing the Venetian fortifications on the River Isonzo without storming them, the Bosnians advanced on a fifteen-mile front, displaying hundreds of heads hoisted on pikes to the refugees holed up in the castles. When they withdrew, eight days later, the final tally was ten thousand people killed or captured, and a hundred and thirty-two villages burned.[22]

A huge disaster. And yet, another similar action "would not be enough", Ludovico il Moro urged: "war" is needed, and not one of a few days but "of three months". It was for this reason that he asked the Sultan to send twelve thousand men to Italy, "whom we shall meet up with in Friuli". The effective Franco-Venetian forces were calculated by Sforza at eighteen to nineteen thousand men: the Turkish contribution, united with the surviving Milanese forces would be sufficient to oppose them. At this point we "will do all that your highness desires", Sforza guaranteed. And the Sultan will understand "that there is no better way of realising great schemes than having at one's service the Duke of Milan, who is also the lord of Genoa".

The instructions also include precautionary measures. First of all, the code word of the mission was to be "Sforza, Sforza, Sforza", if the Duke ever had to send new messengers entrusted with news from Italy: certainly, no great effort of the imagination was made. He then goes on to the use of codes, an indispensable precaution to escape the surveillance of Venice. The letters sent by Ambrogio Bucciardo to Sforza from Scutari in Albania, during his second journey of 1499, had already been intercepted at Dulcigno (Ulcinj). The Sforza court's ability in writing codes has been demonstrated, but it was difficult to protect oneself, seeing as Venice was unbeatable in the art.[23] Correspondence in code was anyway subject to various kinds of interference. As an example from those years, the sisters Eleonora and Beatrice of Aragon, the one Duchess of Ferrara and the other Queen of Hungary, often failed to understand the letters they exchanged: either because the codebook had been modified without informing the other party, or because the only secretary capable of decrypting the code was absent, and so on.[24]

22. See Ricci, *I turchi alle porte*, pp. 26-28.

23. See Senatore, *"Uno mundo de carta"*, pp. 396-417; Preto, *I servizi segreti di Venezia*, pp. 268-279.

24. See *Il carteggio tra Beatrice d'Aragona e gli Estensi*, pp. 43, 194.

The aspects of espionage finished with, Sforza's instructions dealt with another delicate subject, the gifts to be offered of necessity to the Ottoman court. Again, the Duke displayed awareness of the rules in force there, and gave the task of apologising for the inadequate nature of the gifts sent: "we find ourselves where we are, away from home, without any income at all". To tell the truth, perhaps he really was aiming to economise because, in escaping from Milan, he had taken the Ducal treasure away with him. But if things were to reach a positive outcome, Sforza concluded, all the Ottoman dignitaries would not only receive honourable gifts; but they would also be "well remunerated"; in short, paid.

7. The makeshift gifts that Sforza destined for his Turkish interlocutors are not specified. We are well aware of the gifts that the Venetian ambassadors and bailes used to take to Istanbul, on the basis of an ancient experience of local tastes.[25] Instead, we are informed in a more incomplete way about the objects offered by the Italian dynasties.

If we want to form an idea about this, we can turn to a handwritten document of the Duke of Ferrara, Borso d'Este, dated 1464. This is a set of traveling instructions for two of his men sent to Tunis with the task of buying horses. The two brought various gifts destined for the Hafsid sovereign Abu Omar Othman: "things that here in Italy we use for our comfort, and according to the Italian custom". And here is the rather eccentric list, in which, nevertheless, objects that would be useful in war or for hunting predominate: eight embroidered silk caparisons for mules; two hunting horns; two golden silk game-bags; "a buffet of Murano glass"; twelve knives; two seats covered with gold brocade; a box with containers of ivory; two straw hats; twenty-five "large and fine" whole cheeses; a dozen flasks covered with gold leather; a sword with a sheath of gold silk; a dozen collars and chains for dogs. Similar objects were destined for the dignitaries of the court, but in proportion to rank. The important thing was that everything was presented "in such a way as to make a good impression".[26]

The list of gifts sent in 1488 by Lorenzo the Magnificent to the Sultan of Egypt, Qa'it Bey, to gain favour for a mission concerning Prince Cem: sixty-eight cloths, two pieces of brocade, velvet and silk, a decorated bed, a treasure chest and a mirror, both decorated with ivory.[27] Later on we will give an account of an ambassadorial mission sent by Frederick II Gonzaga in 1525 to Suleiman the Magnificent, again for the purchase of horses, and there we will find very similar gifts. The languages of the gift and of hospitality kept channels of communication open between the Christian and the Muslim worlds.[28] But it is true that in the moment of greatest difficulty in his life, Ludovico il Moro, short of money as he was, did not have the chance to present himself in an adequate manner.

25. See Raby, "La Sérénissime et la Sublime Porte".
26. See Foucard, *Relazioni dei duchi*, pp. 11, 13-14.
27. See Meli, "Firenze di fronte al mondo islamico", p. 253.
28. See Zemon Davis, *The Gift in Sixteenth-Century France*, pp. 138, 214.

8. The conclusion of the instructions given by Sforza to his men is an offer to the Turk to become his tributary subject. An offer that is technical and juridical, we might say: "If necessary, promise him a few thousand ducats to be paid as soon as we have regained our state, not once but every year, you will promise this and we will fulfil it".

Sforza does not specify his offer to Bayezid any better, in contrast with what Boccolino da Osimo had done with his numbered paragraphs. Deep down, he still hoped it would not come to this: "if necessary promise him …"; but in short, he is willing to do even this. We do not know the replies of the Sultan, who instead only continued to press Venice in the Levant. The year following this appeal to the Turk, in 1500, Sforza's Swiss mercenaries, with their pay in arrears, refused to fight on the battlefield of Novara. The Duke attempted to flee disguised as Swiss but, incapable of replying to a question in German, he was discovered and captured by the French.[29] The two emissaries of the Sforza, who had remained in the Levant out of caution, were later also arrested by Venice on their return to Italy. The Dukedom of Milan lost its independence forever. Sforza's isolation in the context of the Italian states had condemned him; but his ruin was also a sign of the Italian crisis in the face of nation states. While a part of Europe launched itself towards the domination and Christianisation of the world, a part of Italy was thinking of offering itself as a tributary of the Turk.

Piling one injury on top of another, Sforza's brother, Cardinal Ascanio Sforza, broke with Alexander VI and had to leave Rome to avoid the Pope's rage. The Borgia accused him of "inviting the Turk into Italy", to quote the chronicler from Cesena, Giuliano Fantaguzzi.[30] Secret connivance by the rulers of Mantua, Ferrara and Florence was also suspected: this was the climate in the Italy of the time. Alexander VI in person had done worse with the Turk, as we have seen, during the crisis of 1494. And in 1498-1499 he had also looked on the first anti-Venetian (and anti-French) manoeuvres attempted by Sforza in the East with favour; to the extent that Venice had threatened to request convocation of a general council, in agreement with the French Church subject to Louis XII, and to remove the Pope for the crime of simony. But by this time the Borgia Pope had changed his policy, and launched the crusade of 1500, and in any case on the subject of the appeal to the Turk he was the one to decide the hows and the whens.

The Duke of Milan's Ottoman plans, far from remaining secret, gave rise to a stream of popular rhymes of a derisory tone, in which the inevitable puns on the words Moro and Moors were not absent. This was mostly a Venetian phenomenon that the Republic's censorship willingly allowed to run its course.[31] The nickname Moro lent itself to jokes, whatever its origin had been: the colour of the person himself and of his hair; his habit of appearing accompanied by a black groom; the impulse given to the growing of mulberry that was known in Lombardy as *moron*.[32]

29. See Meschini, *La Francia nel ducato di Milano*, vol. I, pp. 96-108.
30. Fantaguzzi, *Caos*, p. 98.
31. Gürol, *İtalyan Edebiyatinda Türkler*, pp. 172-173.
32. See Benzoni, "Ludovico Sforza", p. 436.

Who knows? And, in any case, it is of no importance: Ludovico il Moro was ripe to be held up to ridicule, dark-skinned like Venetian painters depicted the Turks.[33]

Louis XII, after taking control of Milan, also denounced the scandal of the agreements attempted by the Duke with the Turks; he even accused him of attracting the Turks into Friuli. This was probably false, because the Turks had been familiar with the way to Friuli for some time. To underline his difference with respect to Sforza, the Most Christian King restored to the Knights of Rhodes, crusaders by profession, the Milanese possessions that the Sforza had taken from them.[34] The sovereign was about to depart for the Mytilene crusade, in which Venice did not participate; however calculated it might have been, his attitude had the semblance of coherence. And Louis XII's official historiographer, Jean d'Auton, repeated the concept in a bellicose poem of his: "Everyone is speaking of the agreements between the Turk and Ludovico"… ("Commune voix desclaire, à cri public, l'intelligence du Turc et Ludovic"…).[35]

9. The dossier of appeals to the Turk also includes the aspect of the *damnatio memoriae* against whoever gets himself caught in the act. Boccolino da Osimo had already experienced this by order of Pope Innocent VIII. Then it was Ludovico il Moro's turn, and that of his lineage. If truth be told, the great Italian families were happy to display coats of arms with references to Moors, black men, Saracens and Turks – all words that were vaguely synonymous at the time. Evidently the thing in itself was not considered defamatory, but at times ironic results derived from it. This was the case of the Ferrarese counts, the Turchi, lords of Ariano and Polesine. In honour of their name they delighted in every kind of Turkish object, from scimitars to salt sellers, and books on the subject. Meanwhile, however, between the sixteenth and seventeenth centuries some of their subjects became Turks in Tunis, that is, they converted to Islam, after being captured at sea. One of the apostates from Ariano, by the name of Francesco Guicciardo, found success on the Barbary Coast and became the famous corsair Alì raïs "of the Black Sea". His mother Lucia, who was left in his village, earned the nickname Mora, Moor: Mora because she was the mother of a renegade that she herself had visited in Tunis, while she was still a peasant of the Christian counts, the Turchi. It appears that no one was excessively shocked. And to think that her son's fast galley displayed a standard with the motto: "The Christian faith is false".[36]

Ludovico il Moro and Lucia Mora: two characters placed at the extreme ends of the social scale. If a blind eye could be turned on a peasant who had had dealings with the Barbary, the same could not be done with the ruler who had invited Turkish forces into Italy, and so the epithet of Moro became a heavy one to bear. Sforza had used it plentifully as long as things went well for him – but he never dressed up as a Moor.[37]

33. Kaplan, "Black Turks".
34. See Bognetti, "La città sotto i francesi", pp. 57-58.
35. Dumont, "*Les alarmes de Mars* de Jean d'Auton", p. 130.
36. See Ricci, *Ossessione turca*, pp. 83-94; Ricci, *I turchi alle porte*, pp. 83-84.
37. See McGrath, "Ludovico il Moro and His Moors", pp. 67-85.

Ludovico il Moro died in 1508, a prisoner in the French Castle of Loches, rejecting the accusation of having plotted with the Turk to the end. After mixed fortunes, his son, Maximilian, also called *Moro*, was restored to the throne of Milan by Emperor Charles V's Swiss mercenaries, who drove out Louis XII's army.[38] The adventure of the new Moro lasted until 1515, when his Landsknechts were defeated at Marignano by Francis I of France. Francis would not hesitate to transform himself from a crusading king like his predecessors into a close ally of the Turk, even capable of inviting him to France. But in the meantime he flung himself against the dynasty of the Sforza who (before him) had tried to appeal to the Turk.

10. In 1516, a precious manuscript copy of Psalm 26 (*Dominus illuminatio mea*) was created for Louise of Savoy, mother to King Francis I. The explanatory texts were prepared by the court chaplain, the humanist François Demoulins, while the author of the drawings was the Dutchman Godefroy le Batave.[39] An illuminated medallion is dedicated to every verse of the psalm and presents a recent event closely linked to the subject of the verse. In the centre of almost every scene is Francis I. Verse 2 shows the king on the eve of the Battle of Marignano. The sovereign in arms, standing, with the crusading standard in his hand and a sword, is identified by a very marked monogram: RF, or "Roy de France", or "Roy François". He is facing the Landsknechts led by two knights. These are the Swiss cardinal of Sion (Matthäus Schiner) and a character with black skin, Maximilian il Moro, transformed into a moor (fig. 4). The verse on the circular edge of the medallion reads: "Dum appropiant super me nocentes ut edant carnes meas", while the gloss by Demoulins explains:

> When the Cardinal of Sion, il Moro and the Swiss who came out of Milan advanced so far that their intention was understood, commending himself to God the king began to say: I take the cross in hand and prepare myself for defence.[40]

The assimilation of Maximilian il Moro and a Moor contrasts with the banner with the cross brandished by the king. Maximilian had already been represented as a Moor in the temporary decorative displays put up for Francis I's entry into Lyon in the July of 1515.[41] The appeal sent out to the Turks by the house of Sforza in 1499 was not forgotten by its enemies, even years later.

But who were these enemies of the Sforza? They were Venice and France. The psychological mechanism of projection translated itself into a language of political falsification: the more one plotted with the Turk, the more he accused others of doing so. For some time this had been true for Venice; and this was soon to apply to France.

38. See Schmidt, "Les Suisses en Milanais".

39. See Holban, "François du Moulin de Rochefort", p. 34; Fontaine, "Antiquaires et rites funéraires", pp. 335-336.

40. See Lecoq, *François Ier imaginaire*, pp. 205-207, 315-323.

41. See McGrath, "Ludovico il Moro and His Moors", pp. 85-87.

12. "Better the government of the Turk than of the priests"

1. Appeals to the Turk and proclamations of crusade: two diametrically opposed kinds of behaviour brush against one another strangely, as we have seen on several occasions. But in the era when the appeal to the Turk flourished most of all, the idea of crusade began to fade; the parabolas of the two phenomena were in a certain sense the antitheses of each other. As a consequence, the general political discourse found points of equilibrium that were more and more favourable to the Turk.

Even those who had been the principal beneficiaries of the crusades, the poor and rapacious lower nobility of central-western Europe, displayed "aversion" towards holy war by the end of the Middle Ages. At the same time, in Italy, popular novellas expressed an attitude tending to pacifism towards the Turks.[1] It is hardly surprising then that somebody reached the point of hurling explicit criticisms against the crusade. Recalling the enterprise promoted by Pius II in 1464, the Bolognese chronicler Fileno dalla Tuata did not hold his tongue: in his opinion, the people's money, "collected to set off against the Turks, remained here to fatten the wolves and pigs". Alexander VI's crusade in 1500, in contrast, unfolded right before the chronicler's eyes, and here the priests, "just so that the money comes in, absolve the living and the dead of unheard of sins". Crusades of the past and crusades of the present were all the same: "about this I do not want to say any more, I would have to write things about which I prefer to remain silent so as not to create a scandal".[2]

In the final analysis, it was a subject of unmentionable implications, the crusade. This was confirmed by the Venetian chronicler, Marin Sanudo, in relation to the debates that had accompanied Charles VIII's invasion in 1494. Cardinal *Gurcensis* (Matthäus Lang, bishop of Gurk) had made a concerted effort at the time "to support an expedition against the Turks". But why? "He did this because he was a poor cardinal and had little income; and so in preaching against the infidel a crusade would have been carried out, *ergo* etc.". The translation of this elliptical phrase, "*ergo* etc.": the poor cardinal would have gained by giving sermons for the crusade or taking part in it. It is hardly necessary to add that

1. See Hélary, "Le 'dégoût' de la noblesse française"; Tateo, "Crociata e anticrociata".
2. Fileno dalla Tuata, *Istoria di Bologna*, vols. I-II, pp. 315, 324, 434.

"on our side there was no desire to do it as there was peace with the Turk".[3] The people on "our side" who rejected the crusade were, obviously, the Venetians.

Marin Sanudo expressed the continuity of Venetian policy with the knowledge that he obtained from being a member of the oligarchy. The case of the Bolognese chronicler Fileno dalla Tuata was different. Possessing little education and almost ignorant of Latin, he gave voice to the peculiar popular anticlericalism, imbued with familiarity with the Church and mockery of it, that was deeply rooted in early Renaissance Italy. The scandals of the pontificate of Alexander VI Borgia had only magnified a preexisting negative stereotype.[4] "Better the government of the Turk than of the priests", a rebel declared to the Papal governor of Bologna before being hanged in 1508. "He was right, but it was not prudent to say it to him",[5] Fileno judiciously commented in his handwritten chronicle – and so it had remained until 2005. The words which George of Trebizond had been imprisoned for in 1466 ("how discontented the various peoples were"; the words that Boccolino Guzzoni had sent to Bayezid in 1487 ("how discontented the people subject to the tyranny of factions are" [chapter 8]); the words that Agostino Vespucci had written to Machiavelli in 1501 ("the Turk seems necessary" [chapter 10]); so these words were aired once again in the Bologna of 1508. One cannot say that the condemned man cultivated his thoughts in isolation. But let us preserve his name: Giacomo Rabuini, a tanner.

2. In the middle of all these, there had been a further pronouncement that was still more radical, even if it was drowned in a jumble of Latin verses and so destined for few readers. In 1489, in Florence, the aging poet Pacifico Massimi da Ascoli had published a collection of a hundred elegies (*Hecatelegium*, indeed) with erotic and vaguely autobiographical themes. In his wandering life as a man of letters, Massimi had also spent some time in Rome after 1476. There he had come into contact with Pomponio Leto, one of the members of the Roman Academy plot of 1468. Massimi also had relations with the main figure of the plot, Callimacus, although by then he was to be found in exile in Poland.[6]

The elegies printed in 1489 express a nonchalant eroticism, a strong anticlerical sarcasm, and an implicit naturalistic philosophy; all of this seasoned with recommendations to prudent dissimulation. Admiration for the religious virtue and military organisation of the Turks forms a part of this unconventional way of thinking. The corruption of priests, on the other hand, receives violent gibes: "you who have made a sleazy brothel of dominant Rome". Rome as a whore or a New Babylon was already a *topos* before Lutheran propaganda drew on it abundantly. There was no sanctimoniousness in these affirmations on the part of a man who lived an openly homosexual life, and who in 1501 escaped the persecution against

3. Sanudo, *La spedizione di Carlo VIII*, p. 265.
4. See Niccoli, *Rinascimento anticlericale*, pp. 49-78.
5. Fileno dalla Tuata, *Istoria di Bologna*, p. 529.
6. See Bacchelli, "Celio Calcagnini", pp. 127-131.

homosexuals promoted by Alexander VI (yes, by him indeed). Rather, there is the moralism of one who judges ecclesiastical hypocrisy as deserving of the severest punishment. And so here the scandalous invitation to the Turk to bring his army to Saint Peter's is introduced: "When will your horse graze on the altar of Peter and say with a human voice: 'make yourselves at home?' If the fates keep me in life, I shall see this, if we should give credence to destiny".[7]

We have become familiar with the appeals to the Turk, but we had never before read anything so extreme, certified by 'destiny' even; and we had never met an anticlerical message entrusted to a speaking Turkish horse. The idea of Turkish horses in Saint Peter's was not new, it is to be found in Burgundian political writings in favour of the crusade at the end of the fourteenth century.[8] In any case, even if Turkish horses did not reach Rome, the image was destined to last. On the eve of the Italian elections of 1948, the Jesuit Riccardo Lombardi (known as "God's microphone") was to see Cossack horses ready to drink water in Saint Peter's Square. Who knows if he was aware of having been anticipated by others.

3. Ten years after the memorable Bolognese hanging, and so in 1518, Fileno dalla Tuata heard tell that "the Turk wants to come to Italy". At the same time, the alarm echoes in Machiavelli's comedy *The Mandragola*, in which a woman pretending to be naive asks a monk of dubious virtue: "Do you think that the Turks will invade Italy this year?" To then add: "My word! Heaven help us, then, with those devils! I'm terrified of that impaling".[9] Up to this time there had been little joking about impaling. The chronicler from Cesena who had interpreted the War of Otranto as a punishment for the simony practised at Loreto – and so making a divine instrument out of the Turks – commented on the fall of Lepanto in 1499 like this: "It was said that in that war the Turks had many Venetian prisoners impaled [...] like they had done in Otranto when, having many Christians in their power, they impaled them all".[10] Did celestial vengeance on Christian sinners go as far as this?

Holding Ottoman organization in high esteem, Machiavelli played with the sexual fantasies produced by the Turks, revealing the ability to integrate sex and gender into the reflection that he was developing as a political analyst. And the political analyst devoted an empirical and historical approach to matters of the Orient, without being subject to stereotypes or myths based on providence.[11] The theme developed in this passage of *Mandragola* is the accusation of sodomy made against Muslims: sodomy in the generic sense prevalent at the time, referring

7. Massimi *Hecatelegium*, cc. n2*v*-n3*r* ("Quando tuus media Petri pascetur in ara / et voce humana: 'Sidite' dicet equus? / Haec ego, si vitam servat mihi Parca, videbo, / si qua tamen fatis est adhibenda fides"). Modern editions: Massimi, *Les cent élégies*; Massimi, *Les cent nouvelles élégies*; *Gay and Lesbian Poetry*, pp. 290-302.

8. See Paviot, *Les Ducs de Bourgogne*, p. 28.

9. Machiavelli, *The Mandragola*, p. 33 (III 3).

10. Fantaguzzi, *Caos*, p. 98.

11. See Ruggiero, *Machiavelli in Love*, pp. 109-141; Najemy, "Machiavelli between East and West"; Lavenia, "Turkophilia and Religion".

to anal coitus, both homosexual and heterosexual.[12] But while Machiavelli was amusing himself, others were involved in a serious way.

Just the year before, in 1517, the Fifth Lateran Council had come to an end in Rome. In that solemn session, Cardinal Egidio da Viterbo had reported a prophecy that predicted the imminent conversion of the Turks and the end of their sect, as was said at that time.[13] Almost as a refutation of this, the fall of Mameluke Egypt into the hands of the Ottoman Sultan, Selim I had suddenly occurred.[14] The greatest Muslim power was strengthened still further. Consequently, and with the conversion of the infidels being delayed, Pope Leo X de Medici had decided to initiate a large mobilisation. Beyond strategic considerations, the Pope had been alarmed by the secret despatches arriving from Constantinople via Ragusa (Dubrovnik).[15] In these there was talk of preparations for war in the Ottoman dockyards, while strange Turkish visitors (probably spies) were wandering around in the Italian ports. As if that wasn't enough, in 1516 the Pope in person had only just escaped a Turkish raid when he was hunting on the Roman coast.[16] Presumably the corsairs did not realise how great the target they had missed really was. As for us, we can scarcely even imagine the consequences of the capture of the Pope by infidels: it would require an entire book of counterfactual history.

Until then Leo X had derided the natural wonders that seemed to announce a Turkish invasion. On this topic he went against the prevailing sensibility that attributed an important role to signs in everyday prophecy: charismatic women's visions, evocations of spirits from beyond the grave, sudden winds, flowers and fruits appearing out of season…[17] And still going against the tide, but this time with respect to his experience, Leo X had believed Charles V of Habsburg's promise to put together a Christian league to regain Constantinople. Tired at last of continuous disappointments, in 1515 the Pope had written to Manuel I of Portugal that "the holy and necessary war against the Turks was in general fought with words and the pen rather than with deeds".[18]

Deeds, however, came in 1518, accompanied by significant exchanges of correspondence in code, and by the rehabilitation of the notion of the Christian republic.[19] On the date of 29th April, 1518, the Bolognese chronicler who holds our attention with his perceptiveness, Fileno dalla Tuata, records the arrival in his city of "three cardinals sent by the Pope to different places […] and they wanted to have money to resist the arrival of the Turk". To be precise, the three cardinals were Lorenzo Campeggi, legate to England; Bernardo Dovizi from Bibbiena, legate to France; and Egidio da Viterbo, whom we have already met, legate to Hungary.

12. See Ricci, *I turchi alle porte*, pp. 77-78.

13. See Cantimori, *Eretici italiani del Cinquecento*, p. 24.

14. See *Conquête ottomane de l'Égypte*.

15. See Pfeffermann, *Die Zusammenarbeit*, pp. 174-181; Niccoli, *Profeti e popolo*, pp. 110-114.

16. See Kempers, "*Sans fiction ne dissimulacion*", pp. 381-386.

17. See Casali, *Le spie del cielo*, pp. 195-197.

18. See *Notices et extraits des manuscrits*, p. 599; Bembi, *Epistolarum Leonis Decimi*, s.p.

19. See *I manoscritti Torrigiani*, pp. 189, 201, 205.

Bologna was an obligatory point of transit from Rome to the North; from this place the three prelates would separate. Furnished with a Papal brief and comfortably lodged in the city, the cardinals organised processions and had the most precious relics displayed. But all these initiatives appeared to be only "money traps" to the chronicler.[20] We should like to know whether this ferocious definition was popular as a cliché, or was of Fileno's invention. However, in keeping with tradition, this crusade would not be achieved, despite the offerings collected by the cardinals.

4. Fileno dalla Tuata did not miss the chance to criticise the great ecclesiastics. A couple of months before the cardinals arrived to preach the crusade, another cardinal had stayed in Bologna, one of the richest of the Sacred College: the Neapolitan, Louis of Aragon. It may be true that the cardinal was on a pleasure trip, patron and expert in art as he was, but it was Lent and that applied to him as well. Instead, the cardinal and his retinue showed off scandalously: "they did not eat, if not capons, partridges and pheasants, deriding the believers". You can be no clearer than that.

This is to say that our chronicler was not unaware of the seriousness of the Turkish threat. He lived in an inland city, Bologna, but the Turks (the Muslims) also threatened coasts like those of the Marches that were not so very far away. Still in 1518, on 4th June,

> it was known that five Turkish sailing ships attempted to enter the port of Recanati, but there was such a storm that they did not manage it, one of the five ships sank with all the crew, and then they took a village and sacked it and burned and killed all the inhabitants.[21]

Here the pattern of pirate incursions is presented: the failed attempt to take a small town, the port of Recanati, then falling back on a lesser settlement. In short, with the Turks raiding coasts of the peninsula that were too long to defend, there was little to laugh about, and Fileno knew it. And so how to explain his hostile attitude towards the crusade and his underlying sympathy for the Turks?

5. To attempt to find an answer, let us return to the proud Bolognese condemned man, the tanner Giacomo Rabuini. The tradition of invectives against clerical corruption offered a grounding for his declaration about the government of priests and Turks. No desire for religious apostasy accompanied such political conviction. In this sense, it appears that the tanner reasoned like the Christians in the East who were accustomed to say: "Better the turban than the tiara". The saying is documented, with formal variants and uncertainties of meaning, from the days of the siege of Constantinople. The tiara in question could be that of the Pope or the crown of the Latin Empire of Constantinople, founded after the

20. Fileno dalla Tuata, *Istoria di Bologna*, pp. 741-742.
21. *Ibid.*, pp. 737-738, 747.

Fourth Crusade in 1204.[22] Whatever it may be, the saying can be paraphrased in the following manner: it is better to be governed by Turks, who are willing to concede a statute to non-believers in return for tribute, than by the Catholics who are used to oppressing schismatics with conversion (in addition to tributes). The withdrawal of Venice from the Levant offers many confirmations of this attitude of the Greeks, whose faith, as a consequence, no Catholic could ever count on.[23] The sack of Constantinople carried out by the crusaders in 1204 remained (and still remains to this day) a bitter memory for Orthodox Christians.[24]

Nevertheless, in Bologna in 1508, on the day of a hanging, we have found the echo of such sentiments, even within the Papal States. Or to be more precise: the anticlerical hostility cultivated in some circles seems to be a stronger feeling than any fear of the Turk. Something very serious was boiling away in the depths of Italy, if Cardinal d'Aragona's excesses of gluttony elicited greater expressions of condemnation than did pirate attacks, with their trail of suffering and death. We note that the passage by Fileno dalla Tuata dedicated to the raid on Recanati is an account that is devoid of the deprecation which in this case would have been justified. Yes, something very serious was boiling away in the depths of Italy, where there were those who said that the Turks were less to be feared than priests, Venetians, Florentines and the French.

But this is not all. According to Baldesar Castiglione, in the Italian cities "an infinite variety" of clothing was to be found. Some dressed "after the French fashion", some "after the Spanish", and some even "after the style of Turks". This fad for foreign fashions, indicating the weakening of the identity of the country, was nothing other than an "augury of servitude".[25] Up to this point we quote the famous author of *The Courtier*, but an unknown Ferrarese chronicler viewed the subject in a more complete way. Concerning Charles VIII's invasion of 1494, the chronicler commented: "the people of Ferrara are almost all supporters of the King of France, and many go about wearing clothes, shoes and hats in the French style".[26] To such an extent that, with the return of the King to France, Duke Ercole I d'Este, even though he was a Francophile himself, would have to ban French clothes so as not to irritate the enemies of France. In the Italy of the wars between the European states, foreign clothing indicated a political affiliation, and not merely the superficial following of a fashion. If this applied to the French, (and certainly to the Spanish and the Germans as well), why did it not also apply in some measure to the Turks?

Indeed, the appeals to the Turks that we are analysing cannot be reduced to an accumulation of minor or curious incidents.

22. For the Papal tiara, Zachariadou, "Τα λόγια κι ο θάνατος"; for the Latin Crown, Reinsch, "Lieber den Turban als was?".

23. See Jennings, *Christians and Muslims*; Zachariadou, "Changing Masters".

24. See Gounardis, "L'image de l'autre"; *The Fourth Crusade Revisited*; Ravegnani, *Bisanzio e le crociate*, pp. 113-142.

25. Castiglione, *The Book of the Courtier*, pp. 102-103 (II 26).

26. *Diario ferrarese*, p. 171. See Ricci, *Il principe e la morte*, pp. 52-53.

13. Curious letters between Mantua and Istanbul

1. If the 'Turkophilia' spreading across Italy appears by now to be beyond doubt to us, it would be a mistake to think that it was the rule. But what was the rule? And was there a rule? The most important area of observation for us coincides with northern Italy. Here geographical contact with the Muslim world was less close than along the peninsula; indeed the flow of conversions to Islam was of a lower order, and from halfway through the sixteenth century the number of trials by the Inquisition for apostasy in favour of Islam was to be lower as well.[1] On the other hand, there were numerous rulers in the north of Italy that were actively involved in international politics; autonomous, but generally very fragile rulers who were thus forced by reasons of survival to develop unscrupulous strategies. As a consequence, if the more personal stories reach us from the south, from the north we receive the more political ones.

And so let us stay in the city of the chronicler Fileno dalla Tuata, Bologna. In 1507 the lord of Mantua, Francesco II Gonzaga, sent some of his Berber horses to Bologna to run in the Palio of Saint Petronius "and give honour to the feast". "Our Little Turk" (*Turchetto*) accompanied them".[2] From his name and profession one would say he was a young Muslim groom who was expert in that breed of horse. Characters of this kind, although perhaps not very common, were not so very rare either. For example, in Ferrara in 1559, during the celebrations for Alfonso II d'Este's instalment as duke, an entertainer called "the Little Moor of Lucca" (*Moretto*) performed. This Little Moor also used horses with professional skill: from a mounted position he hurled his "jokes" and then he rode off to yell them out again in another spot.[3]

But if the *Moretto* moved about without danger in Ferrara, employed as he was by the ruler of the place, the Duke of Este, the same could not be said of *Turchetto*, sent from Mantua to Bologna. On the contrary, the idea of his Little Turk being far away raised apprehension in Francesco II. The Gonzaga

1. See Tedeschi, *The Prosecution of Heresy*, pp. 41-42, 100-104; Del Col, *L'Inquisizione nel patriarcato*, p. LXX.

2. Archivio di Stato di Bologna, *Senato, Serie XI, Lettere di diversi da Genova, Milano, Venezia e Lombardia*, vol. 1 (1507-1553), Francesco II Gonzaga to the *Quaranta* of the City of Bologna, Mantova, 24 September 1507.

3. See Ricci, *Il principe e la morte*, p. 41.

Marquis worried how "our servant" would be treated; he asked the Bolognese Senate "that they would respect him, that no one would do him any injury or any insult". Evidently, a visibly Turkish person was not completely safe, even on the streets of Bologna where antipapal ill-will thrived; he was all the less safe during a period of feasting when inhibitions and exterior controls were weakened. The invocation of the Turk by the condemned man in 1508 did not sum up all the sentiments of the city of Bologna, and we are not able to say what the prevalent feelings were.

2. The Berber horses used in the Bologna Palio were the fruit of good relations that had been interwoven between Francesco II Gonzaga and Bayezid II. From 1491 to 1498 the two exchanged numerous letters; later the correspondence lessened, even if there were still ambassadors' despatches. And in 1494 the Turkish messenger, Kasım, robbed in Ancona by Giovanni Della Rovere, found a safe refuge at Mantua. He was also issued with a document of good behaviour, surely requested by him, seeing that the Sultan was not merciful to those who failed in the execution of his orders. The purpose was to certify to the exceptional nature of the ambush suffered in Senigallia. This is what Francesco II wrote to Bayezid on 9th January 1495:

> Cassim-Bey, your ambassador, has behaved faithfully in every circumstance and has done everything possible to him [...] all the more since by his misfortune things have happened to him that had never happened before in any part of Italy to an ambassador of the Great Sultan, as that name is inviolable.

Later in the same year, 1495, relations between the Marquis and the Sultan reached their peak. On 6th July Francesco II, as captain of the League of the Italian States, faced at Fornovo Charles VIII's army on its return to France (without annihilating it, however). The Sultan could do nothing other than rejoice at the blow inflicted on his French enemy, the one who was also planning crusades by exploiting the figure of Cem. Congratulations were written in Istanbul on 16th August 1495 by the inevitable Kasım, clearly entrusted with relations with the Italian courts: "having fought with the King of France [...] you have defeated him and killed a substantial number of French nobles [...] about which news everybody here felt great satisfaction". The request then followed about "the money and possessions" stolen the year before at Senigallia, whether a way had ever been found to get them back:[4] this was Kasim's personal torment. But the league between the Italian States also contained anti-Turkish currents and this, on the contrary, cannot have pleased the Sultan, who toned down his relations with Mantua. The Marquis, at that moment, must have judged his role as hero of Italy after the victory of Fornovo[5] as more profitable than the notoriety of being the Great Turk's friend.

4. In Ferrato, *Il marchesato di Mantova*, pp. 4, 6-7.
5. See Chambers, "Francesco II Gonzaga"; Bourne, *Francesco II Gonzaga*, p. 366.

Everyone knew about the link between Francesco II and Bayezid II: "a very good friend of the Turk" – is the comment of Marin Sanudo – "and they often exchanged gifts as a sign of friendship".[6] On his own part, Alexander VI's son, Cesare Borgia, known as *Valentino*, tried to insinuate himself into this friendship. At the highpoint of his attempt to create a state for himself, in 1503, the Valentino sent an emissary of his, a certain Stefano, to confer with the Sultan. There would have been nothing particularly harmful in this, everyone did it, if it hadn't been for the fact that the mysterious Stefano presented himself as a Mantuan ambassador. This character was recognised at Adrianopolis by acute Venetian representatives and arrested at Ragusa (Dubrovnik) on his return journey. In short, for reasons that remain unclear, Valentino attempted to sully Turkish-Mantuan relations that were already of themselves not very clear. The wide spaces and slow developments of the era easily permitted such deceptions and confusions of identity.

3. The origin of the friendship between the Sultan and the Marquis of Mantua was to be found in the Gonzaga's desire to obtain Turkish horses. They were symbols of wealth and status, these horses, and various courts competed to display them and to cross them with local specimens. In Mantua, horses were also indispensable for the effective functioning of the mercenary army of the Marquis, a war leader upon whose earnings a substantial part of the State's budget was based.[7] Precious economically, and replete with symbolic value, horses could become the target of assassination attempts: in 1501, for political reasons or as personal revenge, an employee of the Gonzaga stables poisoned numerous animals and then escaped.[8]

The Gonzaga, like the Este, and like other Italian princes of the time, also used Turkish or Arab horses as gifts to make to other Christian sovereigns, or even to bequeath to them in their wills.[9] But while the Este tried to obtain them most of all from the Berber lands, the Gonzaga looked directly towards the Ottoman Empire, even if not always to Constantinople: sometimes it was sufficient to go to frontier provinces in Bosnia and Albania. The Medici of Florence, on the other hand, perhaps because of the urban and not feudal nature of their new power, maintained a less intimate relationship with horses. But Lorenzo the Magnificent also had his well-supplied stables. In these a groom by the name of Andrea del Fede was responsible for the Berber horses, who now and again a certain Martino d'Arezzo looked after. We also know the name of the best horse of Lorenzo's Berbers: Orso.[10]

6. Sanudo, *La spedizione di Carlo VIII*, pp. 125, 287.

7. See Belfanti, "I Gonzaga signori della guerra"; In general, Roche, "Les pouvoirs à cheval".

8. See Kissling, *Sultan Bajezid's 2. Beziehungen*, pp. 47-49; Kissling, "Francesco II Gonzaga", pp. 61-63.

9. See Ricci, *I giovani, i morti*, pp. 131-133.

10. See Martelli, "Nelle stalle di Lorenzo", pp. 279-280, 299.

Exports of strategically valuable goods like horses were forbidden by the Ottomans. If one did not resort to smuggling, only high-level agreements could get around the prohibition. Even the Knights Hospitaller of Rhodes, who were just opposite the Anatolian coast, were often forced to obtain stocks from remote Christian lands.[11] In exchange for horses, money was offered to the Turks, but also saddles, textiles and other luxury goods of Italian manufacture; or a sort of bargaining was undertaken using arms and military equipment produced in Christian countries. The exportation of these to Muslim countries was likewise forbidden, or at least it was discouraged by legislation. But in one way or another, princes managed to complete their transactions without getting themselves into trouble. The only ones to pay were socially weak subjects: like the Jew Jacob Gabbay, hanged in Ancona in 1546 for ordering four thousand swords in Brescia to sell on in the Levant.[12]

4. Besides talking about horses, the two sovereigns, Francesco II Gonzaga and Bayezid II, began to exchange news about the political and military events of the time. And here the register changes. A Gonzaga embassy to Constantinople of 1492, in addition to buying horses, had already been supposed to report "certain things and events" to the Sultan. With all written specifications missing, we can only deduce that they must have been delicate issues. In 1493 the Turkish messenger, Kasım, visiting Mantua, returned home with "certain words" to take back to his Great Lord. At the end of the same year, a Mantuan messenger went to Istanbul to carry out "matters entrusted to him", and if this merely had to do with horses there would not have been so much elusiveness. Halfway through 1494 Kasım reappeared in Venice, and from there sent the Gonzaga Marquis forty horses, four of which were gifts, and a precious relic: a shirt supposedly belonging to Jesus Christ. The treasure trove of Christian relics concentrated in Constantinople was by this time available to be used for the Sultan's political activities. In the October of the same year, 1494, the Marquis let the Sanjak of Valona have various items of military equipment for the imminent struggle against the King of France. An outpost pointing towards Italy, both for invasion and to be invaded, Ottoman Albania was fortifying itself in expectation of the French advance. Immediately afterwards, the Sultan wrote to the Marquis with a rather impatient tone, asking him to let him know "what was happening in Italy", and then again "the whole story about his brother".[13] In Constantinople they judged that in Mantua they knew something about Cem's movements.

Naturally we should not exaggerate the intensity of the Turkish-Gonzaga friendship; the warm expressions that are to be found in the Italian translations of the letters correspond to stereotypical formulae of the Ottoman chancery. But we

11. See Luttrell, "The Hospitallers of Rhodes", p. 113; Fleet, *European and Islamic Trade*, pp. 29-30.

12. See Vernelli, "La paura degli 'infedeli'", p. 173.

13. See Kissling, "Francesco II Gonzaga", pp. 38, 41-45, 49.

shall see that this friendship continued to be remembered by the Turks decades later, and so it must have meant something. And then again, beyond any verbal ceremonial, concrete facts are not lacking in the story.

5. A first event occurred in July 1493, and is connected to a visit by Kasım. Marquis Francesco II received two paintings from him, two portraits: unusual gifts, seeing as, if anything, the flow of paintings went in the opposite direction, from the West to the East. The sender was Bayezid in person, a Sultan who was so obedient to Koranic law as to have had the collection of paintings belonging to his father, Mehmed II, dispersed. Perhaps with his gifts the iconoclastic Sultan thought he might obtain a double advantage: he got rid of religiously embarrassing objects and remunerated the Marquis of Mantua. But what was he paying him back for? The date and other circumstances point in one direction: it had to do with yet another attempt to take Cem's life. The Gonzaga court might have colluded for money, going along with what had become an obsession for Bayezid. Charles VIII's invasion of Italy was approaching, and management of the prisoner-guest was becoming a more tense affair. In fact, as we know, Cem did not have much longer to live. As for the two pictures, one represented none other than Cem himself, and the other, the Mamluk ambassador to Rome: "a painting of the likeness of the Turk who is in Rome, and of the ambassador of the Sultan of Egypt". The combination of the two subjects seems strange: the hated half-brother, a rival for their inheritance, and the representative of the hated Mamluks, rivals for hegemony over the Muslim states. We can hypothesise that the portrait of Cem was supposed to help an assassin to recognise him. But was the Mamluk ambassador, who was intriguing to have Cem handed over to him, also in the Sultan's sights? Who knows? After passing to the ownership of Andrea Mantegna, the two paintings are untraceable.[14]

A second event was of the year 1510. Francesco II Gonzaga found himself a prisoner in Venice after joining the coalition against the Republic solicited by Pope Julius II (the League of Cambrai). He was kept for many months in humiliating conditions, which he was unable to resist with great dignity; and further, he had not been captured on the field of honour, but ignominiously, while he slept. At this point, his wife, the vigorous Isabella d'Este, set herself in motion to obtain his liberation.[15] Louis XII of France did not want to commit himself in favour of Gonzaga. Isabella also turned to Julius II, whom the Marquis was serving when he had been captured; and she sent a letter to Constantinople, to the Sultan, who was busy however dealing with a situation of internal chaos. With the delay in the result she sought, Isabella could find no other alternative than appealing to the Sanjak of Bosnia, Feriz bey, so he would intercede with Venice in her favour. Feriz bey had been the Sultan's ambassador in Mantua, where they had smothered him

14. See Kissling, *Sultan Bajezid's 2. Beziehungen*, pp. 22-23, 35-36. Other information in Ferrato, *Il marchesato di Mantova*, pp. 12-13.

15. See Mozzarelli, "Lo Stato gonzaghesco", pp. 402-405; Benzoni, "Francesco II Gonzaga", pp. 778-780.

with attention and gifts. Then, having become the Sanjak of Scutari in Albania, Feriz bey had filtered various embassies of the Gonzaga into the Orient, always addressing the Marquis as "dearest and most beloved brother". Now, from Bosnia, the Sanjak had just offered a hundred armed men to Venice, under pressure from the disaster of Agnadello – which we will talk about a little later on. For this reason he was a reliable intermediary between two friends (or two non-enemies) of the Turks, Mantua and Venice, who were momentarily at odds with each other. And so Francesco II regained his freedom from Venice. He regained it not with the intercession of the Pope or the King of France, his powerful allies. He regained it thanks to Feriz bey, the governor of that very Bosnia from where disastrous raids had swept over Venetian Friuli – and more of these raids were feared.

6. At this point suspicions and pieces of evidence against Francesco II Gonzaga multiplied. Let us add that the Marquis engaged a certain Silvestro da Lucca to teach him the rudiments of the Turkish language. In the autumn of 1493, the teacher prepared a list for him with "most of the verbs necessary" and "most of the nouns [...] to learn Turkish". Thus the same Silvestro declared in asking for payment for his lexicographical efforts. And then the Marquis imposed on his men the battle cry: "*Turco! Turco!*".[16] Perhaps he chose the cry merely to stimulate them to combat and to frighten the enemy by evoking the proverbial Ottoman pugnaciousness. It remains a fact that with that cry, the Italian allies, led by Gonzaga, had the better of the French at Fornovo in 1495: the French who aimed at Constantinople and Jerusalem.

Immediately after the Battle of Fornovo, a Venetian humanist resident in Mantua, Robilio Vitelliano, dedicated a panegyric in verse to the friendship between the Marquis and the Sultan (*Libellus de amicitia Francisci Gonzagae et Belzeti Turcorum imperatoris*). The mangling of the name Bayezid into "Belzetus", in its uniqueness, shows just how far the author was from the corridors of power; besides this, the poem is without usable historical content. In an atmosphere of marked francophobia, there remain, however, lines such as the following: "Francesco loves Bayezid, and Bayezid has recognised/ that Francesco loves him" (*Belzetum Franciscus amat, Belzetus eundem / vidit amatorem*).[17] Such was the situation in the Italy of 1495: they sang the praises of Francesco Gonzaga's love for Bayezid while the Most Christian King Charles VIII was lashing out against him. The assonance, which we may presume was involuntary, between "Belzetus" and Beelzebub, between the Sultan and the prince of evil spirits, caused no embarrassment.

Later, however, things became more complicated in Mantua. It happened well before we reach 1552, when a collateral member of the dynasty, Lucrezia Gonzaga, invited Suleiman the Magnificent to Italy to solve a personal problem of hers. We shall devote an entire chapter to that episode. But indeed earlier than this, in 1526, we find a strange letter sent by Suleiman to Francesco II's son and heir, the Marquis Federico II Gonzaga. We shall also examine this letter very soon.

16. See Kissling, *Sultan Bajezid's 2. Beziehungen*, pp. 25-26.
17. *Ibid.*, pp. 110-111.

14. Venice the "concubine"

1. In 1508, the condemned man who was about to be hanged in Bologna, Giacomo Rabuini, allowed himself the freedom of a man with the noose around his neck. But the comment that the chronicler gives him ("he was right") is much more surprising. It opens a peephole into a popular subterranean sentiment that we can only record the existence of, without evaluating how widespread it was. The year after this intense episode, Venice also found herself with a noose around her neck, at Pope Julius II's behest, and she also started to weigh up the Turkish card. The hangman in this case was the League of Cambrai; the gallows was the defeat of Agnadello of 14th May 1509.[1] While Venice's possessions on the *Terraferma* (mainland domains) were dismembered, cancelling out all the conquests of the previous century, some senators, the younger and more pragmatic ones, proposed inviting the Turks into Italy as allies. Here we are not dealing with mere suspicions as in the times of Otranto, but with proof, certified by votes and official documents.[2] An enemy of the Pope, the Republic, and thus the Sultan's friend? Yes, or then again, no, depending on single moments in history and on the forces active in each given context.

On the other hand, the warlike Julius II, a dyed-in-the-wool Francophile, instead of hurling himself against the Turks, as he had often declared he would, had preferred to fling himself against the city of Saint Mark. He had done so with a peculiar justification: in order to promote the crusade in a serous way, first it was necessary to strike at Venetian ambitions. Otherwise, he said, Venice would profit from the distraction of the powers committed to the Orient to increase her area of domination in Italy. Julius II's bull of excommunication against Venice of 1509 was printed in the vernacular, accompanied by a crude woodcut. This represented the Pope in majesty while he had the warning delivered to the Doge and to two senators dressed in a vaguely Moorish style. In short, it was suggested that against a state that was so sympathetic to the Turk, and almost Turkish itself, every spiritual and worldly weapon became legitimate. This was suggested in the vernacular, with the help of images, so that everyone might understand. As was the custom, Venice reacted by threatening to appeal

1. See Alazard, *La bataille oubliée*.
2. See Preto, *Venezia e i turchi*, pp. 36-45; Pedani, "Venezia e l'Impero ottomano".

to a General Council.[3] But in the end it was the peasants and simple people of the *Terraferma* that were to save the Republic from the threat. To the shout of "Mark! Mark!" they reaffirmed their loyalty, in contrast to the ambiguities or the volte-faces of local aristocrats who wanted to return to the ancient city-states.

2. From his point of view, the Pope was not incorrect in his rather specious anti-Venetian reasoning. At that moment, siding with the Republic meant, in one way or another, mentioning the Turks. After Agnadello, Venetian Lombardy was left under the control of enemy armies up until 1516, while popular insurrections in favour of the Most Serene Republic multiplied. In 1512, the city of Bergamo, after a short-lived expulsion of the French, was occupied by people from the mountains who had come down in arms from the neighbouring valleys. In direct contrast to the city authorities themselves – that is to say, the aristocrats and the bourgeoisie – the people from the mountains went up and down the streets crying in rhymes: "Mark! Mark! Turk! Turk!" (*Marco! Marco! Turco! Turco!*).[4] This is the up-dated version of the most famous cry of 1509. The Turk was not only the official enemy whom Saint Mark the Evangelist guarded against, sculpted in the form of a lion on the fortresses of the Venetian Levant.[5] Translated into iconography, state ideology imposed these shows of strength. But in reality the Turk was also a guarantee of protection for the Republic of Saint Mark that the Christians wanted to crush. For this reason, in Bergamo in 1512 they invoked Saint Mark (Venice) and the Turk together; or perhaps, Saint Mark was being urged to invoke the Turk without hesitating any longer. These mountain people were turbulent and wild, according to the image that people of the cities and the plains had of them:[6] and it was precisely for this reason that they were capable of shouting out what others perhaps did not dare to.

Despite the pressures coming from the *Terraferma* in the dramatic months after Agnadello, Venice did not take the decisive step of appealing to the Turks, because she did not dare to, or did not trust them. But if the affair stalled, it was also due to Bayezid II's unexpected hesitations. While the negotiations with Venice were on-going, a series of earth tremors rocked Constantinople. The plaster that had covered the Byzantine mosaics of Hagia Sophia since the time of the conquest fell off, revealing the grandiose figures of the Evangelists; and a tidal wave submerged the coasts of the capital.[7] The old Sultan was afraid that he had provoked divine rage with his offers of help to the infidels: the culture of premonitions flourished among the Turks no less than among the Christians. And in addition, Bayezid's heirs were already competing for the succession, making the internal situation of the empire unstable. And so Istanbul did not move its armies in favour of Venice.

3. Rospocher, *Il papa guerriero*, pp. 120-128; Seneca, *Venezia e papa Giulio II*, pp. 103-138.

4. See Arcangeli, "Note su Milano", pp. 149-150.

5. See Rizzi, *I leoni di San Marco*.

6. See Cherubini, *L'Italia rurale*, p. 123.

7. See Pedani, *Venezia porta d'Oriente*, pp. 61-62.

3. Lesser things did occur however. The Sanjak of Bosnia, Feriz bey, mediator for the liberation of Francesco II Gonzaga and personal friend of the Venetian nobleman Girolamo Zorzi, allowed the enlistment of a hundred horsemen in his lands. Apart from this, with official military assistance coming to nothing (or perhaps never actually requested), Venice did not refuse the supplies of grain and horses offered by the Turks. Sending arms was again discussed with Bayezid's son and successor, Selim I, even by making use of the Friuli route that the Turks were familiar with; and in this the Republic was playing with fire. In the end, in 1513, the softening of the international stranglehold on Venice caused all plans for Turkish aid to be suspended.

From here on, Venice, incapable of defending herself in the East and even vulnerable in the Adriatic, her own "gulf", assumed more and more unscrupulous modes of behaviour. In Rome this was recognised with resignation. With peace restored between the Papal State and the Republic, in 1515 Leo X asked the Doge Leonardo Loredan to help him arm the galleys in Ancona that were fighting against the "raids and incursions" of corsairs. The request was part of a plan to fortify the coasts of the Marches in defence of the Madonna di Loreto and its treasure:[8] we might remember that Boccolino da Osimo had also been concerned about the safety of the sanctuary. But Venice-Turkish relations were delicate terrain, for which reason the Pope added: "We are well aware that in virtue of the treaties that tie you to the Ottoman Sultan, you cannot undertake any activity against him in the full light of day." Leo X's disappointment with this limitation cannot have been too great, because at the same time he asked the Doge Loredan to look for "certain Greek books which I don't have". Thanks to a colony of Greek émigrés, Venice had become the main market for these "books", which are to be understood as handwritten codices.[9] In short, in the same letter from the Pope, starkly differing needs were mixed: naval armament and the hunt for manuscripts. It is not a letter that brings dishonour to the person who wrote it, even if there were those who criticised the resources the Medici Pope diverted from the crusade towards art and culture.

Two years later, in 1517, Cardinal Giulio de' Medici, a cousin to Leo X, sent the Bishop of Pola, the Apostolic Nuncio in Venice, a despatch that was very understanding about the Republic's motives. The subject of the letter was the plans for crusade that were being aired after the Ottoman conquest of Mamluk Egypt, and Venice's great caution on the matter:

> The Republic has always maintained that she cannot compromise herself, if the enterprise does not really come about. Because she would be left abandoned by the others, having a substantial part of her state nearer and more exposed to danger than the others.[10]

It was inevitable that it was like this, the Cardinal intimated; the geopolitics of the Venetian territories was not open to debate, we might add, as some

8. See Renzulli, "Loreto".

9. Bembi *Epistolarum Leonis Decimi*, s.p. (3 July 1515). See Canart, "Jean Nathanaël", pp. 417-437.

10. "I manoscritti Torrigiani", p. 203.

contemporaries, such as the humanist Paolo Giovio, also believed.[11] And so, at the moment in which Turkish military pressure was growing, Venice continued to promote intense commercial and cultural exchange with the Ottoman Orient,[12] tearing herself apart every time she had to decide between peace or war with the Turk.[13] On many occasions, Venice behaved in such a way as to create an image of herself that spread throughout Europe. "True procurers of the Turks and protectors", "precursors of the Antichrist and procurers of Mehmed", the Venetians, according to French publicists, before Francis I allied himself with the Turk.[14] Spanish diplomats were even less tolerant, they became furious, calling Venice "concubine" or "kept woman" (*amancebada*) of the Sultan. Francisco de Quevedo was to echo this literally in 1617: "indignación contra Venecias [...] que estaba amancebada con el Turco".[15]

Added to this slanderous epithet was the fact that Venice was the only city in Europe to have an Arab name, independent of her original name. Here it is, whatever its controversial origin might be: *madînat al-bunduqiyya*.[16] Deaf to Spanish accusations and incapable of facing the Turks on the open field, Venice tended merely to slow their advance, without however ceasing to keep a watchful eye on her uncomfortable neighbour with diplomacy and espionage. The existence of a Venetian mercantile community in Constantinople produced interactions that neither side neglected.[17] However, there is still a need to interpret the gap between the abundance of manufactured goods exchanged and the ambiguity of texts in which everything, and the contrary of everything can be found: peace and war, alliance and suspicion, curiosity and rejection. Almost as if events occurred independently of words.

11. See Pujeau, "Messer San Marco", pp. 279-288.

12. See *Venezia e Istanbul*; Howard, "Cultural transfer".

13. See *1509-2009, l'ombra di Agnadello*; Poumarède, "Le patriciat vénitien".

14. See Dumont, Lilia florent. *L'imaginaire politique* pp. 315-316; also Rospocher, *Il papa guerriero*, pp. 267-273.

15. See Preto, *I servizi segreti di Venezia*, p. 117; Cappelli, "'La república de Venecia…'", p. 267.

16. See Pedani, *Venezia porta d'Oriente*, pp. 243-244.

17. See Valensi, *Venise et la Sublime Porte*; Andretta, *L'arte della prudenza*, pp. 105-137; Dursteler, *Venetians in Constantinople*; Doumerc, *La paix a-t-elle un prix?*.

15. Mantua-Istanbul, again

1. A letter from Suleiman the Magnificent is not something to be taken lightly. And so here is the genesis of the letter from the Sultan to Federico II Gonzaga, the existence of which we have already mentioned.[1] In the year 1525 the Marquis sent his chancellor, Antiacono Marcelli, better known as *Anconitano* (the Man from Ancona), to Istanbul on two occasions. The intention was the same as ever, buying horses. *Anconitano* had already brought them back previously from Ragusa (Dubrovnik) and other places in the Levant. We can certainly say that negotiations about horses took a privileged position as a form of contact between Christian Europe and the Muslim world. This produced consequences of an artistic order in many places. This can be seen, for example, in Ferrara, the other Italian feudal principality that had a love for horses from the East. The only two equestrian statues that the Este dedicated to themselves (Niccolò III in 1451, Ercole I in 1500) have now disappeared; however it seems that the horses represented were indeed from the East.[2] In Mantua on the other hand, the presence of imported animals in art is still visible to our eyes.

First of all, the six war horses, painted in *trompe l'oeil* by Giulio Romano in a room of Palazzo Te, known appropriately as the Room of the Horses, stand out. These are animals coming from the East and not references to classical models (fig. 5). Next to two of the horses, the script with their names has remained legible: *Morel Favorito* ("Favourite Black") and *Dario*. The pictorial sequence was completed in the years 1527-1530, when importation of horses from the East to the Gonzaga court was flourishing.[3] Around sixty years earlier, by contrast, the charger painted by Mantegna in the *Camera degli Sposi* in the Ducal Palace, rather brings to mind the equestrian statue of Marcus Aurelius in Rome: there is little of the East involved here.[4] The East is significantly involved, on the other hand, in the work of a mysterious Filippo Orso, or Urso, "pictor Mantuanus" ("Mantuan painter") as he described himself. Orso is known above all for having been the first specialist in the depiction of armour, hilts, swords and horses. An

1. See Römer, "À propos d'une lettre de Soliman", pp. 455-463.
2. See Rosenberg, *The Este Monuments*, pp. 50-82, 153-172.
3. See Farinella, "Vizi privati e pubbliche virtù".
4. See Jardine, Brotton, *Global Interests*, pp. 145-151.

album of his, dating back to around 1554, is today in the possession of the Victoria and Albert Museum in London.[5] Among the various breeds of horses presented, two examples stand out, denominated *Un Turco* and *Turcho d'Italia* (fig. 6).

If they really had come from Turkey, the horses must have followed the usual combined route: by land as far as Ragusa (Dubrovnik) and then by sea until Venice or Ancona. And the embarkation of the nervous and cumbersome animals onto the boats of the time cannot have been easy. To understand this, it is enough to observe two rare pictorial documents of these operations. Even if they refer to different places from the ones we are dealing with, and come from a different school of painting, their documentary value is still significant. The Dutch painter, Jan Cornelisz Vermeyen had followed Charles V in his victorious enterprise of 1535 against the den of pirates in Tunis. The 'personal reporter' of the Emperor, in 1548-1550 Vermeyen celebrated the African conquest by producing numerous cartoons for tapestries inspired by the subject. Today the cartoons are preserved in the Kunsthistorisches Museum of Vienna; instead, the series of tapestries that was woven immediately afterwards, in Brussels by Willem De Pannemaker, was divided up, but the majority of the pieces is to be found in the Royal Palace in Madrid (a later series is also in the the Alcázar of Seville).[6] In one of the cartoons in Vienna we can see a scene of the departure from the Tunisian port of Goulette. A horse in a harness is lowered carefully onto the boat of the Marquis Hernando de Alarcon; the small boat, which is already rather full, is clearly directed towards a ship that is anchored in the open sea. In another cartoon, we can see, instead, an arrival of military forces at the port of Carthage: two horses are squeezed into a boat that is overladen with household furniture and people and which is heading towards land. The horses are wrapped in a sheet, perhaps because they risk becoming ill. One of the two is stretching its neck towards the water of the sea: perhaps it had not found enough to drink on board (figs. 7 and 8). Whatever the case may be, the two animals seem quite tested by the sea passage. As for the author of these pictures, Jan Cornelisz Vermeyen, we shall meet him again in Flanders.

2. But let us return to the missions of *Anconitano* in the year 1525. Lombardy, on the borders of the Marquisate of Mantua, was in turmoil following the defeat that Emperor Charles V had inflicted on King Francis I of France at Pavia. The victors had become arrogant, and in the barbershops of Milan it was said that the city should be handed over to anyone who would free it from the Spanish, even the Turks.[7]

Something had also changed in Constantinople. Strengthened by his previous experiences, *Anconitano* noticed this at once when he arrived there for the second time in 1525. He had the obligatory supply of gifts with him: "eight chests with

5. See Ward-Jackson, *Italian Drawings*, pp. 101-105; Campbell, *The Grove Encyclopedia*, p. 39 (entry "Arms"). Other copies of the album are to be found in the Herzog August Bibliothek in Wolfenbüttel and in a private collection in Limerick (Ireland).

6. See Horn, *Jan Corneliusz Vermeyen*, pp. 118-128, 263-264; Deswarte-Rosa, "L'expédition de Tunis", pp. 117-125.

7. See Le Gall, *L'honneur perdu*, p. 349.

gold and silk cloths and some armour, two large dogs and two hunting falcons that are brought to the Turkish Lord". It was the Venetian nobleman, Pietro Zen, on the way to Istanbul to carry out a diplomatic mission, who was to send the information from Ragusa to Venice on 26th December. "And he also brought other presents to the Sanjak", that is to the Sanjak of Bosnia, who was supposed to guarantee the passage across the Balkan interior. Yet again, Ragusa was serving as an obligatory transit point for people, objects, and news between Italy and the Ottoman Empire. Ethnically Slav but culturally Italianised, tributary of the Turk but catholic in religion, the Dalmatian republic conceded something to every adversary in exchange for political autonomy and free commerce. For this reason, there were also those who considered it a nest of vipers.[8]

Anconitano's chests were still sealed in Ragusa, but knowing the list of presents was a subject of interest for diplomacy. Indeed a second letter, sent from Constantinople to Venice from the bailiff Pietro Bragadin, described the contents of the cases that had, by then, been opened: "armour for foot soldiers and knights, saddles, two falcons, cheeses and other things, a caparison for a horse".[9] The two large dogs are not mentioned any more: did they escape, were they stolen, had they been delivered, or had they died? Or perhaps someone had had second thoughts, given the impure nature of dogs according to Islamic Law. So the *Anconitano* was carrying objects and animals that were useful for the hunt and noble warfare, in addition to the ever-present whole Parmesan cheeses which the Imperial House was always greedy for. Despite this, and despite scrupulous respect for the ceremonial in force at the court, the missions were not successful. Now we shall try to find out why.

Before setting off from Constantinople again at the end of the second and fruitless mission, *Anconitano* received a majestic formal letter from Suleiman the Magnificent for Federico II Gonzaga ("you, who are the Lord of the land of Mantua", and continuing on in this vein for more than a metre and a half of text). Dated between 5th and 14th March 1526, the letter is stuffed full of formulae typical of communications sent out in the name of the Sultan (known as *nâme*); and so it is not easy to extract the real contents. Nevertheless, some sentences are not stereotypical at all. Here is the main one:

> You have shown your obedience and your most perfect devotion and your abundant submission and affection towards my throne [...] when you said: "if a service were to be given for us to carry out, our most perfect devotion would be seen in the manner in which we would complete it".

3. "Obedience", "most perfect devotion", "abundant submission and affection": these are all heavy expressions that exceed ceremonial. But above all, a rare fact emerges. Inserted into the Imperial text is a quotation from Gonzaga's letter to the Sultan which had been delivered by *Anconitano* ("when you said: if a service were to be given for us to carry out" etc.). It is a sentence that is very similar to

8. See Di Vittorio, Anselmi, Pierucci, *Ragusa (Dubrovnik)*; Bertelli, *Lucca, Ragusa, Boston*, pp. 51-101; Anselmi, *Mercanti, corsari, disperati e streghe*, pp. 103-110.

9. Sanudo, *I diarii*, vol. XL, col. 689; vol. XLI, col. 190.

those used by Ludovico il Moro when he offered obedience to Bayezid II ("we will do everything that Your Highness desires", "to have at your service a Duke of Milan"); and we know that Sforza, in his desperation, was speaking literally, and not with formulaic expressions.

Let us now see how Suleiman continues, almost replying to Gonzaga's offer:

> Everything that you have said has been presented to my powerful and blessed presence, and your sincerity and devotion have become perfectly known to me, and my illustrious conscience, an ornament of the world, has completely understood them.

The expression to be noted is: "has completely understood them"... And so to arrive at the conclusion, the evocation of the long-standing relations between the two courts:

> Now our illustrious agreement is associated with your friendship and sincerity just as they existed in the time of my grandfather [Bayezid II] and your father [Francesco II]. If the all-powerful and generous God permits, when such a similar service and a similar task present themselves, then it will be announced and indicated on the part of my powerful majesty.

Up to this point we have Suleiman's thinking, authenticated by a spectacular monogram in gold and cobalt-blue ink of the kind denominated *tuğra*: "Shah Suleiman, son of Shah Khan Selim, the always victorious" (fig. 9). Far better than so many words, the majesty of the monogram explains to us why the principal Muslim states have been defined as "calligraphic states".[10] The fact that the young Suleiman as yet devoted himself little to international politics, leaving ample space to the grand vizier Ibrāhīm Pasha, takes nothing away from the value of the document. It was an official document.

4. We should consider, however, the other state involved, the state that was the addressee: the Gonzaga State. What we have read is the original text in Turkish, presented here in a literal translation. There is also a translation into Italian in existence, dating back to the period and preserved, together with the original, in the Gonzaga archives. The Sultan himself had had this prepared on 27th March with this reasoning: "we have written this letter in Turkish but the ambassador of your state has said that the Turkish language is not known among you and therefore we have translated it into Italian, seeing that in our imperial court there are clerks of every language". Clearly, in Mantua Silvestro da Lucca, the teacher of Turkish engaged in his time by Francesco II Gonzaga, had left no heirs. The translation supplied by the Sultan is quite faithful in its formulation, but for the fact that it softens all the words relative to Federico II's offers: this is done systematically. Is this a form of fictitious ceremonial reciprocity between the Great Lord of the East and the little western feudal lord? This is how the publisher of Suleiman's letter interprets the gap between the Turkish original

10. See Messick, *The Calligraphic State*; *Écriture, calligraphie et peinture*; *Turkish Miniature Paintings*, pp. 24-25.

and the Italian translation.[11] But this appears to us as a rather simplistic view. The gap between the two versions involves various aspects of the contents, not only formulaic stereotypes.

Faced with such strange circumstances we are obliged to touch upon daring hypotheses. The tight chronology of the events offers us a basic line to follow. In addition to the letter from Suleiman in Turkish, before leaving Istanbul *Anconitano* received normal ceremonial letters, written in Italian, from each of the three viziers. These are dated 18th April 1526. In exactly those days the imperial army, led personally by Suleiman, was moving from the capital for the Hungary campaign. The war was to culminate on 29th August 1526 with the victory achieved by the Ottomans at Mohács.

Anconitano in his turn set off on his return trip in those April days, as the dates of his letters, sent during his journey as far as Ragusa, reveal. While he complained about not having concluded the deal for the purchase of the horses, *Anconitano* explained the reasons for his failure to Marquis Federico II: the requirements of the Hungarian war had exhausted the market in horses to the point where only those necessary for the journey were allowed to him. *Anconitano* does not say anything more, but we can attempt to go beyond his silence. What overshadowed everything was Suleiman's most ambitious military enterprise; and Hungary was only a step on the way to the great prize, Vienna, the imperial capital of the enemy, Charles V of Habsburg. After Constantinople, which had by then been conquered; after Rome, which the Turks had perhaps given up as an ambition, it was Vienna that was now to be identified as the Red Apple (*Kızıl Elma*), the fabulous country which a Turkish-Byzantine legend promised as a conquest.[12] With Hungary annihilated, Vienna would be besieged by the Turks in the summer of 1529.

It is hardly necessary to remind ourselves that Vienna is not so very far from northern Italy. On the occasions of the two Turkish sieges of the imperial capital, in precisely 1529, and later in 1683, panic spread in this part of Italy. The fleeting appearance in the Julian Alps of detached contingents of the Turkish army was enough to provoke this. In the heart of the Paduan Plain, Mantua occupied a strategic position: equidistant from Milan and Venice, the city was positioned at the origin of the Brenner Road, the main route towards Austria and Germany. Shipping on the Po and on the system of water routes formed by the river Mincio and Lake Garda intersected at Mantua; it was at Mantua that the Italian postal services sorted correspondence directed beyond the Alps;[13] and it was through Mantua that armies, rulers, and personalities made transit. Modest-sized Mantua formed the keystone of northern Italy at that time.

11. See Römer, "À propos d'une lettre de Soliman", p. 457 (the two documents, in Turkish and in Italian, are in the State Archive of Mantua, *Archivio Gonzaga*, b. 794, f° 26bis and ter).

12. See Mandalà, "Tra mito e realtà", pp. 50-54.

13. See Day, "Strade e vie di comunicazione", p. 89; Rodríguez-Salgado, "Terracotta and Iron", pp. 16-23, 58-59.

5. At this point the question cannot be dodged: what did the Marquis really mean when he wrote to the Sultan: "if a service were to be given for us to carry out, our most perfect devotion would be seen in the manner in which we would complete it"? Words that Suleiman returned by quoting them back to him: almost throwing them back in his face, if ever he were to forget having pronounced them. Indeed the Sultan even doubled the dose, adding, on his own part: "when a similar service and a similar task present themselves, then it will be announced and indicated on the part of my powerful majesty". As we can see, the key word is still the same: "service". The Sultan's tone, oscillating between the haughty and the paternalistic, goes well beyond the usual grandiloquence of Ottoman foreign communications. The original letters in Greek, Latin, and even Venetian, written in the half century after the conquest of Constantinople, are a memory. The multilingualism of the Ottoman chancellery was coming to an end.[14] Now the Great Turk is writing in his own language, as linguistic empires always do, and this is almost a sovereign writing to a vassal; but, aware that the recipient is of a lower rank and does not have "clerks of every language" available, he condescends to supply the draft of a translation as well. All of this in an atmosphere of ambiguous allusions, of circumlocutions that were only understandable to someone already informed about the dossier. The affair of the letters from Bayezid II to Alexander VI, stolen from the messenger Giorgio Bucciardo in 1494 at Senigallia, had taught everyone to be suspicious.

And this is why the translation into Italian supplied by Suleiman appears to be a cautious version of the Turkish original. It was preferable that this documentation received from Istanbul did not fall under the gaze of undeserving people. The original in Turkish was certainly not legible to most; the translation in its turn should not compromise anyone. Strictly speaking, there is no appeal made to the Turk in the papers we have examined, and there is not even an appeal made by the Turk; at least, as yet there is neither one nor the other. But what were they preparing for, in Mantua and Constantinople, while Suleiman's attack on Central Europe took shape? In precisely the two-year period 1526-1527, Marquis Federico II's volte-faces between the French and the Imperial side earned him notoriety as a traitor. And a man for sale he certainly was, Gonzaga, if for no other reason than the need to safeguard a weak, ambitious, spendthrift state. To justify himself he also had a supposed argument available to him: from time to time he declared that he was acting as a captain in someone else's pay, or alternatively as Marquis of Mantua, separating the two responsibilities. In the vortex of the Franco-Imperial wars, Italy as a whole was being considered more and more as a land of cowardice.[15] It is hard to think that this was not appreciated by Suleiman's diplomacy. And it is impossible to accuse only Gonzaga of this, seeing that the Most Christian King, Francis I, after the defeat of Pavia, asked the Sultan to intercede for his release.[16]

14. See Veinstein, "L'administration ottomane"; Bruni, "Per la vitalità dell'italiano"; Bruni, *L'Italiano fuori d'Italia*, pp. 9-21.

15. See Benzoni, "Federico II Gonzaga", p. 714; Smith, "Émulation guerrière"; Bruni, *Italia*, pp. 295-306.

16. See Le Gall, *L'honneur perdu*.

6. However things really stood, the affair between Mantua and Constantinople did not finish there. Three years later, in the December of 1529, the dragoman Yunus bey, a Greek from Morea who had converted to Islam, reached Venice on an official mission. He brought from the battlefield of Belgrade letters that extoled the Sultan's victories – among these certainly the failed siege of Vienna was not mentioned. Yunus was accommodated in the Ca' Dandolo, near San Marco, instead of on the island of the Giudecca, which was a little out of the way and where Ottoman emissaries were usually given hospitality. The Most Serene Republic conceded him a two-hour secret audience, confirming the fact that this character knew a lot and could achieve something, as dragomans often could.[17] Yunus also brought letters for the Marquis Federico II, which were sent on to the addressee. The Mantuan ambassador to Venice honoured Yunus with sumptuous presents: fifteen lengths of golden cloth and the same quantity of crimson velvet.[18] Gold and purple, the symbols of royalty.

Nothing more and nothing less: coincidences, plausible contexts, and ceremonial language that are silent and eloquent at the same time. It is not possible to push through this flimsy wall to look at the true facts behind it. It could be objected that this reading of the relationship between Federico II Gonzaga and Suleiman the Magnificent is founded on clues and not proofs. This is true, but what is ever the nature of the proofs that historians usually have available to them? Historiography based on the judicial model is no longer satisfactory, precisely because it obliges us to leave too many layers of the past in the shade.[19] It would be useless to hope to find conclusive proof of an appeal to the Turks every time, in Mantua as elsewhere. Conclusive evidence was offered by the desperate, the defeated and the emarginated, those who had nothing to lose. For others, the appeal to the Turks remained a possibility, a card of last resort, often brandished but rarely used. This said, it should be recognised that the Turkish-Mantuan dossier is the most elusive of those we have inspected. Difficulty in reaching firm conclusions does not, however, justify the lack of attention that historians have given to the fundamental aspect up to now. Not to beat about the bush, the fundamental question is this: was Mantua prepared to act as a bridgehead for the Turks in Italy? We may suspect that the possibility had been weighed up, in a situation of necessity or convenience. In an Italy where rulers didn't hesitate to make appeals to the Turks for the most varied of reasons, had the vassalage of the Gonzaga already been prepared? The later crusading exhibitions by members of the dynasty such as Vincenzo I Gonzaga and Carlo Gonzaga-Nevers, however, were to erase this historical phase that had been so embarrassing.[20]

17. See Ács, "Tarjiumans Mahmud and Murad".
18. See Pedani, *In nome del Gran Signore*, pp. 144-147.
19. Ginzburg, *The Judge and the Historian*.
20. See Viglione, *La Politica antiottomana dei Gonzaga*.

16. Diogo/Salomon calls the Turks to Rome

1. If the Christians behaved in such a way, how can there be surprise at what happened in the complicated world of the converts and reconverted? Here we are not talking about the so-called renegades who had passed over to Islam – catholic in origin, mostly, but also protestants.[1] We are talking about those who existed constantly on the cusp between two (if not three) different faiths, without ever coming to a definitive choice.

Diogo Pires was a New Christian from Portugal. This expression denominated those who had been forcibly converted, or who had only made a pretence at conversion, or who had converted out of calculation, after Portugal, following the Spanish example, had driven out the Jews in 1498. Later, however, Diogo had returned to the Jewish faith with the name of Salomon Molcho. Going to and fro between different identities was not rare at the time. Also not uncommon was the decision taken by Salomon to move to the land of asylum for the Iberian Jews, the city of Salonika, which was subject to the Turks. Here, surrounded only by Jews, Salomon became acquainted with a religious climate rich in millenarian ferment. Immersed in the Kabbalah, he became a prophet and predicted the Sack of Rome in 1527. Then, moving on to action, he straightforwardly proclaimed himself the messiah. In 1530 he had a prophetic dream in which strange birds foretold the flooding of Rome and a country in the North, in addition to an earthquake in his original homeland, Portugal. A little while later the Tiber burst its banks, as indeed it often did. At that time, flooding of the Tiber and lightning strikes on churches and prelates raged without let-up; they offered suitable material for anticlerical speeches, in an atmosphere that was anxious to interpret every sort of divine message. And the Tiber made no mistake: "true and religious, visionary and soothsayer", the Dominican Leandro Alberti defined the river halfway through the sixteenth century.[2]

Next to elements of reciprocal contrast, here connections of images and languages between Christian and Jewish prophesising of the time emerge. In actually coming about, the Roman flood dreamt of by Salomon thus did not remain within the limits of the field of hydrology. It became a sign and a stimulus to action.

1. See Monter, "Calvinistes en turbans"; Bennassar, Bennassar, *Les chrétiens d'Allah*; *Les Convertis*.

2. See Niccoli, *Profeti e popolo*, pp. 186-190; Niccoli, *Rinascimento anticlericale*, pp. 51-52.

This was all confirmed by a flood in Flanders (the country in the North) and by an earthquake that struck Lisbon in 1531: with which the prophetic dream was completely fulfilled.

2. Strengthened in his convictions, Salomon then arrived in Rome. There, dressed in rags, he spent a month outside the walls preaching in apocalyptic tones; and he even reached the point of calling on the Turks to occupy the Papal seat. This really was too much. To tell the truth, the patience of the rulers for a whole month seems incomprehensible, but perhaps the Roman habit of deriding ecclesiastics protected the prophet momentarily. Salomon was nevertheless arrested and his career as a messiah was brought to an end by being condemned to be burned at the stake in 1532. However, in some Jewish circles of Central Europe his mystical eschatology remained alive for more than a century.[3]

Strictly speaking, the case should not be included in our dossier: it was the Jew from Salonika rather than the Portuguese New Christian making prophecies. But an appeal to the Turks, not launched by a desperate, condemned man, but by a man who was still free; not launched secretly but with deafening volume, and in the light of day; not launched from a hidden recess but from the walls of Rome itself: well, an appeal of this kind is something that we could not neglect. To the prophet's misfortune, times were changing, a collective social discipline was being imposed and incidents of impertinence of this kind were less tolerated than before. About forty years previously, the poet Pacifico Massimi, who had invited Turkish horses to Saint Peter's (admittedly in a Latin elegy), came off lightly. Instead, at this juncture it all finished as it was supposed to finish for Salomon, the former Diogo.

3. A homosexual and persecuted as such, the man of letters Pacifico Massimi; a rebel ready to be hanged, the tanner Giacomo Rabuini; a New Christian who had returned to the Jewish faith and so in danger of his life as an apostate, the prophet Salomon Molcho: here are the authors of the most extreme words, of the most fanciful gestures. At this stage it would be tempting to associate the appeal to the Turks with characters that were marginal in various ways; characters subject to particular pressures and, for this very reason, endowed with dislocated and disenchanted views; characters who had some reason not to identify themselves with a society that rejected them; characters that could also easily be accused of treachery, the eternal stigma that accompanies our subject. It might be tempting to establish this association, and we shall retain it a while, because it does contain fragments of truth. But then we think again of the Doges, the Popes, the kings of France who were not necessarily homosexuals, who were never hanged and were never relapsed Jews; we reconsider the varied record of cases we are examining. And then we understand that the subject is more complex, and that we need to continue to explore its intricate aspects.

3. See Scholem, *Sabbatai Sevi*, pp. 562-563; Secret, *Les kabbalistes chrétiens*.

17. France's impiousness

1. If we keep to our plan, we should limit ourselves to Italy; to its geographical plurality and its political mosaic. But from centralised France a fragment of history reaches us that, by its exceptional nature, induces us to pass briefly over the border.

Venice made a virtue of necessity. Despite ambiguities, or hidden favours, the Serene Republic and the Turks disputed the same spaces in the Levant; and so at bottom they were always antagonists, even when they were in agreement. The case of France was different. Distant as they were, the Turks did not directly threaten French interests, except for occasional pirate raids on the coasts of Provence. In contrast, the Turks tormented the Habsburg monarchy on the Balkan land border and along the endless Italian and Spanish coastlines. Ratified in 1536, the Franco-Turkish alliance thus also had a strategic value because it assured France the role of protector of Christians in the Levant and of the churches of Jerusalem, alongside numerous commercial advantages.[1] And yet the alliance had been conceived after the blow inflicted at Pavia in 1525 by the Emperor Charles V of Habsburg on the King of France, Francis I of Valois. The king himself had been captured and had endured a scarcely honourable imprisonment in Spain, which only the payment of a huge ransom had brought to an end.[2]

By this stage France was surrounded by Habsburg possessions: Spain, the Low Countries, Germany. The gold and silver that was flowing in from the New World permitted Charles V to finance the most ambitious policies. A dramatic phase was opening for the very survival of France as a nation. Faced with such a threat, it was not difficult to predict extreme reactions on the part of the French.

Before all this began, it was prefigured by a conversation picked up by a Mantuan diplomat in the French Court in 1516. The subject of the exchange was the fate of the Duke of Urbino, Francesco Maria Della Rovere, whom Pope Leo X had deposed in favour of his own nephew, Lorenzo de' Medici. King Francis declared that Della Rovere did "exactly the right thing in pursuing every way" to regain his state; he himself, "if he were to find himself in his place, would give himself to the devil to get back that which was his".[3] Again the devil, already

1 Bérenger, "La collaboration militaire franco-ottomane"; Poumarède, "Justifier l'injustifiable"; De Rosa, "Le capitolazioni franco-ottomane"; Veinstein, "Les capitulations franco-ottomanes"; Pellegrini, *Guerra santa contro i Turchi*, pp. 181-235, 325-354.

2 Le Gall, *L'honneur perdu*, pp. 399-402.

3 See *Federico Gonzaga alla corte di Francesco I*, p. 274.

invoked by Ludovico il Moro at the time of the invasion of Charles VIII: and from then on we know that the option of the devil implied the Turkish option.

2. Francis I of Valois was the territorial heir of Charles Martel, who had stopped the Arabs of Al-Andalus at Poitiers in 732. He was the dynastic heir, if not by bloodline, of Saint Louis IX, the most famous crusader of the Middle Ages. The saintly king had gone on crusade not in word but in deed, and on two occasions. He had been taken prisoner in Egypt in 1250; and he had met his death in infidel territory, at Tunis in 1270.[4] Like all the kings of his nation, Francis I bore the title, *Très Chrétien*, most Christian,[5] which his last two predecessors, Charles VIII and Louis XII, had confirmed by committing themselves to departing for the crusade. Francis I had recognised his responsibilities as Most Christian as much as he could. In December 1515, loaded with glory thanks to his victory over the Swiss at Marignano, he had met Leo X in Bologna. There he had assured the Pope that he considered it his duty to go on crusade against the Turks. And the Pope had offered him the reliquary of the True Cross, an explicit allusion to the enterprise in the Holy Land.

In those times, Henry Tudor, King Henry VIII of England, who had not yet declared autonomy from the Church of Rome, thought in a similar way. In his opinion, "the kings of France and England were young and impressive figures and since the time of Charlemagne there had not been seen in Christendom sovereigns who could prosecute a war against the Turks better". Thus reported the French ambassador to London, Robert de Bapaume, writing to Louise of Savoy, Queen Mother and regent of France while her son was waging war in Italy.[6] The association between the two young kings (and also, later on, the Emperor Charles V) was a recurrent theme in European propaganda.[7]

Honouring the promise made in Bologna, in 1518, Francis I had joined the crusade called after the Ottoman conquest of Mameluke Egypt.[8] De facto, the eastern Mediterranean had been transformed by this time into a Turkish lake dotted by residual Venetian and Genoese islands. We have already spoken about this particular mobilisation for crusade, also quoting the ironic reactions it generated, both at the popular and at the educated level. But Francis I's adhesion had been real. In contrast to Catholic Spain, in France the tenths planned for the crusade had been collected. Symbolic gestures had also been added: in 1519 the kings of France and England had decided not to shave until they had fulfilled their crusading vows – according to other versions, for the Frenchman the reason was, instead, to conceal a burn sustained in a rough game.[9] In so doing, Francis I hoped to gain some merit in his attempt to obtain the imperial crown. But in 1519 the crown went to Charles of

4 See Le Goff, *Saint Louis*.

5 See Gabriel, "François Ier 'rex christianissimus'".

6 See *Letters and Papers*, p. XLVIII.

7 See Burke, "Images de trois rois".

8 See Setton, *The Papacy and the Levant*, vol. III, pp. 173-179; *Conquête ottomane de l'Égypte*.

9 See Le Gall, *Un idéal masculin*, p. 30.

Habsburg, supported by the money of the Fugger banking family, which the grand electors found more convincing than the crusading promises of the French King. Perhaps the king knew in his heart of hearts that the crusade had, by that stage, little of chance of really coming about, as indeed it turned out on this occasion as well. It remains that in 1520 he sent a fleet to assist the Knights Hospitallers of Rhodes when they were being besieged by Suleiman, though without being able to prevent the island falling into Turkish hands.[10] After the defeat of Pavia, however, and with the capitulations of 1536, the centuries-old eastern policy of France, the favourite nation of the Roman Church, was reversed.

The Most Christian King is the new incarnation of the Antichrist, thundered the imperial propaganda when it heard of the Franco-Turkish alliance. Through Habsburg suggestion the traditional iconography of Europe as a young maiden in distress was enriched with new features that were both anti-Turk and anti-French. This was balanced out by the fact that in France the until-then-flourishing production of polemical images representing the Turk as a dragon or a snake faded away.[11]

3. No longer young nor physically impressive as Henry Tudor had described him, in 1543 Francis I invited the admiral Khayr ad-Din to winter in the port of Toulon. Playing on the assonance of his name (which is better understood using the transliteration Hayreddin), the French called him "sieur Hardi". All in all, they wrapped him in respect and admiration. But for other Christians, Italians and Spanish in particular, Khayr ad-Din was the most feared corsair, Barbarossa. From Toulon, Barbarossa was to recommence operations in the spring against Spain and in the meantime he needed a base in the western Mediterranean. No Christian ruler had ever dared offer so much to an infidel: it just had to fall to the Most Christian King. During the approach to France, Barbarossa made a stop at Antibes and, with the French, started an unsuccessful siege of Nice, the Duke of Savoy's main port.[12] This Franco-Ottoman joint action caused great scandal.

Then there was the arrival at Toulon. There the raids previously carried out by Barbarossa on the surrounding coasts had not been forgotten. But this time it was different. The peaceful entry, on 14th October, of 200 Turkish galleys with 30,000 men into the Provencal port was spectacular. For the whole winter the port was at the disposition of the Turks and the Algerian and Tunisian pirates. With the exception of ten heads of family, the Christian population was evacuated to reduce the risk of undesirable contacts, which were not removed completely, nonetheless. A market for selling the booty grabbed during raids on Christian shores, slaves included, was set up. The cathedral of Notre-Dame-de-la-Sède was temporarily turned into a mosque, without the agreements having foreseen this. The admiral and his officers took residence in the best houses of the port, while the crews camped outside the walls. The reception was what it was in a town that had around a thousand inhabitants.

10 See Vatin, "La conquête de Rhodes".

11 See Prosperi, *America e Apocalisse*, pp. 127-152; Sorce, "Il drago come immagine del nemico", p. 183.

12 See Bérenger, "La politique française en Méditerranée", pp. 14-16.

With the winter past, it was not easy for the King of France to rid himself of his awkward guest. To induce him to leave, a huge sum had to be paid to which were added precious cloths, jewels, equipment from the arsenal, besides four hundred Turkish oarsmen freed from their chains. The difference compared to the payment of a ransom for a conquered city was little more than nominal. The sea journey home was an opportunity for more raids on Christian shores, while the French galleys that escorted the Turkish convoy looked on passively. Meanwhile, in Toulon the damage was calculated. For the town to recover it was necessary to grant it a ten-year tax exemption.[13] The Cathedral converted into a mosque harked back to sinister precedents: at Otranto a short time earlier, not to mention the drama of Hagia Sofia in Constantinople. Like Alfonso di Calabria in Ferrara before him, Francis I at Toulon realised that appealing to the Turks had a definite cost while the advantages remained uncertain. For more than a century, the town celebrated the day of departure of the Turks with a large banquet known as "the dinner of the lanterns".

4. Nevertheless, Francis I, more than any of his predecessors, continued to lay emphasis on Turkish themes, figures and costumes during his solemn entry processions. And the Turks, or Moors, were often (but not always) presented in conditions of inferiority, as those defeated, as slaves. This was the way in Paris in 1518 and in 1530 at least, and it was the same in Caen in 1532, and in Orléans in 1539. On this last occasion, provocatively, the performance was organised for the benefit of a guest who answered to the name of Charles V of Habsburg, the one who with his excessive power had forced France to move closer to the Ottomans.[14] The Emperor had been permitted to cross France to go to Flanders in order to punish the rebel city of Ghent.

But meanwhile the eastern ally of the Most Christian King of France enjoyed equal and opposite spectacles. In 1582 the celebrations for the circumcision of the son of Murad III, the future Sultan Mehmed III, lasted fifty-five days. First official invitations were sent to the King of France, the Doge of Venice and the courts of Warsaw and Vienna. The Turkish delegation that arrived in Paris to deliver the invitation stimulated such curiosity that the sovereign who hosted it, Henry III, earned the nickname "the Turkish king". Then, in Istanbul, when the jubilee celebrations had begun, the recent conquest of Cyprus was commemorated with public scenic enactments. Other battles between Christians and the Ottomans were represented, some that had really taken place, others that were pure fantasy. It is unnecessary to ask ourselves who always had the better of these encounters, while from the conquered Christian cities herds of pigs escaped for the pleasure and scandal of the Muslim spectators.[15] The bestial nature of infidels, be they dogs or pigs, was reaffirmed in the wake of a

13 See Vergé-Franceschi, *Toulon*, pp. 30-34.

14 See Chartrou, *Les entrées solennelles*, p. 116.

15 See Terzioğlu, "The Imperial Circumcision Festival", pp. 86-87; Atasoy, *1582 Surname-i Hümayun*; Eunjeong Yi, *Guild Dynamics*, pp. 4-5.

tradition that had equivalents on the Christian side: no-one rejected a rhetoric of otherness based on supposed animal natures.[16] And it is worth noting that at that moment there was no Turkish-Christian war in progress. The year before, even the Spain of Philip II had drawn up an armistice with the Ottomans: not a peace, because this word, when referred to infidels, was incompatible with the ideological system of the Catholic Monarchy.[17]

5. With the celebrations in Istanbul of 1582 over, a series of commemorative miniatures created by the great artist Nakkaş Osman remained.[18] The miniatures are inserted in the manuscript of the official history, *Şehinşāhnāme* (Book of the king of kings) by the court man-of-letters Seyyıd Loḳmān. In the miniatures various representations of Christians are to be seen, recognisable by the form of the faces, by the colour and cut of the beards and moustaches, and by the head coverings: all in rigorous agreement with the prevailing fashion of that moment. But these forms were only large puppets, similar to modelled funeral urns, made with inflammable materials and stuffed with sticks of explosive. The puppets had been made so as to blow up with pyrotechnical effects, among houses, castles, trees, horses, cockerels, horned monsters, all of which were also designed to explode (fig. 10). The effort to reproduce the bodily features of Europeans on the part of Nakkaş Osman was notable for a figurative culture that was even accustomed to Ottomanising subjects inherited from Persian painting, which was much closer and more similar.[19] Together with other threads of Occidentalism,[20] these images in part balance out the overwhelming documentary evidence of European *Ottomanesque* themes of the time. The practice of exoticism, both ideological and aestheticizing, was not the prerogative of Europeans.

But in 1582 Turkish Occidentalism served to deride those same Christians who allied themselves with the Turk. If neither the King of France nor the Doge of Venice had been present at the celebrations for the circumcision, the delegations accredited by the two governments were of a high level. The Turks thus gratified the Most Christian King with the (undeserved) title of "emperor", *pâdişah*, just like the Sultan, while the Habsburg Emperor was only the "King of Vienna" and the tsar of Russia the "bey of Moscow"; and the first chronicle in Turkish about the kings of France had just come out, in which they were denominated precisely by the term *pâdişah*.[21] In private, however, in Istanbul they called their French allies "new Turks", a pejorative expression that was a calque from the other phrase, "New Christians", used in Spain for converted Muslims and Jews.[22] The border

16 See Hampton, "Turkish Dogs", pp. 67, 80; Zemon Davis, "Cannibalism and Knowledge", pp. 16-18; Ricci, *I turchi alle porte*, pp. 69-71.

17 See Skilliter, "The Hispano-Ottoman Armistice"; Rodríguez Salgado, *Felipe II*.

18 See Çağman, "Nakkaş Osman".

19 See Bağci, "From Translated Word".

20 See Lewis, *The Muslim discovery*.

21 *La première histoire de France*.

22 See Rodríguez Salgado, "¿Carolus Africanus?", p. 514.

between Christians and Turks, perforated by the toing and froing of politics, was continually reconstructed in people's minds. But during the celebrations of 1582, more than the French ally, it was the Venetian Republic, expelled from Cyprus, that was explicitly mocked. The same Venice that in 1571, in the aftermath of Lepanto, had exulted in the very same way, setting light to figures of Turks: "puppets resembling Turks and the Pasha were made in many locations, and were burnt in triumph".[23] An identical celebratory language operated in all climates.

6. On the occasion of the Franco-Ottoman alliance, even the obligatory Islamic aniconism was challenged openly. Around 1570, in Istanbul, the court artist, Haydar Reis, known as Nigārī, produced a watercolour copy of the portrait of Francis I by Jean Clouet, today in the Louvre – it might be claimed to be this one, even if the hat recalls rather more the portrait by Joos Van Cleve in the Musée Carnavalet in Paris. The king is perfectly recognisable despite the orientalising translation of his facial features. The painting is now to be found at Harvard, together with a portrait of Charles V that Nigārī copied from Lucas Cranach.[24] Nigārī never went to the West, and for this reason he had to base himself on prints or drawings taken from Clouet and Cranach. The Turkish inscription beneath the figure of the King explains that he, along with the Emperor, visited Sultan Selim II to receive one of his decrees. An obviously false event, all the more so as Selim reigned from 1566 to 1574, when Francis and Charles had been dead for some time. Of the two Christian sovereigns, Francis appears by a long way the more orientalised: an allusion to his status as a "New Turk"?

7. After the unfortunate events at Toulon, no Turkish fleet received invitations to visit France. But, *politique d'abord*: much more was required to suffocate the Franco-Turkish convergence which was, on the contrary, destined to last for centuries. In 1551, France looked on in a benevolent way at the conquest of Tripoli by the pirates Dragut and Sinan Pascià. The city was snatched from the Knights of Malta who had received it from Charles V: these Maltese were none other than the ex-Knights Hospitaller of Rhodes, aided in 1520 by Francis I when he was still an enemy of the Sultan. It is true that there were criticisms from inside France itself: criticisms based on philosophy, religion and history.[25] But the absolute monarchy, if it did not have the strength to impose itself unconditionally in internal matters, where opposing forces offered resistance, had power over international policy decisions which everyone recognised as its prerogative. All the more so as the influential Calvinist minority in France supported a strategy which, with the help of the Turks, put the brakes on the ambitions of the Hispanic-Papal block. And thus no French galley took part in the epic naval engagement at Lepanto.

23 Nubilonio, *Cronaca di Vigevano*, p. 338.

24 See Binney, *Turkish Treasures*, pp. 24-25; Renda, "Les portraits des sultans ottomans", p. 41.

25 See Malettke, "Die Vörstosse der Osmanen im 16. Jahrhundert".

From this point on, friendship with the Turks became a mainstay of French international strategy. In 1660, at the moment of bringing aid to Venice during the War of Cyprus, Louis XIV's minister, Cardinal Mazarin, recommended that this be done "without making it obvious that this comes from His Majesty, this crown not intending to break openly with the Turk".[26] Some years later, in 1672, Louis XIV replied thus, contemptuously, to Leibniz: "Holy wars have been out of fashion since the time of Louis IX, Saint Louis". The philosopher had written a collection of notes as a petition in Latin (*Consilium Ægyptiacum*) in the hope of inducing the sovereign to give up on expansion in Germany; he advised him instead to turn his attention to Egypt, the Ottoman granary on which the supplies of Constantinople itself depended.[27] Thanks to the intercession of the Elector of Mainz, Leibniz had succeeded in presenting the petition to Louis XIV in the castle of Saint-Germain. But the result was as related above, despite the fact that the brief assigned the main benefits of the dismemberment of Ottoman power to France.

It is very informative, this squabble between Leibniz and the Sun King; informative because of the rank of the two contenders and because it shows how the subject of the Turk followed a logic that was by then completely secular. It is particularly interesting when we think that, among the various images of majesty he indulged in, Louis XIV loved to represent himself as his predecessor and namesake, Louis IX, the perfect example of the crusading king.[28] The seductions of dynastic holiness were not to be evaded quite so easily, especially because the French monarchy based a part of its mythology on it. But it is unlikely that the saintly ancestor would have rejoiced like the Sun King did a decade after the meeting with Leibniz, when a Turkish army besieged Vienna, the capital of the hated Habsburgs; it is unlikely that the ancient Most Christian King would have manoeuvred as the early modern king was to do, leaving the Holy Roman Emperor alone in the face of danger. The four bombardments unleashed by the French fleet between 1682 1688 on Algiers and on Tripoli did not contradict the basic principle: they were only warnings given to pirates who did not respect the rules established between Paris and Istanbul. Until, in 1698, an "eternal peace" was even stipulated with the Berber corsairs.[29]

If eternal peace was always a utopia, this bulwark of French policy was confirmed in actions and in memory. In the aftermath of the Arab-Israeli War of 1967, General Charles de Gaulle declared that he intended "to resume the same policy of friendship and cooperation with the Arab peoples of the East that had been typical of France in that part of the world for centuries".[30] It had all started in 1536…

26 See Poumarède, *Pour en finir avec la croisade*, p. 415.

27 See Djuvara, *Cent projets de partage*, pp. 221-224; Robinet, *G.W. Leibniz*, pp. 251-252.

28 See Gouzi, "Louis XIV en Saint Louis".

29 See Peter, *Les Barbaresques sous Louis XIV*, pp. 10-50, 77-128.

30 Paris, "La 'politique arabe' de la France".

18. The Franco-Ottoman alliance and Italy

1. The potential duration of the Franco-Ottoman alliance was certainly not predictable when it first took shape. For observers of the time it was enough to evaluate its immediate effects. From the outset, Italy appeared to be the chosen victim, and this has not been adequately stressed by the plentiful literature on the subject, both past and modern historiography. Italy, the chosen victim, for many reasons: for being part of the imperial sphere of influence, with the exception of Venice; for its closeness to the Levant and to the Ottoman Balkans, and here Venice was included; for the indefensible length of its coasts.

This was understood in 1534, when the fleet belonging to the feared Barbarossa (Khayr ad Dyn) met the emissaries of Francis I in the south of France and then set off for the conquest of Tunis. Along the way it spread terror on the Genoese, Corsican, Tuscan, Roman and Neapolitan coasts.[1] The immediate reconquest of Tunis on Charles V's part, demonstrating the power of the Emperor, did nothing other than consolidate Franco-Ottoman ties. Indeed, in 1536 a permanent ambassador was installed at Constantinople in the person of Jean de la Forêt, and this is considered the formal beginning of the alliance. The year 1537 marked large joint operations against the Italian States and their possessions. In the summer an Ottoman fleet, which also carried de la Forêt himself along with it, assembled in the Albanian port of Valona. From there a landing in Puglia was organised, at Castro, not far from Otranto: everyone feared that this was a new attempt to conquer Italy. Withdrawing after two weeks, the Ottomans took with them thousands of slaves from a devastated region. In August followed the siege of Venetian Corfu, where twelve French galleys, commanded by Bernard d'Ornesan, Baron of Saint-Blancard, joined with the Turks. Saint-Blancard tried to persuade the allies into new offensives against Puglia, Sicily, and the March of Ancona, but the threat of the plague and the arrival of autumn induced Suleiman to have his fleet return to Istanbul. After which, for two years Saint-Blancard criss-crossed the seas with Barbarossa.[2] If, in general, the French did not take part in atrocities vented on the Christian coasts, they were always present and did not prevent them.

1. See *Inventario delle fonti manoscritte*, vol. 5, pp. 18-19; Kumrular, "Ispanyol ve İştalyan Arşiv".

2. See Garnier, *L'alliance impie*, pp. 128-154; Varriale, *Arrivano li Turchi*, pp. 103-120.

The Peace of Nice of 1538 between Charles V and Francis I interrupted actions against Italy. But the assassination of the French ambassador Antonio Rincon on imperial orders, which took place in Pavia in 1541, caused war to break out again. In 1542, a Florentine mercenary in the pay of France, Piero Strozzi, cousin to Caterina de' Medici, took control of the Adriatic port of Marano, on the border between Venice and the Habsburg dominions; he then sold it to the Republic with the threat of ceding it to Barbarossa.[3] The next year, 1543, was the one in which it could be better understood just how much of a danger the Franco-Ottoman alliance posed to Italy, because in this year there was the siege of Nice and the prolonged stay at Toulon. During the winter, to kill time, Barbarossa launched attacks against nearby Liguria, sacked San Remo and reached the point of threatening the proud capital, Genoa. As the humanist Paolo Giovio wrote to the Duke of Florence, Cosimo de' Medici, if Barbarossa had wanted "to see Genua, we certainly would have felt such a fire in our pants as to make us run".[4] Nevertheless, in the May of 1544 Barbarossa left Toulon to fall back on Istanbul. The crossing was accompanied by other raids on the Italian coast (Porto Ercole, Talamone, the islands of Giglio and Lipari), while the French galleys that escorted the Turkish convoy followed it all passively.[5]

2. Without doubt, serious damage to Italy and a permanent threat. However, reactions were not all so bitter as one might expect. The geography of the Franco-Turkish raids allows us to understand the reasons for this. Most of all, it was Spanish Italy, or pro-Spanish Italy that was affected: the Kingdom of Naples, with Sicily and Sardinia; the Republic of Genoa and Corsica. The papal coasts were less involved, perhaps because of the surveillance of the French galleys that often flanked the Turks with precisely this purpose. In its turn, the Republic of Venice came out of things almost unscathed – with the noticeable exception of the siege of Corfu.

Let us begin to observe the behaviour of the Papal State, a universalist institution by this time led exclusively by Italians who were also the temporal sovereigns of an Italian state. In defining the Franco-Ottoman alliance as "impious", the Hispanic-Habsburg front continued to apply pressure, and it asked the Pope to deprive King Francis of the title of "Most Christian King". A gesture that was difficult to bring about, even if there was the desire to do so, seeing as it had to do with a customary title; the title of the Catholic Kings was very different, conceded as it had been to the Spanish sovereigns in 1494 by an act of Alexander VI. Even if regretful of a development that, in one blow, rendered the idea of crusade and every hope of Christian universalism out of date,[6] the Papacy did not make great efforts to denounce France. In Rome there was fear of the excessive power of Charles V, and the counterweight of Paris was considered necessary; the sack of the city carried out

3. See Jacquart, *François Ier*, pp. 212-215, 339.

4. Cited by Bonora, *Aspettando l'imperatore*, p. 101.

5. See Bérenger, "La politique française", pp. 14-16; Crowley, *Empires of the Sea*, pp. 74-79.

6. See Poumarède, *Pour en finir avec la croisade*; Pellegrini, *La crociata nel Rinascimento*, pp. 156-176.

in 1527 by the imperial Landsknechts, in part Lutherans, had marked an era. And so in 1533, when the Franco-Ottoman convergence was already emerging, Pope Clement VII gave the hand of his own niece, Catherine de' Medici, to Francis I's son, the future King Henry II. On the other hand, it was easy to accuse of treason those desperate enough to turn to the Turks, not knowing another way to obtain justice for a wrong suffered; it was easy to condemn some unscrupulous Italian prince; it was difficult, though, to express annoyance with the King of France.

What occurred in the first years of the 1540s, during the central phase of the pontificate of Paul III Farnese, is exemplary. At that time, international turbulence made the Franco-Ottoman alliance blatantly obvious. In 1540, after the disastrous war of Prevesa, Venice was preparing the peace treaty with the Turks, a treaty supported by Francis I, and feared by Charles V. Charles, in the meantime, as we have seen, launched the Algiers enterprise to destroy a nest of pirates and keep faith with his obligations of crusade, coming out heavily defeated. In 1542, while the war between the King and the Emperor raged, Paul III declared his neutrality. Up to then, the papal sovereigns had got themselves disastrously mixed up in the Italian wars. Instead, from that moment onwards, neutrality was to be the ideology (if not always the practice) upon which their strategy of survival was to be based. The new development was significant, but many princes, prelates and ambassadors did not believe it.[7] There was talk of secret understandings between the Pope and France, who would nevertheless guarantee the defence of the lands of the Church from the Turks; and, by the concept of transitive property, treating with France meant treating with the Turks in some way. All the more since the Pope also remained neutral after the Franco-Turkish attack on Nice of 1543; and even after the hospitality accorded to Barbarossa in the port of Toulon. Genuine or simulated as it may have been, pontifical neutrality, in the face of such scandal, sounded offensive to the supporters of Charles V.

3. And what is to be said of Venice? In 1532, a tiara to offer to Suleiman was commissioned from the goldsmiths of the city on Francis I's behalf: this was an ornament worthy of a universal authority.[8] Thus a triangulation between the traditional Franco-Venetian friendship, the planned Franco-Ottoman alliance and the ambiguous Turkish-Venetian cohabitation declared itself. Theorising the new international order came immediately afterwards, in 1535. Francis I in person explained his intentions "openly" to the Venetian emissary Francesco Giustinian:

> Ambassador, it cannot be denied that I want the Turk to remain powerful; not only for his usefulness, because he is an infidel and we are Christians; but to force the emperor to commit his resources, and with such a great enemy make him less, and give greater security to every potentate.

7. See Prodi, *Il sovrano pontefice*, pp. 337-344; Tallon, "Conflits et médiations"; Bonora, *Aspettando l'imperatore*, pp. 62-63, 101-103, 114-115, 123.

8. See Kurz, "A Gold Helmet"; Necipoğlu, "Süleymân the Magnificent"; Concina, *Dell'arabico*, pp. 57-76.

The ambassador Giustinian added that the matter seemed "quite infamous" to the French and for this reason they tried desperately to justify it "with every kind of argument".[9] Even while he noted the embarrassment of France, the ambassador showed great indulgence, while everything continued to go well for the Republic: others had become the target.

The Franco-Turkish siege of Corfu of 1537 upset this equilibrium. And in 1538 France did not participate in the league of Christian princes assembled in preparation for the War of Prevesa. Then, for the first time, a pro-Venetian (but anonymous) pamphlet advised Francis I "to get out of the friendship he has with the Great Turk". Along the lines of Habsburg propaganda, the pamphlet put the title of Most Christian King in doubt, and asked God to forgive the grave error. With the Corfu-Prevesa crisis over, things started to operate as before. Giovio, who was not an out-an-out pacifist, adjudged Venetian pragmatism as inevitable because of geopolitical constraints ("not to allow Lord San Marco to be impaled", he wrote to Federico II Gonzaga in January 1540). This also applied when France was more favourable to the Bosphorus than to the Lagoon, as it was during the peace negotiations in progress at the time.[10]

Then the Franco-Venetian-Ottoman triangle was enriched with other sides, transforming itself into a polygon. The crucial year is 1547, or rather, its first months. In February, the new French ambassador to the Sublime Porte, Gabriel Luetz d'Aramon, stopped in Venice on the way to Istanbul. At the time there was talk of a possible anti-imperial alliance made up of Venice, France, England, the Lutheran princes and the Turks, while all the Italian heterodox circles were in ferment. But Henry VIII of England died that same month, in March Francis I died, and in April Charles V defeated the Lutherans of the Schmalcaldic League at Muhlberg[11] The political-religious climate changed at a stroke. Venice found herself forced to withdraw from excessively explicit involvements with France and with the Turks. The German reformers also had to realign themselves.

And to think that later on it would be they, the German reformers, threatened by the expansionism of Louis XIV, who would theorise a specific sin of princes: alliance with infidels. The exemplification was to be taken from Francis I's notorious "impious crime" (*impium facinus*); and the consequent misfortunes of France, from the violent death of Henry II in a tournament to the Wars of Religion, all of which were to be seen as just punishment.[12] Moral theology is not an abstract discipline, but Venice had known this for a long time.

4. When France embarked on the scandalous policy, the Italian princes' actions towards the Turks already constituted a substantial dossier. In this context, was

9. *Relazioni degli ambasciatori veneti*, ed. by Alberi, pp. 166-168; see Knecht, *Francis I*, p. 225.

10. See Pujeau, *L'Europe et les Turcs*, pp. 49, 228-229.

11. See Paviot, "Autour de l'ambassade de d'Aramon"; Tommasino, *L'Alcorano di Macometto*, pp. 87-128.

12. Fritsch, *Princeps peccans*, pp. 345-351; see De Benedictis, "'Peccat princeps qui...'".

there anyone who could cast the first stone without the fear that it could rebound on him? All the more so, as not even Charles V was innocent in the matter; even he was making – or was thinking about making – impious alliances. On 25th August 1525 the Emperor replied to a letter from the Sofi of Persia, Ismāʿīl, who exhorted him to war against the "common Ottoman enemy". Charles informed the Safavid ruler that the King of France, defeated, "found himself in his power, and alive"; and as things stood, he asked for further information before "combining their respective forces".[13] The Persian option was thus not refused in principle. By weakening Turkish pressure with the help of the Sofi, the victory over France obtained at Pavia would be consolidated.

Pressing the Ottomans from the east and from the west was a dream that Venice had cultivated for a long time, in parallel with her pro-Ottoman manoeuvres in Europe. Between 1463 and 1479 the Republic had sent the Turcoman sovereign of Persia, Uzūn Ḥasan, numerous ambassadors (Lazzaro Querini, Caterin Zeno, Giosafat Barbaro, Ambrogio Contarini), but without result.[14] With the arrival of the Safavids, a new attempt was entrusted to the Cypriot dragoman Michele Membré. The Shah Ṭahmāsp welcomed the emissary benevolently, but he had to flee when news of the Venetian-Ottoman peace of 1540 arrived.[15] The enormous distances made these machinations unrealistic: Ismāʿīl had already been dead for a year when Charles V wrote to him, and the less friendly Ṭahmāsp was seated on the throne of Persia.

5. After the death of Francis I in 1547, Franco-Ottoman actions against Italy and its surrounding areas continued with unchanged intensity. In 1551 ambassador d'Aramon accompanied the corsairs Dragut and Sinan in the conquest of Tripoli, which Charles V had handed over to the Knights of Malta; seeing as he was there, Dragut devastated the island of Gozo and carried off the population in chains. Then French galleys supported Turkish galleys in attacks on Calabria and they clashed with the Hispanic-Genoese squadron of Andrea Doria at Ponza. D'Aramon also supported the lonely affair of Charles V's rebel subjects in the south of Italy, such as Ferrante Sanseverino, Prince of Salerno, who managed to have himself received by Suleiman so as to ask him to intervene in Italy.[16] In 1553 Sinan's fleet repaid the French by helping them to occupy Corsica, while joint actions were carried out against the island of Elba and the Neapolitan, Sicilian and Sardinian coasts.[17] In light of all this, in 1554 a new Venetian ambassador to Paris, Giovanni Cappello, summarised the situation thus:

13. See *Correspondenz*, pp. 168-169.

14. See *I viaggi in Persia*, pp. 97-100; Piemontese, "L'ambasciatore di Persia".

15. See Membré, *Relazione di Persia*; *Mission to the Lord Sophy*. See Mahmoud Helmy, "Membré, Michele".

16. See Tommasino, *L'Alcorano di Macometto*, pp. 122-123.

17. See Yerasimos, "Les relations franco-ottomanes"; Alonso Acero, "El norte de África", pp. 395-397; Serrelli, "Sardinya Kralliği'nin Savunma Sistemleri".

> His Most Christian Majesty is a friend of the sovereign of the Turks only to the purpose of reducing the forces of the Emperor: and yet he makes use of the Turkish army, with which he threatens a great part of the imperial possessions. And although the French are very displeased at this friendship, it not being honourable that His Most Christian Majesty uses infidels […] nevertheless his majesty wants thus to show he will spare no expense nor spiritual or material effort to defeat or overcome the imperial forces.[18]

The more moralistic tone than that of the ambassador Giustinian twenty years earlier betrays the new Tridentine climate, but the understanding attitude on the part of Venice has not changed, a power compromised with the Turks a hundred times over. All things considered, at that time, people were rather used to it. The Piedmontese jurist, Pierino Belli, in a tract of his on the laws of war, admitted that in certain, limited cases one could make an alliance with the Turk[19]. Instead, in the Venice of the north, in Amsterdam and in Holland, the Calvinists who had rebelled against Spain could permit themselves to speak more freely. In 1574 they coined a medal in the form of a half-moon on which was written: "Liever Turks dan Paaps", rather Turks than Papists, that is, the Spanish of King Philip II.[20] The fame of the stubborn *gueux* (the Sea Beggars of the Dutch Revolt) was not usurped. Meanwhile the other great antipapal figure, Elizabeth I of England, made public and secret agreements with the Ottomans.[21] The two great monarchies of the west, France and England, each in its own way, had by now repudiated the medieval myth of the *Res publica christiana*.

18. In *Relazioni di Ambasciatori Veneti*, ed. by L. Firpo, pp. 284-285.
19. See Le Gall, *Les guerres d'Italie*, p. 198.
20. See *L'empire du sultan*, p. 120.
21. See Brotton, *The Sultan and the Queen*.

19. Lucrezia Gonzaga writes to Suleiman

1. The behaviour of the Turks in the allied city of Toulon had not been edifying: but when is the behaviour of a billeted and idle army ever edifying? And still the Italian princes did not give up. The Turk, perhaps without knowing it, offered an opening for their manoeuvres. Except that, by definition, the Turk was powerful while the princes were small and were playing with fire.

Even a lady notable for her religiosity and culture, Lucrezia Gonzaga, got involved. We will surprise her now in a moment of peculiar intellectual weakness: or perhaps of singular boldness? Belonging to a lesser branch of the family of the Marquises of Mantua, the Gazzuolo branch, Lucrezia had received an excellent education from such a tutor as Matteo Bandello, who was later to dedicate a short story to her. In 1541 she was given in marriage to Giampaolo Manfrone, a Venetian mercenary leader and lord of Fratta in the Polesine. However violent and vulgar her husband was, Lucrezia always remained faithful to him. Having lost all sense of limit, in 1546 Manfrone conspired against Ercole II d'Este because he disapproved of the marriage of a sister of his that the duke had encouraged. As a result, the rebel was imprisoned in the dungeons of Ferrara Castle, where, in 1552, he went mad and died in circumstances that remained unclear. In the same year, a collection of 312 of Lucrezia Gonzaga's letters was printed in Venice.

Now a widow, Lucrezia gathered around her at Fratta a small court of intellectuals inspired by Erasmus. Erasmus' attitude to the Turks tended towards pacifism, in the conviction that the exercise of prayer and virtue would eventually prevail over the errors of their faith. The radical circles of Zurich and Basel had positioned themselves in the same political direction, influenced however by phases in the theological debate and the demands of the struggle with Rome. Luther himself believed that the Turks were a great threat for Christians, but also the only force capable of striking at the Papacy seriously. Hope of a peaceful conversion of the Muslims stayed in the air, as was the case in the medieval period, except that now it was mainly the reformers, and not the Catholics who cultivated it.[1] Whether the heterodoxy of Lucrezia was genuine or false, her proximity to characters inclined to Erasmian positions put her in danger. She underwent a trial

1. See Margolin, "Érasme et la guerre"; Segesvary, *L'Islam et la Réforme*, pp. 203-210; Bietenholz, "La minaccia turca"; Felici, "Una nuova immagine dell'Islam".

by the inquisition which was concluded in 1568 with the admission of her errors and her abjuration: a private abjuration in consideration of the rank of the guilty party.[2] Having carried out her sad obligation, Lucrezia lived in retreat until her death eight years later.

2. But let us return to the anti-Este plot hatched by Manfrone. Duke Ercole II was not willing to show clemency to someone who rebelled against him. The style of "Renaissance despotism" (as it is known nowadays) required a calculated dose of generosity and of cruelty.[3] Lucrezia knocked on all doors without success. She wrote to the signori of northern Italy, to the leaders of the Gonzaga, the Pio, the Bentivoglio, the Roverella families; she wrote to the Emperor, Charles V, to the King of France, to popes, cardinals, bishops and abbots and abbesses. In the end, nothing was left to her but the extreme decision of writing to the Sultan.

The form of address to the recipient of the message read like this: "To Suleiman emperor of Constantinople and of Trebizond, lord of Syria, Egypt, Phrygia, Cilicia, Cappadocia, Judea, Pamphylia, and of other kingdoms and very large provinces, at Constantinople"; the date given on the text is 20th September of an undefined year during the incarceration of Manfrone. The inspiration for the appeal is the usual one, even if it is made much clearer here: since I can find neither mercy nor pity among the Christians, who should be the true source of such things". In the way it is formulated, the phrase manages at the same time to injure Christians, who abdicate from their duties of virtue, and Muslims who would be less inclined to these obligations out of principle. Regarding Suleiman, not only are "many great victories" eulogised, which no-one contested, but also "many generous wars", and here again somebody might feel aggrieved. Then comes the request: "that you would also be pleased to use your arms, victorious in the world, in favour of my unhappy consort, who is a prisoner in the hands of a Ferrarese Duke who is inferior to you in power by a long way".

On this last point no-one had any doubts.

Lucrezia then launches into giving operational advice for the Sultan. She proposes enrolling into the enterprise "your cherished son-in-law, Rüstem Paşa", or, secondarily, "Salah Rais or Türgüt Rais, both indeed bold and courageous". Each of the people in question is not named at random. The first, the Bosnian, Rüstem Paşa Opuković, was the husband of Suleiman's the favourite daughter, Mihrimah, in whose honour the Sultan would later have the Great Mosque built by his architect, Sinan.[4] In addition to being "Royal Son-in-Law" (*dâmâd*), at that moment Rüstem Paşa held the post of Great Vizier, which was often the prerogative of those who had renounced their faith. While she looked to the east, she also looked up very high, our Italian lady from the provinces. As for the two raïs, or rather the two admirals and corsairs, the most famous was Türgüt Alì,

2. See Ridolfi, "Gonzaga, Lucrezia".
3. See Gundersheimer, *Ferrara: The Style of a Renaissance Despotism.*
4. See Gennaro, *Istanbul*, pp. 32-35.

better known in Europe as Dergut or Dragut. The successor to Khayr ad-Din (Barbarossa) in the regency of Algiers, Dragut was the author of violent raids along the Italian peninsula, on Sardinia and on Corsica: "Avenging sword of Islam" was the epithet attributed to him by the Ottomans. But Salah was hardly joking either in his actions at every corner of the Mediterranean.[5]

3. Lucrezia's invocation of Dragut forces us to pause. Thanks to the grim fame of his actions, in the Italian theatre of the time the name Dragut was synonymous with a Turkish barbarian. "Brè, brè, brè", Dragut irrupts shouting in the comedy, *La turca* by Giovan Battista dalla Porta, published in 1606. On his appearance all the Christian characters run away, moaning: "Turks, Turks, Turks", "Look, the Turks, dear me", "Uproar, they slaughter, they kill, they steal", "A Turk is violating me" (the voice of a young girl, *à propos* of sexual fantasies about the Turk). Meanwhile Dragut continues to shout in his vaguely canine way. On the other hand, weren't dogs infidels by definition? Turks seen by Christians, just like Christians seen by Turks?

The stuttering "brè, brè, brè" used to denote the Turkish language must have been typical. Certain fakers also bellowed in the same way ("bran, bran, bran, bre, bre, bre"), when claiming to have been ransomed from Turkish slavery. They are described in Rome in 1595, as part of an investigation into the "secret companies" of beggars.[6] Doubts about the reliability of this legal document take nothing away from our linguistic hypothesis, whether the tricksters really made the barking noise, or if it was simply attributed to them. Meanwhile the incomprehensible language of Dragut in the comedy was enriched with threatening variants: "Cangiabroc, sveglias, abricos".[7] And about these other forms we can say nothing, if not that they remind us of the growl of some of the guards of Dante's hell, from Minos to Pluto.[8] Only the finale of the comedy, which is consolatory for the public gallery, would not have pleased Lucrezia Gonzaga. Because the character Dragut reveals himself to have been born a Christian, he returns to his faith and leaves for the war against the Turks. The real Dragut was also of Greek origins, but it does not seem that he ever gave signs of reconversion.

4. We must indeed accept that this is literature, but the negative, animal-like, or infernal mythology that crystallised around the name of Dragut should nevertheless have some meaning. For this reason, we begin to doubt how well we have been reading the text. A Gonzaga lady, struck by misfortune but hardly the most desperate outcast, on the contrary blessed with privileges and income, invites

5. See Vergé-Franceschi, Graziani, *La guerre de course en Méditerranée*; Serrelli, "Sardinya Kralliği'nin Savunma Sistemleri".

6. See *Il libro dei vagabondi*, p. 352; Ginzburg, "Prefazione", p. 7.

7. Dalla Porta, *La turca comedia nuova*, p. 43*r*. See Lohse, "L'immagine degli Ottomani", pp. 203-204.

8. *Hell*, V 4; VII 1.

the most feared corsairs to Italy. At the very moment in which she violates one of the most deeply-rooted taboos of the era, she finds herself describing the corsairs as "bold and courageous". And yet, we have indeed read the text accurately, even if the risks of the appeal to Suleiman were not underestimated by Lucrezia: "I beg your great power to command your servants that as soon as they have conquered the castle where the Duke resides, they leave at once without damaging the coasts of the Christians". In short, once the service at the castle of Ferrara was done, the Turks were supposed to move on, leaving the Christians in peace. In 1551, the year before the publication of Gonzaga's letter, Dragut had carried out one of his cruellest exploits. Before conquering Tripoli, he had attacked the Maltese island of Gozo, hauling away five thousand slaves. Like everyone else, Lucrezia must have been informed of the action, but that was not enough to dissuade her from her appeal. As confirmation of his notoriety, in 1553 Dragut would also attack the Medici defences of the island of Elba.

Concern that the exotic allies would give themselves over to pillaging had also tormented Boccolino Guzzoni, and it was certainly not a fear without foundation. But at least Boccolino offered Bayezid something of inestimable value, a bridgehead for the conquest of Italy, while here it is not clear why Suleiman should inconvenience himself at all. Ah, certainly, glory: "you will earn more praise with this" than for every other feat achieved by the "fortunate and virtuous Ottoman house", including "breaking the horns of (humiliating) Hungary". Here the imperial mythology current at the court of Suleiman is summarised, Suleiman, legislator and messiah, new Solomon (the assonance between the two names also helped);[9] Suleiman, rival to Charles V and to the Pope at the level of universal sovereign, as the sumptuous tiara ordered by him in Venice in 1532 showed. There was no pity from Lucrezia for the Hungarian Christians crushed by the disaster of Mohács; no pity for King Ludovic II Jagiellon (Louis II of Hungary), who died on that day, nor for the aristocracy and high clergy of the kingdom who were also exterminated. On the contrary, for them there was a contemptuous, almost vulgar expression ("breaking the horns" – *humiliating*), certainly not fitting with the Erasmian irenics which the lady aspired to in her inner circle. "So do it as soon as it is possible for you to do so, I beg you with my hands clasped", this is the final invocation to Suleiman.

A habitual offender, a little later Lucrezia asked Baldassarre Altieri, secretary to the English embassy in Venice and friend to Luther and Melanchthon, "if the Turk will arm in the spring".[10] The question is suspect; the interlocutor is suspect, given the attitude of the reformers towards the Turk.

5. Lucrezia Gonzaga's letter to Suleiman is written in Italian, like most of the letters addressed to the Great Turk that we have met up until now (only a few were in Latin). The persistent international standing of the Italian language, at least on the Mediterranean chessboard, receives confirmation before the decline

9. See Fleischer, "The Lawgiver as Messiah"; Necipoğlu, "Süleymân the Magnificent".
10. Gonzaga, *Lettere*, pp. 179-181.

of the Italian States produced a similar contraction of the Italian linguistic space. The Turks had already absorbed Negroponte (Euboea), Venetian Albania, and the Morea, and soon it would be the turn of the Aegean Archipelago, of Chios, of Cyprus, of Crete. Later Corsica, Malta, Corfu, Zante, Istria, Dalmatia would also pass under changed sovereignty. But in the meantime Lucrezia could still permit herself to write to Suleiman in Italian, even if hers was an enforced choice, since it does not seem that she knew other modern languages of the time. By contrast, the ruling Italian princes were already equipping themselves to face up to the incipient decline of Italian. Without straying too far off on a tangent, we can say that Duke Alfonso II d'Este, son of Lucrezia's enemy, spoke perfect French and Latin, and understood Spanish sufficiently well. In addition he had learned German "with great and assiduous effort", a language that was not learned "for pleasure, being most barbarous": thus the Venetian representative at Ferrara, Emilio Maria Manolesso, noted in 1575.[11] As for Suleiman, by this time he was tending to abandon the Venetian-Italian, Greek and Latin used by his predecessors in their contacts with Italy, in favour of passing over to the empire's own language. We have seen that the letters sent by Suleiman to the Marquises of Mantua, Lucrezia's relatives, had already switched to Turkish.

In Lucrezia's words to Suleiman we can sense rage and stupefaction. Perhaps love, or something that resembles it in the terms of the age, had developed within her arranged marriage. Perhaps we are in the presence of a manifestation of Mediterranean "amoral familism",[12] that unique form of ethics that does not retreat in the face of any difficulty or offence purely to protect the family's core. But the wide family clique of the Gonzaga, which was much more attentive to political considerations, did not follow Lucrezia's extreme familism in any way. Precisely because it was generated by affections that were difficult to control (conjugal love or amoral familism, or both), the letter is full of political and ceremonial gaffes. Some better diplomatic counsellor might not have been without his usefulness to the supporting actors of Italian life of the time. This is true for the adventurer Boccolino Guzzoni, and we can hardly be surprised about it. But it also applies to the lady who, addressing Suleiman, does not sign herself, Manfronia, as she was called, but, proudly, Gonzaga. Perhaps to remind Constantinople of the good relations once shared between Bayezid II and Marquis Francesco II, and later between Suleiman himself and Marquis Federico II.

6. The authenticity of Lucrezia's correspondence remains in doubt.[13] According to some historians, Ortensio Lando, secretary to the noblewoman, might have been the author, or at least responsible for heavy alterations: the language, purified of streaks of northern Italian, is too standardised to have come from a Venetian-Mantuan pen. The paradigmatic model of a secretary, Lando was not alien to

11. *Relazioni degli ambasciatori veneti*, ed. by Alberi, vol. I, p. 45.
12. See Banfield, *The Moral Basis*.
13. See Gonzaga, *Lettere*, pp. XIII-XXVII (*Introduzione* by R. Bragantini).

unscrupulous editorial operations, even to the point of piracy. However, since there is no trace of protests by the supposed female author, the falsification, if it ever took place, must have been accepted by her. Then again, the climate of the victim created by the author is found in other women's correspondence of the time.[14] But in this case it goes far beyond this, even as far as to celebrate the cancellation of Christian Hungary. Surprising, truly surprising.

The appeal to Suleiman is thus of value because it was published under the name of Gonzaga and because it was not repudiated by her: this is the level of factuality that interests us and not other questions of authenticity. Sill in that same year of 1552, which seems to be the crucial year in the biography of Gonzaga (the death of her husband, the printing of her correspondence), the faithful Ortensio Lando published a panegyric of his mistress. Here we read how she reacted "when the harsh news reached her that her consort had fallen into the hands of his enemy", in other words, Ercole II d'Este. An allusion follows, but the appeal to Suleiman is sufficiently clear given the delicacy of the implicit subject: "What did she not do? What did she not say? What did she not attempt to regain for him the liberty he had lost?"[15]

Last of all, we would like to know if the letter, considered as genuine, was ever forwarded to the Sultan. And in what way did it get there, if not by the usual means, controlled by Venice? And it is unlikely that Venice would have enjoyed finding the Turks on her borders, in a moment in which no-one in Italy was threatening her. In this situation, the lady's initiative has the air of a message in a bottle, entrusted to a lateral branch of the Po in hopes that its currents would carry it as far as the Bosphorus. Such a lack of realism makes one even think that the letter was not written as a letter and that, imaginary vendetta against the Este Duke as it was, it never even left. Or rather, at the point in which we find ourselves, let us believe that we have identified a sort of minor literary genre: letters to the Great Turk that were never delivered. Written from Rome, from Rimini, from Osimo, from Napoli, from Milan, from Fratta in the Polesine and from who knows how many other places in Italy, about which we no longer have any information.

14. See Campanini Catani, "Dal manuale alla raccolta"; Campanini Catani, "Le forme dell'io", pp. 550-551.

15. Lando, *Due panegirici*, p. 51.

Fig. 1 Matteo de' Pasti, *Arabica machina ad expugnationem urbium*, in Roberto Valturio, *De re militari* (Rome, Biblioteca Apostolica Vaticana, *Reginense lat.* 1946, f. 136*v*).

Fig. 2. Matteo de' Pasti, *Forma bombarde machina*, in Roberto Valturio, *De re militari* (Rome, Biblioteca Apostolica Vaticana, *Reginense lat.* 1946, f.. 148*v*).

Fig. 3. Alfonso II of Aragon with the Turkish ambassadors, in Ferraiolo, *Cronaca* (New York, Pierpont Morgan Library, ms. M.801, f. 104*v*).

Fig. 4. Godefroy le Batave, Maximilian il Moro as a Moor, in François Demoulins, *Interprétation du Psaume XXVI* (Paris, Bibliothèque Nationale de France, ms. fr. 2088, f. 2).

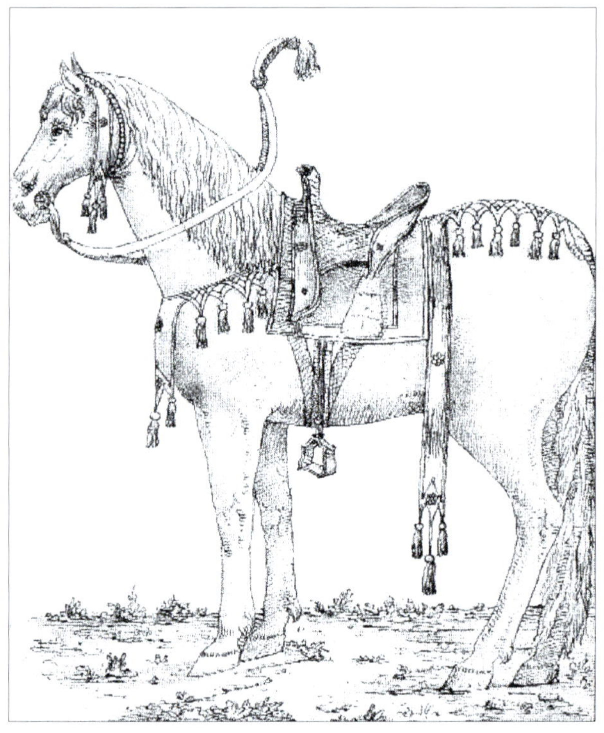

Fig. 5. Giulio Romano, Hall of the Horses, detail (Mantua, Palazzo Te).
Fig. 6. Filippo Orso, *Turcho d'Italia* (London, Victoria and Albert Museum, E. 1725-1929).

Figs 7-8. Jan Cornelisz Vermeyen, *Conquest of Tunis*, detail (Vienna, Kunsthistorisches Museum).

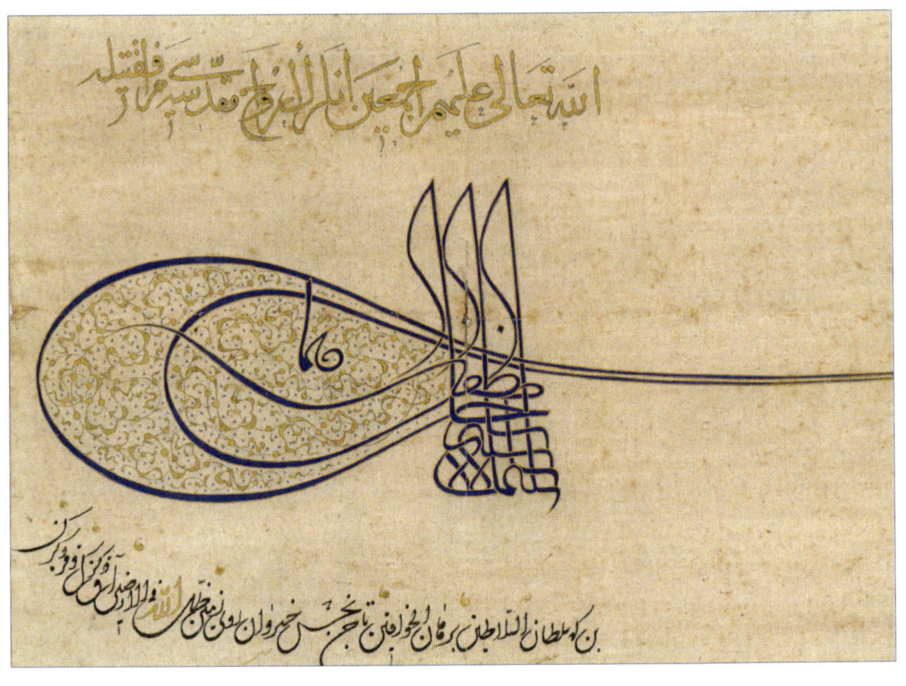

Fig. 9. Monogram of Suleiman the Magnificent (Mantua, Archivio di Stato, *Archivio Gonzaga*, b. 794, f. 26bis).

Fig. 10. Nakkaş Osman, Celebrations for the imperial circumcision of 1582, in Seyyid Lọkmān, *Şehinşāhnāme* [Book of the King of Kings] (İstanbul, Topkapı Sarayı Müzesi, ms. B 200, f. 59a).

Fig. 11. Jan Cornelisz Vermeyen, *Mulei Ahmet princeps africanus filius regis Tunesi*, Rotterdam, Museum Boijmans van Beuningen.

Fig. 12. Silvester van Parijs, *Cecy est le Roy de Thonis contrefaict a la vie*, Antwerp, Museum Plantin-Moretus.

20. Threatening and faking

1. The Turks made no effort to take the castle of Ferrara. But, a little later, the Este family line was to have a headache of Turkish origin, all the same. It began with Luigi, younger son of Renée de Valois and of the same Ercole II who had imprisoned the rebel Giampaolo Manfrone. In 1558, the eighteen-year-old Luigi was in France, a country Este princes travelled to willingly, seeing as they were related to the royal dynasty. From France Luigi informed his father that he had no intention of returning to Ferrara, a place he had no affection for; he would rather, he declared, escape "to Turkey if he had no other choice". A veiled threat of apostasy? Followed, perhaps, by a return to Ferrara in the company of the Turk, just as Lucrezia Gonzaga had hoped.

Other characters of high rank did the same, or were to do the same, to avenge abuses that were otherwise irremediable. Such had been the case with the famous Alvise Gritti, the natural son that Andrea Gritti, the future Doge, had conceived in Istanbul, perhaps with a Greek woman. An apostate or not (doubts remain on the issue) Alvise lived lavishly as a Turk in Istanbul, in this way overcoming the accusations of illegitimate origins that were thrown in his face in Venice. He also collaborated in the logistics of Suleiman's great offensives against the Christian powers: the Hungarian War of 1526 and the siege of Vienna of 1529.[1] No less famous than Gritti was the French count, Claude-Alexandre de Bonneval. A general in the Habsburg army who had fallen into disgrace in the Emperor's eyes, in 1720 he was to become a Turk with the name of Ahmet, being nominated pasha of Rumelia and head of the Ottoman artillery.[2] Perhaps Luigi d'Este did not press so far ahead with his thinking; perhaps his comment was simply a reply to a rhetorical topos that referenced the word 'Turk' to indicate an extreme firmness of conviction. However things stood, Ercole II decided not to take any risks, even though he was furious with that "miserable wretch, Luigi", as he wrote to Cosimo de' Medici.[3] He already had to deal with the scandal of his Calvinist wife, Renée de Valois; and to refute the accusations of having offered protection to the Jews exiled from the Iberian peninsula and from the Spanish Low Countries. So, thanks

1. See Nemeth Papo, Papo, *Ludovico Gritti*, pp. 42-48; Ricci, "Bâtards princiers".
2. See Benedikt, *Des Pascha-Graf Alexander*.
3. See Campori and Solerti, *Luigi, Lucrezia e Leonora d'Este*, pp. 7-10.

to his blackmail, the Este prince stayed in France. Brandishing the Turkish card as a young man did not impede Luigi later becoming an influential member of the Sacred College of Cardinals.

2. After thunder comes the rain: but it was false rain. To go beyond the metaphor: almost by dint of invoking him, the Turk did come to Ferrara, but he was a fake. In the January of 1576, a visitor dressed as a Turk offered Duke Alfonso II d'Este the crown of Jerusalem in the name of Sultan Murad III. Suspicions about the bearer of the proposal were hardly lacking, but it must have had some credibility as he was accommodated in the Castle of Ferrara. In the end he was unmasked by the arrival of updated news from Constantinople. It was all false, as the kingdom of Jerusalem had been extinct for centuries, Palestine had become an Ottoman province and the crown of Jerusalem was, by that time, merely nominal. Only the motive of the dissimulator – a subject of the Kingdom of Naples, as was later to be discovered – remained uncertain. Was he acting on his own behalf, to gain some personal profit? Or was he an agent of the Medici of Florence, eager to make fun of the Este, their rivals in the competition for prestige among the Italian princes? No-one would ever know, because the indomitable Neapolitan, even if he had been put in shackles, twice managed to escape: the first time he was retaken, the second he disappeared forever.

In falling into the trickster's trap, Alfonso II showed that he did not refuse the proposals of the Turks out of hand, while never actually invoking their arrival. But, at the same time, he continued to offer his troops for crusading enterprises. He did this to gain the benevolence of the papacy, the titular sovereign over Ferrara, who could blackmail the House of Este because of the absence of a male heir. And so Alfonso participated in the crusade in Hungary launched by the Habsburgs against Suleiman the Magnificent in 1566 – a crusade that was soon halted by the death of the Sultan. Then he took to behaving like all his contemporaries, approving a crusade in words and trying to make sure others actually fought it. Without armed galleys, Alfonso sat out the Lepanto campaign, but in 1595 he promised to take part in a new Hungarian war against Murad III. And this time he did not even set off.[4]

Receiving royal crowns from Murad, becoming his vassal when he was already a vassal of the Pope; waging war (for real or in pretence) against Suleiman or against Murad himself: the Duke of Ferrara did not reject any kind of contact with the Turk. In the meanwhile he continued to cherish the epic knightly poems written in his city, where the Moors were systematically focussed on as Turks. Political dependence on the papacy only added a further risk to his manoeuvres. But he certainly did not equal his great-grandfather, Ercole I, who in 1496, we should remember, had sent Ambrogio Bucciardo to Constantinople to incite the Turks against Venice. The Council of Trent was, by this time, imposing a new discipline on the behaviour of the Catholic world, and Alfonso II d'Este understood this perfectly well; the season of explicit appeals to the Turk was about to come

4. See Ricci, *Ossessione turca*, pp. 59-64.

to an end. "The Turks are at our gates", the Neo-Platonist philosopher, Francesco Patrizi, would proclaim in 1594.[5] Professor at the University of Ferrara, but native of the Dalmatian island of Cherso (today, Cres), and having lived for a long time on Cyprus, Patrizi was an expert in border relations with the Turks. And he was right to say that they were at the gates of Italy. Indeed it is true that many people, for more than a century, hoped or feared that they would make their entrance.

And since we have made mention of the great renegade, the Count of Bonneval, we should also like to report his opinion on the phenomenon of the appeal to the Turk. In the summer of 1729, Bonneval was manoeuvring to take Hungary from the Habsburgs and return it to the power of the Sultan. And this is how he justified his actions, in a letter to the French ambassador to Istanbul, Louis Sauveur de Villeneuve:

> So many popes and Catholic kings have allied themselves with Saracen sultans and Turkish emperors that I should be a fool to have any scruples about it. Do our princes not align themselves every day with protestant sovereigns whom the Church condemns and treats as if they were Muslims? Being cured of the prejudices of my wet nurse, my conscience and honour do not reprove me in any way in the matter.[6]

It can be no clearer than this: to be shocked was equivalent to not being freed from the "prejudices of the wet nurse".

5. Patrizi, *Paralleli militari*, p. 3*r*. See Gorris, "'*Prudentia perpetuat*'".
6. See Gorceix, *Bonneval Pacha*, pp. 146-147.

21. "To do Justice, the Turk and the Great Sultan"

1. In 1571 the War of Lepanto provoked waves of emotion. The Turks had just laid siege to Malta, which had barely avoided being taken; they had conquered the Genoese island of Chios, the Latin dukedoms of the Cyclades and, with some difficulty, the Venetian island of Cyprus.[1] From the time of the Fall of Constantinople, if not earlier, the Christian world did little other than retreat, one phase after another. Fears of a return to Turkish expansionism produced yet another Holy League consisting of Spain, the Papacy, Venice and other lesser signatories. The Catholic propaganda apparatus was mobilized, driven on by inquisitors and Jesuits and by the determined Pope Pius V,[2] exploiting the opportunity to discipline the improper conduct of soldiers and sailors.[3] "Pilgrimages and fasts" were announced in all churches, and the prayer against pagans (*contra paganos*) was recited, having been modified into a prayer against the Turks (*contra Turcas*): the Turks, the new pagans.[4] But the bottom line was that, above all, military costs were rising. Fiscal crackdowns came as a consequence, and popular discontent spread, just as in the times of the last crusades.

A little before the outbreak of the war, halfway through the year 1570, Doge Pietro Loredan had died. The Doge had been at one and the same time the author and victim of this costly foreign policy: he had not been the one to awaken the Turks after a thirty-year period of peace between the two powers, and this time no-one could accuse Venice of trouble-making or concubinage with the Turk. During the Doge's funeral, people had protested in an unheard-of manner. The cry: "Long live San Marco, long live the Signoria / as the Doge of famine is dead", had echoed through the streets. And only the driving rain had prevented still more serious defiance. Indeed, hundreds of men wanted to throw loaves of the millet bread they were forced to feed themselves with at the corpse of the Most Serene Doge.

1. See Brogini, *Malte, frontière de Chrétienté*, pp. 176-205; Argenti, *The Occupation of Chios*; Slot, *Archipelagus turbatus*, pp. 66-72; *Cipro-Venezia: comuni sorti storiche*; Costantini, *Il sultano e l'isola contesa*, pp. 43-74; Skoufari, *Cipro veneziana*.

2. See Ricci, *Papa Pio V*.

3. See Civale, *Guerrieri di Cristo*.

4. See *Episcopale Bononiensis Civitatis*, p. 96*v*.

2. In these circumstances an anonymous versifier composed a *Lamento dei pescatori veneziani* (Lament of the Venetian fishermen) that represents a harsh attack on warlike sentiments. The modest poem focusses on the themes that exploded on the day of Doge Loredan's funeral. Chiming in with the tradition of popular egalitarianism, oligarchs who "are scared that the melons and water melons will be pinched / by the Great Turk" are derided. And, in keeping with religious millenarianism, the sins of Christians are stigmatized and religious reform is hoped for: "It is not the Turks but the good Lord who makes war, / for all our numerous sins or wickedness / it is a wonder the earth does not open up".

Later on, the verses mention, precisely "that hard millet bread [...] that the Doge had sold [...] that was the cause of so many illnesses." And they reach their conclusion with a scandalous appeal to the Turk, in which the English translation does not do justice to the expressiveness of the original, in Venetian dialect:

> But because the Lord does not desire tyrants/ to rule too much in the world, he has placed/ the Turks and their great Sultan in the field. / These steal what the others have stolen, / and he prepares war and hardships for them [...] / Afterwards we shall all be dear brothers, / and we shall all go together bare-assed to catch fish, / soft-shell crabs, and shrimps.[5]

It was to be the Turk, then, who would bring back equality and fraternity to the body of the Republic: afterwards, in a friendly way, everyone would go fishing "bare-assed". The popular and lagoon-inspired context is continued right up to the last line. Paradoxically, the atrocities committed by the Turks on Cyprus had the effect of making people continue to attribute the role of avenger of the vices of Christians to them.

Despite these widespread sentiments, war broke out. We know that the victory at Lepanto was clear, but that disagreements between Venice and Spain prevented them from obtaining adequate fruits from this victory. Although tested, the Turks quickly realised that the equilibrium in the Mediterranean would not change, and the Republic hurried to sign a lasting peace.[6] Notwithstanding this, anti-Turk passions became wildly popular; astrology, iconography and denigratory publishing reached their peak, to the point of creating the topos of Lepanto as the New Salamis.[7] A contribution to the publishing on the subject was given by a singular character, the poet Luigi Groto, known as *il Cieco d'Adria* (The Blind Man of Adria), who was involved in another story. He had been a member of Lucrezia Gonzaga's circle of intellectuals, the one that had invited Suleiman into Italy. But the trial before the Inquisition endured by his protector in 1568 must have clarified his ideas; and Lepanto offered him the chance of redemption. He published a hundred and forty pages of celebratory verses in Latin, Neo-

5. *Il fiore della lirica veneziana*, pp. 441-449. For the tradition of laments in general, see Alazard, *Le lamento dans l'Italie de la Renaissance*.

6. See Yildirim, "The Battle of Lepanto".

7. See Gorris Camos, "La stella delle meraviglie", pp. 562-565; Sorce, "Metafore in bianco e nero"; Alonso, "Lepanto como Nueva Salamina"; Garcia Hernán, *Consecuencias politico-culturales de la batalla de Lepanto*.

Greek, Italian, and the dialects of Friuli, Padua, Bergamo and Bologna:[8] it was a phenomenon that, in terms of sheer quantity, was without equal in the Italian literature of the century. And in this way the Blind Man of Adria paid his debt to orthodoxy by celebrating the victory of Lepanto, which an exile from Lucca in France, Niccolò Franciotti, defined ironically as a "rhetorical victory".[9]

Meanwhile in 1572, some rebels in the city of Urbino had little concern at all for anti-Turkish sentiments of the moment. Following a well-established script, they declared that, to reach their goals, "they would even give themselves over to the Turk".[10] The appeal to the Turk, yet again…

8. Groto, *Trofeo della vittoria sacra*. See Dionisotti, "La guerra d'Oriente"; Formica, "La Porta e la Tiara", pp. 179-187.

9. See Adorni Braccesi, "La relazione inedita di Niccolò Franciotti", p. 67.

10. See De Benedictis, *Tumulti*, p. 90.

22. And the appeal to Christians?

1. Do not let us think that the Turks did not do the same, in their turn. Quite the contrary, on their side too, in extreme circumstances, the habit of appealing to non-believers, Christians, was commonplace. We have already met Prince Cem, the younger brother of Bayezid II. After losing the struggle for the throne, Cem evaded the policy of royal judicial fratricide by asking for help in turn from the Knights Hospitallers of Rhodes, the Duke of Savoy, the King of France and the Pope. Becoming much more a hostage and a pawn rather than a manipulator, he eventually got involved in, and became victim of, a game that was far bigger than him. On this occasion the appeal to Christians emanated from within the Ottoman Imperial House itself. There were no other Cems after this, despite the periodical crises caused by the uncertainty of succession procedures: from time to time it was seniority that counted, or primogeniture, or simply being the first to take possession of the imperial treasure. Although often tormented internally, the Ottoman Empire cultivated an idea of self-sufficiency that impeded it from involving Christians in its own convulsions.[1]

Other episodes reach us from marginal areas with respect to the main Muslim powers, or from areas on the frontier between Christianity and Islam.[2] We shall speak of them now, including both the level of high politics, where international alliances are put together, and the level of simple everyday life, where individual destinies are fulfilled. What we are not able to provide, however, is a quantitative evaluation of the phenomenon. Or rather: was the violation of the ideological-religious barrier an action that was more common among Turks or Christians? To tell the truth, we suspect that it was more common among Christians. We suspect this based on the whole dossier of evidence presented in this book, of course. In addition, we cannot neglect, by analogy, the greater frequency with which Christians renounced their faith compared to the Muslims doing this: whatever the reasons may have been for this and whatever the absolute numbers, the imbalance between the two trickles of conversions remains evident. Nor was the phenomenon of the Moorish saints – converted slaves, for the most part

1. Vatin, Veinstein, *Le Sérail ébranlé*, pp. 81-182.

2. To be published in the proceedings of the conference *Os territórios de fronteira entre a Cristandade e o Islão. Novas abordagens*, held in Lisbon, June 2011.

– which spread across the Catholic Mediterranean from the sixteenth century, enough to even out this difference.[3] But let us accept that this is too little to offer a convincing answer to the question posed above: who appealed to the infidel more willingly, Christians or Muslims?

2. The Muslim region that had a greater tendency to appeal to Christians seems to have been the Maghreb, the Barbary Coast, as it was known at the time. The Christian kingdoms of the Iberian peninsula were only separated from North Africa by narrow straits. This was well-known to fugitive slaves from one side and the other, so they often managed to get away on makeshift boats: the pages of *Don Quixote* devoted to the attempts of the slave Cervantes to escape from Algiers are famous.[4] And how narrow that sea is, indeed is well-known today to the illegal immigrants from Africa who attempt to reach the shores of Europe that are in sight, using any means possible. At the end of the *Reconquista* against the Arabs, the Christians continued their advance, eventually settling on the opposite shore of the Mediterranean and along the Atlantic coast (the so-called Western Barbary). There a situation of endemic anarchy favoured foreign penetration. Before the mirages of the New World and the oceans had redirected energies elsewhere, the Portuguese took Ceuta in 1415 and Tangiers in 1475; the Spanish followed with Melilla in 1495, Mers El Kébir in 1505, Cazaza in 1506, Peñón de Vélez de la Gomera in 1508, Oran in 1509, Bugia (now Béjaïa) and Peñón de Argel in 1510.[5] Not all of these possessions lasted very long; some, however, are under Spanish sovereignty to this day, as a permanent sign of an era of weakness of the Maghreb in comparison with the Iberian peninsula.

Classic frontier locations surrounded by Muslim populations, the Christian garrison towns on North Africa were real sources of turncoats. An unjust punishment, or one considered as such, an act of revenge, or personal resentment was enough to induce the most adventurous to cross over to the other side with a simple leap. It happened most of all to those who did not have a family or a social network waiting for them, as was often the case with men catapulted into such faraway places.[6] By a peculiar paradox, the frontier between Christianity and Islam, precisely because it was officially inviolable, produced such tensions as to make violation of it attractive. If this was true for the Christian soldiers stuck there, it was also true for the Muslims of the surrounding areas. For them the temptation of an agreement with the Christians, should one become necessary, was offered by the bastions of the Spanish or Portuguese garrisons. Intense spying activity completed the ambiguous atmosphere of these places.

3. See *Il santo patrono e la città*.

4. Cervantes, *Don Quijote de la Mancha*, vol. I, pp. 39-41. See Lloréns, "Historia y ficción"; Teijeiro Fuentes, *Moros y turcos*; Smith, "'The Captive's Tale'"; *Cervantes y la Berbería*.

5. See García Arenal, Bunes, *Los españoles y el Norte de África*; Unali, *Ceuta 1415*; Maffi, "'Il problema dell'altro'"; Bello León, "La cruzata en el Atlántico Medio".

6. See Bennassar, Bennassar, *Les chrétiens d'Allah*; Alonso Acero, *Orán-Mazalquivir*, pp. 154-164, 421-437; Ricci, *Ossessione turca*, p. 168.

3. All this was helped by the fact that while Ottoman power was distant, unifying forces were not in operation in the region. Claims of Ottoman possession were made over Algiers from 1515, Tripoli from 1551 and Tunis from 1574, but they met strong local resistance and were not without jurisdictional uncertainties. Only Morocco stayed beyond the sphere of Ottoman control; only Morocco did not receive orders and governors from Istanbul.[7] But Morocco was troubled by tribal and religious conflicts, in addition to dynastic tensions connected to the absence of the law of primogeniture. And from Morocco the defeated or the weak often turned their attention across the straits of Gibraltar. In short, for many geopolitical reasons North Africa was the ideal land for appeals to the Christians made by Muslims.

The Nasrid Emirate of Granada, the last Arab stronghold in Spain, fell into Castilian hands in 1492. Meanwhile, in Morocco the Marinid dynasty gave way to the rise of the Saadian dynasty, originally from the Sahara and strongly imbued with religious values. During this changeover, elements linked to the Marinids did not delay in allying themselves with the Christian sovereigns of the Iberian peninsula, even if the most important of them, the Kings of Castile, held the formal title of Catholic Kings thanks to their victory over Granada. And apart from the struggles of the Marinids and Saadians, things did not develop any differently between the African and Iberian the coasts. In 1512, the Abdelwadid Sultan of Tlemcen, Muley Abdallah, personally travelled to Burgos to meet Ferdinand II of Aragon. It was the first time that an Arab sovereign had touched Spanish soil since the fall of Granada. Laden with gifts (among these many freed Christian slaves), Muley Abdallah made an alliance with the Catholic Kings to defend himself against the unruliness of his coreligionists. In reality, it was an act of submission to infidels.[8]

With the Marinids defeated once and for all, some Saadians then turned to Spain on the occasion of disputes within their family line, or in the attempt to resist Ottoman pressure.[9] The claim, on the part of all contenders, of direct genealogical descent from the Prophet did not impede anyone from making deals with unbelievers. The defeated Arab dynasts who found refuge in Spain converted sooner or later, receiving baptism in sumptuous ceremonies. We cannot always be sure if the illustrious origins of the refugees were genuine, nor whether the conversions were all sincere, but this is of little consequence now.

Besides certain rare cases of belated changes of mind, marked by a return to the faith and to the land of their forefathers, the assimilation of the refugees was complete. Or, almost complete, seeing that in their titles the memory of their origin was preserved: Carlos de Africa, Felipe de Africa (the most numerous when the kings of Spain were called Felipe), Francisco de Africa, Josefa de Africa, Pedro de Marruecos, Infante de Fez, Regina de Fez, Fernando de Bugía, Ana dc Bugía, Felipe de Orán...[10] And in this way, next to the local *moriscos*, another group of new Christians settled on Spanish soil. The Nasrid leaders who had been baptised

7. See Dakhlia, Valensi, "Le spectacle de la cour".

8. See Cour, *L'établissement des dynasties*, pp. 51-52; García Arenal, "Mahdī, Murābīt, Sharīf"; *Maroc médiéval*, pp. 541-557..

9. See Alonso Acero, *Sultanes de Berbería*, pp. 61-109.

10. See Fiume, *Schiavitù mediterranee*, pp. 268-274.

when their city had fallen had set the example, giving origin to the Christian family line of the Granada. Although the marker of difference represented by a name remained, the exiles of high rank were exempted from the statute of the purity of the blood which would otherwise have limited the careers of their descendants. In these individual destinies, the theme of the appeal to infidels mixes with the theme of conversion to Christianity, a subject which is distinct in itself.

4. The political convulsions of the Maghreb and the anti-Ottoman feelings flourishing there also had repercussions in places that were internal to the Christian world, places that, on the whole, should have remained extraneous to events. We shall now take a look at an example. A Muslim sovereign struck by misfortune asked for help from Duke Ercole II d'Este, the father of the Alfonso II who was to receive the offer of the crown of Jerusalem from a supposed emissary of Sultan Murad III. The person requesting help was the King of Tunis, Mohamed-Hassan V, better known as Muley Hassan. Belonging to the Berber dynasty of the Hafsids, in 1542 Muley Hassan had been blinded and sent into exile by his son, Ahmed III Ahmida, known in his turn as Muley Ahmed; he was to reign until 1569.[11] A fugitive in Christian lands, on 19th March 1548 Muley Hassan arrived in Ferrara.

We do not know the previous sojourns of the invalid. We do know, however, that his final destination was Germany. At Mühlberg, Emperor Charles V had just defeated the Lutherans of the Schmalkaldic League, who were intriguing with the Turks and France. He had then brought the Diet of Augsburg to a close, obtaining other successes, in memory of which he had been depicted in glory by Titian (the painting is today in the Prado Museum in Madrid). Following Charles was no easy task, seeing as the Emperor spent a quarter of his days travelling, and changed his bed 3,200 times in Germany, Spain, the Low Countries, Italy, France, England and Africa;[12] but however that may have been, Muley Hassan wanted to meet him to make his case. The Emperor (and King of Spain) never ceased worrying about North Africa, where continuous threats to the Spanish and Italian coasts came from. To anyone who disapproved of such a waste of energy, Charles replied that he was accurately continuing the policy of the Catholic Kings towards Islam. The emblem of this continuity was the palace that the Emperor had built in Granada on the hill of the Alhambra, right behind the residences of the defeated Nasrids.

Charles V had already supported Muley Hassan in internal Tunisian disputes. In 1535, so as to block Barbarossa, the ally of France, who had driven Muley Hassan out of his kingdom, Charles V had conquered Tunis; and the Hafsid sovereign had been reinstated as a vassal of the Christian Emperor. As the completion of his African victory, between 1535 and 1536 Charles V had gone on a majestic ceremonial

11. See Doumerc, *Venise et l'émirat hafside*, pp. 45-76; Alonso Acero, *Sultanes de Berbería*, pp. 139-141; Valensi, *Ces étrangers familiers*; Varriale, *Arrivano li Turchi*, pp. 67-86, 120-126.

12. See Lapeyre, *Charles Quint*, pp. 13-14; Anatra, "Itinerari di Carlo V".

journey across Italy, from Sicily to Piedmont.[13] This happened while Francis I of Valois was negotiating his alliance with Suleiman: the contrast between French and Habsburg policy could not have been more obvious. Despite the crusading glory earned in Tunis, Charles V's subsequent expedition to Algiers in 1541 turned out to be a disaster. The Emperor withdrew from North Africa forever, while Barbarossa was left a free hand on the seas. And from that moment Algiers had taken off as the corsair capital, thanks also to the contribution given by the refugees from Andalusia.[14] Afterwards Charles V had seen the landing of his Turkish enemies at Toulon and the renewed banishment from Tunis of his vassal Muley Hassan, a victim of his son, on this occasion. The figurative commemoration of the conquest of Tunis in 1535, commissioned from Jan Cornelisz Vermeyen around 1548-1550, was nothing more than a symbolic compensation for the Emperor's most recent failures in Africa.

5. But let us return to Ferrara in the days of Muley Hassan's presence in the city. Duke Ercole II "willingly received and saw" the dispossessed Arab sovereign, as a local chronicler noted. He had him accommodated in the Palace of Count Costabili, one of the most sumptuous residences in the city.[15] After five days, Muley Hassan left for Mantua, where he was received as a guest by Duke Francesco III Gonzaga. From Mantua it was easy to travel up towards the Brenner Pass and Germany, where Charles V was currently to be found. Muley Hassan had already had friendly relations with the Gonzaga on the basis of the alliance between Tunis and Palermo. Ferrante Gonzaga, *Signore* of Guastalla and a valiant captain, had taken part in Charles V's expedition to Tunis thanks to which Muley Hassan had returned to the throne. Then, from 1535 to 1546, Ferrante had taken the role of Spanish viceroy in Sicily, and so collaboration with the Tunisian sovereign had been consolidated in an anti-Ottoman form.[16] Muley Hassan thus had a certain habit of making appeals to infidels. And Ferrante Gonzaga's family line no less so. Ferrante was the brother of the Marquis Federico II, friend to Suleiman, and son of Marquis Francesco II, friend to Bayezid II. But Ferrante, far from compromising himself with the Turks like his relatives – and before Lucretia Gonzaga raised the stakes beyond all measure – had dedicated himself to fortifying the Sicilian coasts threatened by the corsairs.[17]

As soon as he arrived in Mantua, on 27th March 1548, the refugee Muley Hassan wrote a formal and imploring letter to Ercole II d'Este. The wretched exile was counting on the excellent Jewish doctors who lived in Ferrara as a consequence of the shelter offered by the Este to the Jews expelled from the

13. See Rodríguez Salgado, "¿Carolus Africanus?", pp. 503-507; Visceglia, "Il viaggio cerimoniale di Carlo V".

14. Nordman, *Tempête sur Alger*.

15. Massa, *Memorie di Ferrara*, p. 91.

16. See Odorici, "Lettere inedite di Muley-Hassen"; Brunelli, "Gonzaga, Ferrante", pp. 736-737.

17. See Dufour, "Città e fortificazioni"; Bazzano, "La Sicilia di Ferrante Gonzaga", pp. 119-138; Favarò, *La modernizzazione*, pp. 38-42.

Iberian peninsula together with the Moors.[18] Perhaps he had also met one of these doctors during his stay in the city. We possess the original of Muley Hassan's letter in Arabic, but we do not know whether it was written by the sovereign in person, given the condition of his vision. The document was accompanied by a halting translation in Spanish produced by a companion of the sovereign, a certain Giovanni Navarette de Caravagiolo. The letter begins with great praise for "the great, benign and generous Duke of Ferrara"; and it concludes with the hope that he would like "to have me given a good cure for my eye, nothing else do I wish from the prince". The signature, "Mahamet Lasen King of Tunis", is nothing other than a mangled version of the official name of the king, Mohamed-Hassan.[19]

6. Leaving Mantua, the blind man from Tunis slowly reached Charles V's court which in the meantime had moved on to Brussels. In the province of Flanders, less accustomed than Italy to the presence of Turks, the appearance of Muley Hassan stimulated great curiosity. This also because as a person he was already known there, both on the basis of accounts of the conquest of Tunis, and through certain iconographic sources. At the time of the African expedition of 1535, Charles V's official illustrator, Jan Cornelisz Vermeyen, had painted a portrait of Muley Hassan's son, prince Muley Ahmed. Today the painting has disappeared, while an analogous watercolour survives, which Vermeyen produced as soon as he had returned to Flanders (fig. 11).

These images did not take long to produce effects. Almost at once, in 1536, a French artist naturalised as a Fleming, Silvester van Parijs (Sylvestre de Paris) saw the painting or the watercolour by Vermeyen; starting from the facial features of the son, Muley Ahmed, he engraved a portrait of the father, Muley Hassan, in wood. The new identity was certified by a false title, because Silvester van Parijs had certainly not reproduced Muley Hassan from the life ("contrefaict à la vie"), since he was in Africa.[20] Representing "from life" people, cities, and places was a very popular skill with the public because it promised reliable and up-to-date images.[21] But in reality, Silvester van Parijs simply aged the portrait: he made him heavier, and he added a marked cross-eyed appearance to him (fig. 12). This ocular defect of Muley Hassan, which must have been in the public domain, in a sinister way anticipates his future blinding by Ahmed.

Thus, in Flanders an iconographic current was established regarding the two members of the Hafsid dynasty. Gradually this was enriched with other contributions. We shall not survey them here, but we cannot neglect the endpoint because it even culminates in Rubens. In about 1620, the Master from Antwerp made a copy of the portrait of Muley Ahmed that Vermeyen had painted almost a century before.

18. See Raspadori, "La Facoltà medica di Ferrara", pp. 265-267; Nutton, "The Rise of Medical Humanism"; Bacchelli, "Antonio Musa Brasavola".

19. Archivio di Stato di Modena, *Archivio Segreto Estense*, *Carteggi con principi esteri*, b. 1621, «Tunisi, Re». See anche Foucard, *Relazioni dei duchi*, pp. 33-35.

20. See Horn, *Jan Corneliusz Vermeyen*, pp. 15, 19-20, 74, 78.

21. See Ricci, "'Verare la città'".

On the basis of an inventory made after his death, it appears that the painting was part of Rubens' private collection (today it is in the Boston Museum of Fine Arts). Although it is missing a title, the sources and tradition confirm that Rubens also changed the identity of the person depicted: not Muley Ahmed, a rebel against Charles V, defenestrated in 1569 and weighed down by a dreadful reputation, but instead Muley Hassan again, the faithful vassal of the Emperor. Rubens did not even make the effort to age the subject, as Silvester van Parijs had done in his time; he limited himself to inverting the image, following a method of concealing plagiarisms that was common at the time. The King of Tunis stands out against a background of ancient ruins (perhaps the ruins of the aqueduct of Carthage), while to the sides scenes of combat between Christians and Muslims can be seen. These are the most obvious signs of Rubens' dependence on the iconography of Vermeyen. Idealised after the event, Muley Hassan has been transformed into the symbol of victorious Christianity. And for this reason Rubens also inserted him into some of his Adorations of the Magi in the form of Balthasar, the Black King.[22]

As far as the historical figure of Muley Hassan is concerned, successes with artists were unlikely to have an influence on the chances of saving his eyes. His later life among Christians is little documented. It appears that he was present at the imperial abdication of Charles V in Brussels in 1556. Immediately following this, he left traces of his presence from Naples to Sicily, where he lived supported financially by the Spanish government. We are tempted to think that he converted, and his posthumous glorification by a Catholic painter like Rubens reinforces the theory. Anyway, his misfortune has allowed us to witness a kind of Mediterranean triangulation: a Muslim who asks for military aid from Christians and medical assistance from Jews. If the Muslim documentation presented in this book is less copious than the Christian documents, it offers us this rare episode: a multiple appeal to infidels.

22. See Held, "Rubens 'King of Tunis'".

23. The clash of civilizations or the Mediterranean Alternative

1. We have come to understand that all the actors in the Mediterranean, divided as it was, were capable of turning to infidels against their own coreligionists. But this book is principally devoted to the appeal to the Turks made by Christians as a consequence of conflicts developing within their own world.

With the exception, perhaps, of the invasion of Otranto, appeals made from Italy were not given any serious weight by the Turks. Wiser than those who invoked them, or perhaps less daring than they were conventionally judged to be, the Turks avoided a quantity of mourning for themselves and others. The history of the appeal to the Turks is thus a collection of mutilated fragments, of secret thoughts, of abortive attempts, of justified accusations or unfounded smears, of blackmail on all sides, of letters never sent, replies never written or which never reached their destination, of coded messages that were not always authentic, of gifts intercepted, of informers in constant alarm, of ambushes in the ports of the Levant or on the Italian coast. Faced with such discontinuous material, early modern historians, who are used to dealing with documents in abundance, find themselves in a situation that is similar to historians of earlier and more reticent periods. Like them, they have to refine their role as restorers of fragments, as creators of a narrative that is compatible with the underground courses of factual data.[1] In this perspective, the concept of plausibility takes on a central role, so as to make even silences and absences fruitful.

But this is also the history of a rhetorical *topos* that is intermingled with reality in a changeable way, from one episode to the next. In attempting to distinguish the weight of the two ingredients, rhetoric and reality, it seems to us that rhetoric prevails when the protagonists are isolated, desperate, poorly informed, and capable only of uttering illusory threats; the reality principle, on the other hand, takes precedence in cases that are more political, less naïve and involving high social rank. Scandalous as ever, the appeal to the Turks indicates both the global level of operations that still emanated from Italy and, at the same time, the increasing impotence of this activity.

Even if they were often left without response, appeals were made from Italy, or attempted appeals at least, and this is what is important for us. Paradoxically, the

1. See Ricoeur, "L'écriture de l'histoire".

requests and the refusals both contribute to negating the image of an insuperable opposition between the two most numerous power-blocks of Mediterranean monotheism. Requests, because they show Christians (some Christians, but not of secondary importance) prepared to ally themselves with the Turks even to the point of finding them on their own soil; refusals, because they reveal the Turks to be so little inclined to warmongering as to decline the offer of bridgeheads in Italy. Questions that belong to counterfactual history[2] (in our case: what if the Turks had conquered Italy?) are not merely an intellectual game for posterity, straddling philosophy and futility. The same questions must have been posed by those responsible for the choices made, Christians no less than Turks; never so much as in this instance was the line of demarcation between factual and counterfactual so provisional, awaiting verification.

It should be emphasised that everything happened without visible implications of religious disavowal such as to weigh down the events ideologically. In the episodes we have analysed, religion is relatively unimportant, merely serving as a kind of obligatory background, as a stereotyped language that accompanied every human action at that time.

2. Our dossier could easily be enlarged, even though many events, by their very nature, have left no mark and are destined to escape us forever. But in light of what we have described, the historical bases of the theory of the clash of civilisations appear to be factually inaccurate. In particular, they do not take into account the porosity introduced on the frontier by popular and élite anticlericalism: both these modes of behaviour, to be found at the extremes of the social scale, were widespread in the Italy of the Renaissance.

At the geographical centre of the Mediterranean, Italy was not just one place among many in the system of relations between Christianity and Islam, and this for two powerful reasons. In the first place, Italy was the location of the headquarters of Latin Christianity. It was in Rome that doctrines were developed, information was gathered, and strategies were put together that were capable of influencing international politics. In the second place, however, the Italian peninsula was a borderland, and had been since Arab expansion in the High Middle Ages had shattered the religious unity of the Mediterranean.[3] And from then on the rift had done nothing other than become more marked. While Christianity spread in the West (the conquest of Granada and of the New World), in the East Islam was expanding (the conquest of Constantinople and the Balkans). Arab Islam was master of North Africa, a short step away from Sicily; Ottoman Islam overlooked the Adriatic-Ionic Sea from Albania and, in Bosnia, was approaching Friuli, a mere stone's throw from eastern Italy. If Venice was only maintaining its positions in the Levant with difficulty, the whole of the long Italian coastline was exposed to piracy and privateering.

2. *What if?*; *More what if?*.
3. See Pirenne, *Mohammed and Charlemagne*.

The theory of the clash of civilisations, in its turn and in its own terms, marks the peculiarity of the Italian situation. It tells us that historical inheritance has left deep fault lines around Italy: to the south, the frontier between western and Islamic civilisations; and to the east, the tripartite frontier between Western, Islamic and Orthodox civilisations.[4] Three of the nine planetary civilisations listed by the theory come into contact near Italy. Few corners of the globe enjoy at one and the same time such aspects of centrality – universal religious authority – and of such marginality – numerous fault lines. The centre of gravity of Roman Christianity, and yet at the periphery, Italy is a unique laboratory for our object of study. It is not by chance that the majority of the stories we have narrated are set on the eastern edges of the peninsula: along the most problematical of the frontiers that surround Italy.

3. Recently a theory known as the "Mediterranean Alternative" has been contrasted with the theory of the clash of civilisations. Being formulated by European and Arab historians, the Mediterranean Alternative is, almost by definition, less well-known and influential than the theory of the clash of civilisations of American provenance, but this does not mean that it is not worthy of attention. The theory of the Mediterranean Alternative hinges on the capacity for cooperation that characterised the inhabitants of this landlocked Sea over the centuries, before the explosion of nineteenth century nationalisms and twentieth century ideological and religious fundamentalisms.[5] For reasons of survival for all the parties involved (the Mediterranean coastlines measure fifty-thousand kilometres, perfect security is an illusion), official conflict permitted narrow openings of peaceful mediation. In this view, the term "alternative" becomes a synonym of de facto compromise. There is no philosophical ambition, no pure reason in all this, just like the genesis of the idea of tolerance that we mentioned at the beginning of this book; only practical reason imbued with empiricism, and accustomed to cultural plurality. The result has not been insignificant, since the cultural and religious variety of the Mediterranean has been preserved over the centuries without excessive homogenisation.

The theory of the Mediterranean Alternative appears to be confirmed by a historical piece of linguistic data: the development of the Mediterranean lingua franca. The lingua franca was a horizontal communicative instrument, and so not something coming from above like the imperial languages (in the early modern and modern ages, with the decline of Latin, Spanish, French and English, in this order). In contrast, in the centuries of its greatest expansion (thirteenth to eighteenth centuries), the lingua franca was made up of simplified contributions from all the coastal cultures. Religious barriers had no effect, even if, with the Romance element being predominant, for many Muslims it was considered a "Christian"

4. See Huntington, *The Clash of Civilizations*.

5. See *L'alternativa mediterranea* (especially the contributions di Zolo, "La questione mediterranea" and Cassano, "Necessità del Mediterraneo"); see also Bono, *Un altro Mediterraneo*, pp. 79-110; *Adriatico contemporaneo*. But also earlier: *Dialogue de civilisations en Méditerranée*.

language, or one useful for trading with Christians. Indeed, Venetian, Genoese, Neapolitan and Sicilian, or rather, regional variants of Italian, accounted for 80% of the lingua franca; after this Catalan, Occitan, Greek, Arabic and Turkish were its other main components, in proportion with the importance of their respective naval traditions. The phonetics, morphology, syntax and lexis of the lingua franca are quite well-known, naturally within the limits permitted by a language that was spoken much more than it was written.

Stifled by nineteenth century colonialism (the critical date is the French conquest of Algiers in 1830), the lingua franca does not cease to surprise us in its fundamental social and philosophical meanings. And now, quite rightly, its memory is being reevaluated with appropriate research.[6] Even more so, considering that no group of people claims its inheritance, in contrast to other extinct or dying languages that enhance the linguistic variety of modern Europe.[7] Is it a sign of nobility, to be without heirs in an era of hardening identities? This was, indeed, the language of people on the borderline, of sailors, corsairs, slaves and the redeemers of slaves, of renegades and of merchants; it was the language of intermediaries, of people who were generally of pliable religious conviction.[8] It was not, on the other hand, the language of admirals and of official military fleets; and least of all the language of men of letters or of religious hierarchies.

In historical fact, the Mediterranean Alternative has not survived the globalisation of political, economic and cultural processes; it has not survived the passing of the central importance of the Mediterranean Sea. The emergence of compact power blocks has gradually substituted the mosaic patchwork, also causing the extinction of the lingua franca, to the benefit of one imperial language or another.

4. If the *lingua franca* summarises the Mediterranean Alternative, a fragile island myth does no less. It is worthwhile dedicating some space to it.

For a long time, on the Mediterranean coast, stories were told about a hermit who lived in a cave on the island of Lampedusa. This strip of land is geologically a part of Africa and is nearer Tunisia than to Sicily. Here the hermit had a duplicate series of holy furnishings and holy books, with which he gave advice to Christian and Muslim sailors, each according to their law.[9] Unifying factors (monotheism, the relationship with the sea) prevailed over other factors of historical division. The offerings received by the holy man also made his home into a centre of supply and mercantile exchange on the deserted island. Among other things, the cave contained an image of the Madonna that was venerated both by Christians and Muslims: devotion to Mary was not rare in Islamic lands, due to the praise which the Koran bestows on the mother of the

6. See Kahane, Kahane, Tietze, *The Lingua Franca in the Levant*, pp. 10-29; Cortelazzo, *Venezia, il Levante e il mare*, pp. 388-397; Cifoletti, *La lingua franca mediterranea*; Cifoletti, *La lingua franca barbaresca*; *Trames de langues*; Dakhlia, *Lingua franca*, pp. 147-191.

7. See Burke, *Languages and Communities*.

8. See *Le commerce de captifs*.

9. See Scaraffia, *Rinnegati*, pp. 15-19; Kaiser, “Zones de transit”.

prophet Jesus.[10] The cave actually exists and is today enclosed within the small church of the Madonna di Porto Salvo. However, the original icon of Mary is missing because at a certain moment it was taken away by the Sicilian nobles, the Tomasi (the ancestors of the author of the famous novel, *The Leopard*). They held the title of Princes of Lampedusa from 1664 until 1843, when Ferdinand II, King of the Two Sicilies bought the island out of fear of a surprise attack by the English. Malta was nearby, and British imperialism at its height.

But did the syncretic hermit really exist? A place like Lampedusa, remote and populated in an erratic way, can only produce ephemeral documentary traces. An unexpected indication reaches us from 1726, in the report of the redemption from slavery of a sailor. Originally from Ferrara, and having previously embarked on a Maltese pirate ship, the man was captured and reduced to slavery in Tunis. He was called Lorenzo Pavini and we read that he was freed in the place of another slave who had died "upon the rock of Lampedusa" while he was waiting for the final details of the agreement to be reached; in the circumstances an ill-defined role was carried out by the "Father Clemente, hermit, inhabitant of that rock". Was Father Clemente the venerated hermit whom everyone talked about? Or had Father Clemente inherited his mission? Or should the Ferrarese origin of the report make us think of a literary calque? In the *Orlando furioso* a hermit receives the shipwrecked Moor, Ruggiero, on an island.[11] The theme in itself was not rare, seeing as the *Isolari* (Books of islands) of the Renaissance tended to fill the Aegean Sea with rocky outcrops inhabited by only one monk.[12] In this case, however, the difference is that Ariosto's hermit set down to baptising the Moor at once, while our hermit was devoted to a two-fold form of worship.

Whether the hermit of Lampedusa really existed or not, he was definitely important for sailors; but for us the follow-up to the story is more interesting. Because nothing is given forever. With the passage of time, all frontiers have hardened and the idea of neutrality between the Law of Christ and the Law of Allah has lost its meaning. Both parties involved may have been responsible for this hardening of attitudes, the origin of which is probably to be found outside the Mediterranean. In fact, popular Sicilian dialect has ended up attributing the title of *romito di Lampedusa* (hermit from Lampedusa) to anyone who cannot choose, who is always in a state of doubt, or who is not worthy of our trust because he has a dual faith.[13] With hermit becoming a negative paradigm, the meaning of the myth has been lost: it appeared to be a shining, illuminating fable and instead it finishes in darkness. Analogously, on the level of reality, the function of being a bridge between Christianity and Islam performed by Lampedusa and its surrounding islands has been lost, where once slaves from one side and the other were delivered, ready for ransom. Today, by contrast,

10. See Keriakos, "Les apparitions de la Vierge en Égypte".

11. *Nel riscatto di Giuseppe Antonio Benedetto Dotti*; Ariosto, *Orlando Furioso*, pp. 905-906 (XXXVII 51-54). See Ricci, *Ossessione turca*, p. 160

12. See Lestringant, *Le livre des îles*, pp. 62-84.

13. See Calcara, *Rapporto del viaggio scientifico*. The current linguistic usage was confirmed to me by Giovanna Fiume, whom I thank.

slaves of the 21st century land there, refugees and illegal immigrants. With this the finale becomes even darker.

5. The Mediterranean Alternative also meant this: the existence of intermediate spaces, of intermediate languages, and of intermediate people who could only be trusted to some extent. It meant the capacity to share specific holy places without worrying too much about the barriers raised by religious professionals; it meant popular indifference towards notions of purity and contamination.[14] If religious crossovers in the strict sense of the term were peculiar to areas in the Byzantine-Ottoman tradition, in more general terms Italy was deeply shaped by the Mediterranean Alternative; Italy, at once at the centre and at the margins of Latin Christianity, Italy, immersed in a sea where the religions of the Book come into contact. The conceptual alternative implies, in addition, an alternation in time between differing phases: phases dominated by a collision between states and armed religions; or phases characterised by daily and pragmatic arrangements between individuals whose interests did not always fit with those of the group they were a part of.[15] This dialectic of opposition and engagement, unfortunately, was not able to interrupt the vicious circle of fears that had chained the Christian north coast and the Muslim south coast of the Mediterranean together: a sea that was united and divided at the same time.

And as far as the future is concerned, if in the case of the theory of the clash of civilisations the prediction of an era of wars is perhaps unwise, in the case of the idea of a Mediterranean Alternative, the prediction of an era of peaceful exchange is certainly ingenuous and fanciful. On the other hand, we have criticised the clash of civilisations not so much because it is excessively centred on war, but rather because it draws borders that are too clearly delineated. The stories that we have collected are themselves stories of clashes, but, far from respecting a clear-cut partition between Christians and Muslims, they reveal more complicated alliances and entanglements. Whatever the meaning of a word like "hybridity" may be, conflict is always threatening.[16] In the introduction we have said that we are not overlooking the acts of violence inflicted reciprocally in the past; it is all the more true that we do not underestimate present and future tensions.

In discussing the Mediterranean Alternative, other limitations could be introduced. Despite this, the historical analysis that supports this idea works in concert with a minute Mediterranean geography, made up of islands, peninsulas, isthmuses, harbours, canals, and straits; in the Mediterranean world, from land you can often see the sea, just as from the sea you can often see land. By contrast, the theory of the clash of civilisations appears to reflect the Anglo-Saxon imperial experience of large land masses and open seas, rendered self-

14. See Couroucli, "Le partage des lieux saints".
15. See Ricci, *Türk Saplantisi*, pp. 7-8.
16. See Burke, *Cultural Hybridity*.

referential and universalist by their very immensity. And so intricate, indented earth-water margins might present themselves to us as a mental alternative to oceans and continents, because, historically, a different life was led there, one well-practised in differences, in intimacies, and in reciprocal yielding. More explicitly than ever, differing political visions of the future bring with them differing readings of the past – and vice versa.

Bibliography

1509-2009, l'ombra di Agnadello: Venezia e la terraferma, ed. by G. Del Torre and A. Viggiano, Venice, Ateneo veneto, 2011

Abulafia D., "Mediterraneans", in *Rethinking the Mediterranean*, ed. by W.V. Harris, Oxford, Oxford University Press, 2006, pp. 64-93

Ács P., "Tarjiumans Mahmud and Murad. Austrian and Hungarian Renegades as Sultan's Interpreters", in *Europa und die Türken*, pp. 307-316

Adorni Braccesi S., "La relazione inedita di Niccolò Franciotti su Venezia e la battaglia di Lepanto", *Archivio veneto*, 6 (2013), pp. 51-68

Adriatico contemporaneo. Rotte e percezioni del mare comune tra Ottocento e Novecento, ed. by S. Trinchese and F. Caccamo, Milan, FrancoAngeli, 2009

Agapiou N., "Enea Silvio Piccolomini et les Grecs", in *Pio II umanista*, pp. 145-164

Airaldi G., "Oltre le frontiere. Genovesi e Turchi tra Medioevo e età moderna", in *Incontri di civiltà nel Mediterraneo. L'impero ottomano e l'Italia del Rinascimento*, ed. by A. Naser Eslami, Florence, Olschki, 2014, pp. 19-30

Akasoy A., "Mehmed II as a Patron of Greek Philosophy: Latin and Byzantine Perspectives", in *The Renaissance and the Ottoman World*, ed. by A. Contadini and C. Norton, Surrey, Ashgate, 2013, pp. 245-256

Alazard F., *La bataille oublié. Agnadel 1509: Louis XII contre les Vénitiens*, Rennes, Presses Universitaires de Rennes, 2017

Alazard F., *Le lamento dans l'Italie de la Renaissance*, Rennes, Presses Universitaires de Rennes, 2010

Albanès J.H., *Gallia christiana novissima. Histoire des archevêchés, évêchés et abbayes de France*, ed. by U. Chevalier, 7 vols., Valence, Imprimerie Valentinoise, 1899-1920, vol. III

Alberti L., *Descrittione di tutta Italia*, Venice, Avanzi, 1568

Alonso A., "Lepanto como Nueva Salamina: un tópico hispano-italiano entre Mal Lara y Viruès", in *Oriente e Occidente*, pp. 475-485

Alonso Acero B., "El norte de África en el ocaso del emperador (1549-1558)", in *Carlos V*, pp. 387-414

Alonso Acero B., *Orán-Mazalquivir, 1589-1639. Una sociedad española en la frontera de Berbería*, Madrid, Consejo Superior de Investigaciones Científicas, 2000

Alonso Acero B., *Sultanes de Berbería en tierras de la cristiandad. Exilio musulmán, conversión y asimilación en la Monarquía hispánica (siglos XVI y XVII)*, Barcelona, Bellaterra, 2006

L'alternativa mediterranea, ed. by F. Cassano and D. Zolo, Milan, Feltrinelli, 2007

Álvarez Palenzuela Á.V., "Alfonso V, rey de Nápoles: regulación de la sucesión y reconciliación con el Pontificado", in *XV Congreso de Historia de la corona de Aragón*, 3 vols., Zaragoza, Departamento de educación y cultura, 1996, vol. I, pp. 509-522

[Amasaei H.], *Vaticinium quo praedicitur universum orbem terrarum christianae religionis imperium subiturum*, Venetiis, [Manutius] 1499

Anatra B., "Itinerari di Carlo V", in *Storia sociale e politica. Omaggio a Rosario Villari*, ed. by A. Merola, Milan, F. Angeli, 2007, pp. 138-150

Andenna G., "Un tragico punto di svolta: l'occupazione turca di Otranto", in *Otranto nel Medioevo tra Bisanzio e l'Occidente*, ed. by H. Houben, Galatina, Congedo, 2007, pp. 243-279

Andretta S., *L'arte della prudenza. Teorie e prassi della diplomazia nell'Italia del XVI e XVII secolo*, Rome, Biblink, 2006

Anselmi S., *Mercanti, corsari, disperati e streghe*, Bologna, Il Mulino, 2000

Anselmi S., *Storie di Adriatico*, Bologna, Il Mulino, 1996

Anselmi S., *Ultime storie di Adriatico*, Bologna, Il Mulino, 1997

Antonaci A., *Otranto. Testi e monumenti*, Galatina, Pajano, 1955

Arcangeli L., "Note su Milano e le città lombarde nelle guerre di Luigi XII (1499-1515)", in *Città in guerra*, pp. 135-142

Argenti Ph., *The Occupation of Chios by the Genoese and their Administration of the Island. 1346-1566*, 3 vols., Cambridge, Cambridge University Press, 1958

Ariosto L., *Orlando Furioso secondo la princeps del 1516*, ed. by M. Dorigatti, Florence, Olschki, 2006

Atasoy N., *1582 Surname-i Hümayun: An Imperial Celebration*, İstanbul, Kocbank, 1997

Babinger F., "Lorenzo de' Medici e la corte ottomana", *Archivio storico italiano*, 121 (1963), pp. 305-361

Babinger F., *Mehmed the Conqueror and His Time*, Princeton, Princeton University Press, 1992

Babinger F., "Maometto il Conquistatore e l'Italia", *Rivista storica italiana*, 63 (1951), pp. 465-505

Bacchelli F., "Antonio Musa Brasavola archiatra di Ercole II duca di Ferrara", *Micrologus*, 16 (2008), pp. 323-346

Bacchelli F., "Celio Calcagnini, Pacifico Massimi e la simulazione", *I castelli di Yale*, 7 (2005-2006), n. 8, pp. 1-28

Bağci S., "From Translated Word to Translated Image: The Illustrated Şehnāme-i Türkî copies", *Muqarnas. An Annual on Islamic Art and Architecture*, 17 (2000), pp. 162-176

Baldi B., *Pio II e le trasformazioni dell'Europa cristiana (1457-1464)*, Milan, Unicopli, 2006

Banfield E.C., *The moral basis of a backward society*, New York, The Free Press, 1968

Barreto J., *La majesté en images: portraits de pouvoir dans la Naples des Aragon*, Rome, École française de Rome, 2013

Baskar B., "L'anthropologie méditerranéenne en Adriatique du nord-est: de l'ethnologie 'monothéiste' à l'anthropologie des frontières", in *La Méditerranée des anthropologues. Fractures, filiations, contiguités*, ed. by D. Albera and M. Tozy, Paris, Maisonneuve & Larose, 2005, pp. 227-241

Bazzano N., "La Sicilia di Ferrante Gonzaga (1535-1543): uno schizzo storiografico", in *Ferrante Gonzaga. Il Mediterraneo, l'impero (1507-1557)*, ed. by G. Signorotto, Rome, Bulzoni, 2009, pp. 119-138

Bear M., Makdisi U. and Shryock A., "Tolerance and Conversion in the Ottoman Empire: A Conversation", *Comparative Studies in Society and History*, 51 (2009), pp. 927-940

Belfanti C.M., "I Gonzaga signori della guerra (1410-1530)", in *La corte di Mantova*, pp. 61-68

Bellini and the East, ed. by C. Campbell and A. Chong, London-Boston, National Gallery Company-Isabella Stewart Gardner Museum, 2005

Bello León J.M., "La cruzata en el Atlántico Medio: repercusiones en Canarias y la Berberia de Poniente", in *Proceedings of the International Congress Guerra santa y paz cristiana a fines de la Edad Media*, Malaga (forthcoming)

Bembi P. *Epistolarum Leonis Decimi Pontificis Maximi [...] libri*, Venetiis, ab Ioanne Patauino & Venturino de Roffinellis, 1535

Benedikt H., *Des Pascha-Graf Alexander von Bonneval. 1675-1747*, Graz, H. Bohlaus, 1959

Bennassar B., Bennassar L., *Les chrétiens d'Allah*, Paris, Perrin, 2001

Benzoni G., "Federico II Gonzaga", in *Dizionario Biografico degli Italiani*, Rome, Istituto della Enciclopedia italiana, vol. 45, 1995, pp. 710-722

Benzoni G., "Francesco II Gonzaga", in *Dizionario Biografico degli Italiani*, Rome, Istituto della Enciclopedia italiana, vol. 49, 1997, pp. 771-783

Benzoni G., "Ludovico Sforza detto il Moro", in *Dizionario Biografico degli Italiani*, Rome, Istituto della Enciclopedia italiana, vol. 66, 2006, pp. 436-444

Bérenger J., "La collaboration militaire franco-ottomane à l'époque de la Renaissance", Revue Internationale d'Histoire Militaire, 68 (1987), pp. 51-66

Bérenger J., "La politique française en Méditerranée au XVIe siècle et l'alliance ottomane", in *La guerre de course en Méditerranée (1515-1830)*, ed. by M. Vergé-Franceschi and A.-M. Graziani, Paris-Ajaccio, Presses de l'Université Paris-Sorbonne, 1999, pp. 9-26

Bernardi A. (Novacula), *Cronache forlivesi. Dal 1476 al 1517*, ed. by G. Mazzatinti, 3 vols., Bologna, R. Deputazione di storia patria, vol. I, 1895

Bertelli S., *Lucca, Ragusa, Boston. Tre città mercantili tra Cinque e Seicento*, Rome, Donzelli, 2004

Bertozzi M., "George Gemistos Plethon and the Myth of Ancient Paganism: From the Council of Ferrara to the Tempio Malatestiano in Rimini", in *Proceedings of the International Congress on Plethon and his Time*, ed. by L.G. Benakis and Ch.P. Baloglou, Athina-Mystras, International Scientific Society for Plethonic and Byzantine Studies, 2003, pp. 177-185

Bietenholz P.G., "La minaccia turca e Johannes Oporinus, editore basileese nella metà del Cinquecento", in *Oriente e Occidente*, pp. 115-126

Binney E., *Turkish Treasures from the Collection of Edwin Binney III*, Portland, The Museum, 1979

Bisaha N., *Creating East and West: Renaissance Humanists and the Ottoman Turks*, Philadelphia, University of Pennsylvania Press, 2004

Bitossi C., "Genova e i turchi. Note sui rapporti tra genovesi e ottomani fra medioevo ed età moderna", in *Italien und das Osmanische Reich*, pp. 87-117

Blanchard J., "Political and Cultural Implications of Secret Diplomacy: Commynes and Ferrara in the Light of Unpublished Documents", in *The French Descent*, pp. 231-247

Bloch M., *Les rois thaumaturges. Étude sur le caractère surnaturel attribué a la puissance royale particulièrement en France et en Angleterre*, Paris, Gallimard, 1983

Bognetti G.P., "La città sotto i francesi", in *Storia di Milano*, 17 vols., Milan, Fondazione Treccani degli Alfieri, 1953-1966, vol. VIII, pp. 1-80

Boiardo M.M., *L'inamoramento de Orlando*, ed. by A. Tissoni Benvenuti and C. Montagnani, 2 vols., Milan-Naples, Ricciardi, 1999

Bono S., *Un altro Mediterraneo. Una storia comune fra scontri e integrazioni*, Rome, Salerno, 2008

Bonora E., *Aspettando l'imperatore. Principi italiani tra il papa e Carlo V*, Turin, Einaudi, 2014

Bourne M., *Francesco II Gonzaga. The Soldier-Prince as Patron*, Rome, Bulzoni, 2008

Braudel F., *The Mediterranean and the Mediterranean World in the Age of Philip II*, London, Collins, 1976

Brogini A., *Malte, frontière de Chrétienté (1530-1670)*, Rome, École Française de Rome, 2006

Brunelli G., "Gonzaga, Ferrante", in *Dizionario Biografico degli Italiani*, Rome, Istituto della Enciclopedia italiana, vol. 57, 2001, pp. 734-744

Bruni F., *Italia. Vita e avventure di un'idea*, Bologna, Il Mulino, 2010

Bruni F., *L'Italiano fuori d'Italia*, Florence, Franco Cesati, 2013

Bruni F., "Per la vitalità dell'italiano preunitario fuori d'Italia. Notizie sull'italiano nella diplomazia internazionale", *Lingua e stile*, 42 (2007), pp. 189-242

Burckhardt J., *La civiltà del Rinascimento in Italia*, Florence, Sansoni, 1984

Burke P., *Cultural Hybridity*, Cambridge, Polity, 2009

Burke P., "Images de trois rois. François Ier entre Charles Quint et Henri VIII", in *François Ier*, pp. 24-43

Burke P., *Languages and Communities in Early Modern Europe*, Cambridge, Cambridge University Press, 2004

La caduta di Costantinopoli, ed. by A. Pertusi, 2 vols., Milan, Fondazione Lorenzo Valla, A. Mondadori, 1976

Çağman F., "Nakkaş Osman in Sixteenth Century Documents and Literature", in *Art Turc / Turkish Art. 10e Congrès International d'art turc*, Genève, Fondation Max van Berchem, 1999, pp. 197-206

Calcara P., *Rapporto del viaggio scientifico eseguito nelle isole di Lampedusa, Linosa e Pantelleria*, Palermo, R. Pagano, 1846

Caleffini U., *Croniche. 1471-1494*, Ferrara, Deputazione provinciale ferrarese di storia patria, 2006

Campana A., "Una ignota opera di Matteo de' Pasti e la sua missione in Turchia", *Ariminum*, 1 (1928), 1, pp. 106-108

Campanini Catani M., "Le forme dell'io nella scrittura epistolare", in *L'auteur à la Renaissance*, ed. by R. Gorris Camos and A. Vanautgaerden, Turnhout, Brepols, 2009, pp. 543-556

Campanini Catani M., "Dal manuale alla raccolta: Teoria e pratica della scrittura epistolare attraverso i *secrétaires*", in *"Il segretario è come un angelo"*, ed. by R. Gorris Camos, Fasano, Schena, 2008, pp. 327-337

Campbell G., *The Grove Encyclopedia of Decorative Arts*, 2 vols., Oxford, Oxford University Press, 2006, vol. I

Campori G., Solerti A., *Luigi, Lucrezia e Leonora d'Este*, Turin, E. Loescher, 1888

Canart P., "Jean Nathanaël et le commerce des manuscrits grecs à Venise au XVIe siècle", in *Venezia, centro di mediazione tra Oriente e Occidente (sec. XV-XVI). Aspetti e problemi*, ed. by HG. Beck, M. Manoussacas and A. Pertusi, Florence, Olschki, 1977, pp. 417-437

Canfora L., *La storia falsa*, Milan, Rizzoli, 2008

Cantimori D., *Eretici italiani del Cinquecento*, ed. by A. Prosperi, Turin, Einaudi, 1992

Cappelli F., "'La república de Venecia…' 1617 attribuita a Francisco de Quevedo", *Rivista di filologia e letterature ispaniche*, 6 (2003), pp. 259-274

Cardini F., *In Terrasanta. Pellegrini Italiani tra Medioevo e prima età moderna*, Bologna, Il Mulino, 2002

Carlos V y la quiebra del humanismo politico en Europa (1530-1558), ed. by J. Martínez Millán and I.J. Ezquerra Revilla, 4 vols., Madrid, Sociedad Estatal para la conmemoracion de los centenarios de Felipe II y Carlos V, 2001, vol. I

Caro Baroja J., *Las falsificaciones de la historia (en relación con la de España)*, Barcelona, Seix Barral, 1992

Le carte del sultano nell'Archivio di Stato di Venezia, ed. by M.P. Pedani and P. Bortolozzo, Venice, Archivio di Stato, 2010

Il carteggio tra Beatrice d'Aragona e gli Estensi (1476-1508), ed. by E. Guerra, Rome, Aracne, 2010

Casali E., *Le spie del cielo. Oroscopi, lunari e almanacchi nell'Italia moderna*, Turin, Einaudi, 2003

Caselli C., "Spie italiane nell'impero ottomano: la *Deposicio Antonii de Corsellis* (1485) conservata presso l'Archivio di Stato di Modena", *Studi medievali*, III s., 51 (2010), 2, pp. 779-815

Cassano F., "Necessità del Mediterraneo", in *L'alternativa mediterranea*, pp. 78-110

Castiglione B., *The Book of the Courtier*, ed. L. Eckstein Opdycke, New York, Scribner, 1903

Catalano F., "La crisi politica e sociale di fronte al 'barbaro'", in *Storia di Milano*, 17 vols., Milan, Fondazione Treccani degli Alfieri per la storia di Milano, 1953-1966, vol. VII, pp. 1-539

Cattaruzza M., *L'Italia e il confine orientale*, Bologna, Il Mulino, 2007

Cecconi G., *Vita e fatti di Boccolino Guzzoni da Osimo capitano di ventura del secolo XV*, Osimo, V. Rossi, 1889

Certa G.P., *Delle cose del Regno di Napoli dal tempo del re Alfonso II al tempo del re Ferdinando cattolico*, Naples, Officina tipografica, 1840

Cervantes M. de, *Don Quijote de la Mancha*, ed. by F. Rico, 2 vols., Barcelona, Instituto Cervantes, 1998

Cervantes y la Berbería. Cervantes, mundo turco-berberisco y servicios segretos en la época de Felipe II, ed. by E. Sola and J.F. de la Peña, Mexico, Fondo de cultura economica, 1995

Cessi R., "Per la storia della guerra di Ferrara (1482-83)", *Archivio veneto*, V s., 44-45 (1949), pp. 57-76

Chambers D., "Francesco II Gonzaga, Marquis of Mantua, 'Liberator of Italy'", in *The French Descent*, pp. 217-229

Chartrou J.-M., *Les entrées solennelles et royales à la Renaissance (1484-1551)*, Paris, Presses Universitaires de France, 1928

Cherubini G., *L'Italia rurale del basso Medioevo*, Rome-Bari, Laterza, 1984

Chong A., "Gentile Bellini in Istanbul. Myths and Misunderstandings", in *Bellini and the East*, pp. 106-129

Chrétiens et musulmans à la Renaissance, ed. by B. Bennassar and R. Sauzet, Paris, Champion,1998

Cifoletti G., *La lingua franca barbaresca*, Rome, Il calamo, 2004

Cifoletti G., *La lingua franca mediterranea*, Padova, Unipress, 1989

Cipro-Venezia: comuni sorti storiche, ed. by C.A. Maltezou, Venice, Istituto Ellenico di Studi Bizantini, 2002

Città in guerra. Esperienze e riflessioni nel primo '500. Bologna nelle "guerre d'Italia", ed. by G.M. Anselmi and A. De Benedictis, Bologna, Minerva, 2008

Civale G., *Guerrieri di Cristo. Inquisitori, gesuiti e soldati alla battaglia di Lepanto*, Milan, Unicopli, 2009

Le commerce de captifs. Les intermédiaires dans l'échange et le rachat des prisonniers en Méditerranée, XVe-XVIIIe siècle, ed. by W. Kaiser, Rome, École française de Rome, 2008

Concina E., *Dell'arabico. A Venezia tra Rinascimento e Oriente*, Venice, Marsilio, 1994

Conquête ottomane de l'Égypte (1517). Arrière-plan, impact, échos, ed. by B. Lellouch and N. Michel, Leiden-Boston, Brill, 2013

La conquista turca di Otranto (1480) tra storia e mito, ed. by H. Houben, 2 vols., Galatina, Congedo, 2008

Contamine Ph., "Découverte et conquête: le roi de France, les Français et le 'voyage de Naples' (1494-1495)", in *De l'Italie à Chambord, François Ier: la chevauchée des princes français*, ed. by C. Arminjon, Paris, Somogy, 2004, pp. 9-21

Les Convertis : parcours religieux, parcours politiques, ed. by P. Martin and Eric Suire, Paris, Garnier, 2016

Corio B., *Storia di Milano 1499*, ed. by A. Morisi Guerra, 2 vols., Turin, Utet, 1978

Correspondenz des Kaisers Karl V, ed. by K. Lanz, 3 vols., Leipzig, Brockhaus, 1844, vol. I

La corte di Mantova nell'età di Andrea Mantegna: 1450-1550. The Court of the Gonzaga in the Age of Mantegna: 1450-1550, ed. by C. Mozzarelli, R. Oresko and L. Ventura, Rome, Bulzoni, 1997

Cortelazzo M., *Venezia, il Levante e il mare*, Pisa, Pacini, 1989

Costantini M., "Le isole ionie nel sistema marittimo veneziano del Medioevo", in *Venezia e le isole ionie*, ed. by C. Maltezou and G. Ortalli, Venice, Istituto Veneto di Scienze, Lettere ed Arti, 2005, pp. 141-163

Costantini V., *Il sultano e l'isola contesa. Cipro tra eredità veneziana e potere ottomano*, Turin, Utet, 2009

Cour A., *L'établissement des dynasties des chérifs au Maroc et leur rivalité avec les Turcs de la Régence de Alger. 1509-1830*, Paris, E. Leroux, 1904

Couroucli M., "Le partage des lieux saints comme tradition méditerranéenne", in *Réligions traversées*, pp. 15-25

Cristea O., "La pace tesa: i rapporti veneto-ottomani del 1484", *Annuario. Istituto romeno di cultura e ricerca umanistica*, 5 (2003), pp. 277-286

Una cronaca napoletana figurata del Quattrocento, ed. by R. Filangieri, Naples, L'arte tipografica, 1956

Crowley R., *Empires of the Sea. The Final Battle for Mediterranean: 1521-1580*, London, Faber and Faber, 2009

Cusin F., *Il confine orientale d'Italia nella politica europea del XIV e XV secolo*, Trieste, LINT, 1977[2]

D'Ascia L., *Il Corano e la tiara. L'epistola a Maometto II di Enea Silvio Piccolomini (papa Pio II)*, Bologna, Pendragon, 2001

Dakhlia J., *Lingua franca. Histoire d'une langue métisse en Méditerranée*, Arles, Actes Sud, 2008

Dakhlia J., Valensi L., "Le spectacle de la cour: éléments de comparaison des modes de souveraineté au maghreb et dans l'Empire ottoman", in *Soliman le Magnifique*, pp. 145-157

Dalla Porta G.B., *La turca comedia nuova*, Venetia, Ciera, 1606

Day J., "Strade e vie di comunicazione", in *Storia d'Italia*, ed. by R. Romano and C. Vivanti, 6 vols., Turin, Einaudi, 1972-1976, vol. V, pp. 87-120

De Benedictis A., *Tumulti: moltitudini e ribelli in età moderna*, Bologna, Il Mulino, 2013
De Benedictis A., "'Peccat princeps qui…'. Principî di governo cristiano nella letteratura politico-giuridica tedesca di fine '600", in *La pathologie du pouvoir: vices, crimes et délits des gouvernants*, ed. by P. Gilli, Leiden-Boston, Brill, 2016, pp. 525-547
De Rosa L., "Le capitolazioni franco-ottomane tra politica ed economia nell'età di Carlo V", *Nuova rivista storica*, 85 (2001), pp. 61-76
Del Balzo C., *L'Italia nella letteratura francese dalla caduta dell'impero romano alla morte di Enrico IV*, 2 vols., Rome-Turin, 1905-1907
Del Col A., *L'Inquisizione nel patriarcato e diocesi di Aquileia. 1557-1559*, Trieste, Edizioni Università di Trieste-Centro Studi Storici Menocchio, 1998
Denis A., *Charles VIII et les Italiens. Histoire et mythe*, Genève, Droz, 1979
Deswarte-Rosa S., "L'expédition de Tunis (1535): images, interprétations, répercussions culturelles", in *Chrétiens et musulmans*, pp. 75-132
Di Bernardo F., *Un vescovo umanista alla corte pontificia. Giannantonio Campano (1429-1477)*, Rome, Università Gregoriana, 1975
Di Vittorio A., Anselmi S., Pierucci P., *Ragusa (Dubrovnik) una repubblica adriatica. Saggi di storia economica e finanziaria*, Bologna, Cisalpino, 1994
Dialogue de civilisations en Méditerranée. Première rencontre internationale de dialogue culturel Nord-Sud, ed. by M. Hadhri, Tunis, CETIMA, 1997
Diario ferrarese dall'anno 1409 sino al 1502 di autori incerti, ed. by G. Pardi, Bologna, Zanichelli, 1928-1933
Dionisotti C., "La guerra d'Oriente e la letteratura veneziana del Cinquecento", in *Venezia e l'Oriente tra tardo Medioevo e Rinascimento*, ed. by A. Pertusi, Florence, Sansoni, 1966, pp. 471-493
Djuvara T.G., *Cent projets de partage de la Turquie (1281-1913)*, Paris, Librairie F. Alcan, 1914
Documentos sobre relaciones internacionales de los Reyes Católicos, ed. by A. de la Torre y del Cerro, 6 vols., Barcelona, Consejo Superior de Investigaciones Científicas, 1950
Doumerc B., "Il dominio del mare", in *Storia di Venezia*, 15 vols., Rome, Istituto della Enciclopedia italiana, 1996, vol. IV, pp. 113-180
Doumerc B., "La paix a-t-elle un prix? Le doge face au sultan (fin XVe-début XVIe siècle)", in *Proceedings of the International Congress Guerra santa y paz cristiana a fines de la Edad Media*, Malaga, december 2010 (forthcoming)
Doumerc B., *Venise et l'émirat hafside de Tunis (1231-1535)*, Paris-Montréal, L'Harmattan, 1999
Drévillon H., *L'Individu et la Guerre. Du chevalier Bayard au Soldat Inconnu*, Paris, Belin, 2013
Ducellier A., *Chrétiens d'Orient et Islam au Moyen Âge (VIIe-XVe siècle)*, Paris, Armand Colin, 1996
Dufour L., "Città e fortificazioni nella Sicilia del Cinquecento", in *La città e le mura*, ed. by C. De Seta and J. Le Goff, Rome-Bari, Laterza, 1989, pp. 106-127
Dumont J., "*Les alarmes de Mars* de Jean d'Auton. Édition et commentaire", *Annuaire-Bulletin de la Société de l'Histoire de France*, 13 (2012), pp. 97-166
Dumont J., "Entre France, Italie et Levant. Philippe de Clèves et la *Croisade de Mytilène* (1501)", in *Bourguignons en Italie, Italiens dans les pays bourguignos (XIVe-XVIe s.)*, ed. by J.-M. Cauchies, Neuchâtel, Centre Européen d'Études Bourguignonnes, 2009, pp. 51-68
Dumont J., Lilia Florent. *L'imaginaire politique et social à la cour de France durant les Premières Guerres d'Italie (1494-1525)*, Paris, Champion, 2013

Dursteler E.R., "Power and Information: The Venetian Postal System in the Early Modern Eastern Mediterranean", in *From Florence to the Mediterranean*, pp. 601-623

Dursteler E.R., *Venetians in Constantinople: Nation, Identity, and Coexistence in the Early Modern Mediterranean*, Baltimore, Johns Hopkins University Press, 2006

Eco U., "Tipologia della falsificazione", in *Fälschungen im Mittelalter*, 6 vols., Hannover, Hahnsche Buchhandlung, 1988-1990, vol. I, pp. 69-82

Écriture, calligraphie et peinture, *Studia islamica*, 96 (2003)

Edgerton S.Y., *Pictures and Punishment. Art and criminal prosecution during the Florentine Renaissance*, Ithaca-London, Cornell University Press, 1985

L'empire du sultan: le monde ottoman dans l'art de la Renaissance, ed. by R. Born, M. Dziewulski and G. Messling, Bruxelles-Tielt, Bozar Books, 2015

L'envers du décor. Espionnage, complot, trahison, vengeance et violence en pays bourguignos et liègeois, Neuchâtel, Centre européen d'études bourguignonnes, 2008

Episcopale Bononiensis Civitatis et Diocesis. Raccolta di varie cose che in diversi tempi sono state ordinate da mons. [...] cardinale Paleotti, Bologna, Benacci, 1580

Épistolaire politique II. Authentiques et autographes, ed. by B. Dumézil and L. Vissière, Paris, Presses de l'université Paris-Sorbonne, 2016

Ertaylan İ.H., *Sultan Cem*, Istanbul, Edebiyat Fakültesi Basımevi, 1951

Estudios sobre Málaga y el Reino de Granada en el V Centenario dela conquista, ed. by J.E. López de Coca Castañer, Málaga, Diputación provincial de Málaga, 1988

Eunjeong Yi, *Guild Dynamics in Seventeenth Century Istanbul. Fluidity and Leverage*, Leiden-Boston, Brill, 2004

L'Europa dopo la caduta di Costantinopoli: 29 maggio 1453, Spoleto, Fondazione Centro italiano di studi sull'alto medioevo, 2008

Europa und die Türken in der Renaissance, ed. by B. Guthmüller and W. Kühlmann, Tübingen, Max Niemeyer Verlag, 2000

Fábregas A., "Redes. El espacio de actuación internacional del comercio nazarí", in *Italie et Espagne entre Empire, cités et États*, ed. by A. Carette, R.M. Girón-Pascual, R. González Arévalo and C. Terreaux-Scotto, Rome, Viella, 2017, pp. 25-42

Falcioni A., "Malatesta, Sigismondo Pandolfo", in *Dizionario Biografico degli Italiani*, Rome, Istituto della Enciclopedia italiana, vol. LXVIII, 2007, pp. 113-114

Fantaguzzi G., *Caos. Cronache cesenati del secolo XV*, ed. by D. Bazzocchi, Cesena, Arturo Bettini, 1915

Farinella V., "Vizi privati e pubbliche virtù: Federico II Gonzaga a Palazzo Te", in *Il principe inVisibile*, ed. by L. Bertolini, A. Calzona, G. Cantarella and S. Carotti, Turnhout, Brepols, 2015, pp. 225-244

Farinelli F., "Storia e geografia dell'Adriatico", in *Adriatico mare d'Europa. La geografia e la storia*, ed. by E. Turri, Cinisello Balsamo, Silvana editoriale, 1999, pp. 15-98

Favarò V., *La modernizzazione militare nella Sicilia di Filippo II*, Palermo, Associazione Mediterranea, 2009

Federico Gonzaga alla corte di Francesco I nel carteggio privato con Mantova. 1515-1517, ed. by R. Tamalio, Paris, Champion, 1994

Felici L., "Una nuova immagine dell'Islam (e del cristianesimo) nell'Europa del XVI secolo", in *Encountering Otherness. Diversities and Transcultural Experiences in Early Modern European Culture*, ed. by G. Abbattista, Trieste, EUT, 2011, pp. 43-66

Fernández Lanza F., "1500'de Türklerin Modon'u Kuşatmasi ve Işgali" [The Turkish siege and occupation of Methoni in 1500], in *Türkler ve Deniz*, pp. 201-229

Ferraiolo G., *Cronaca*, ed. by R. Coluccia, Florence, Accademia della Crusca,1987
Ferrato P., *Il marchesato di Mantova e l'impero ottomano alla fine del secolo XV*, Mantua, Stabilimento tipografico Mondovì, 1876
Fileno dalla Tuata, *Istoria di Bologna*, ed. by B. Fortunato, 3 vols., Bologna, Costa, 2005
Il fiore della lirica veneziana, ed. by M. Dazzi, Venice, N. Pozza, 1956
Fiume G., *Schiavitù mediterranee. Corsari, rinnegati e santi di Età moderna*, Milan, Bruno Mondadori, 2009
Fleet K., *European and Islamic Trade in the Early Ottoman State. The Merchants of Genoa and Turkey*, Cambridge, Cambridge University Press, 1999
Fleischer C.H., "The Lawgiver as Messiah: The Making of the Imperial Image in the Reign of Süleimân", in *Soliman le Magnifique*, pp. 159-177
Flores M., *Traditori. Una storia politica e culturale*, Bologna, Il Mulino, 2015
Flori J., *L'Islam et la Fin des Temps. L'interprétation prophétique des invasions musulmanes dans la chrétienté médiévale*, Paris, Éditions du Seuil, 2007
Fontaine M.M., "Antiquaires et rites funéraires", in *Les funérailles à la Renaissance*, ed. by J. Balsamo, Genève, Droz, 2002, pp. 329-356
Formica M., "La Porta e la Tiara. Immagini e dinamiche identitarie nella cultura italiana del XVI secolo", in *Italien und das Osmanische Reich*, pp. 169-198
Fornari F., *Psicoanalisi della guerra*, Milan, Feltrinelli, 1979
Foucard C., "Fonti di storia napoletana nell'Archivio di Stato in Modena. Otranto nel 1480 e nel 1481", *Archivio storico per le province napoletane*, 6 (1881), pp. 74-176, 609-628
Foucard C., *Relazioni dei duchi di Ferrara e di Modena coi re di Tunisi*, Modena, Pizzolotti, 1881
The Fourth Crusade Revisited, ed. by P. Piatti, Vatican City State, Libreria editrice vaticana, 2008
François Ier: pouvoir et images, ed. by B. Petey-Girard and M. Vène, Paris, Éditions de la BnF, 2015
Freely J., *Jem Sultan: the adventures of a captive Turkish prince in Renaissance Europe*, London, HarperCollins, 2004
The French Descent into Renaissance Italy 1494-95, ed. by D. Abulafia, Aldershot, Variorum, 1995
Frioli D., "Per la tradizione manoscritta di Roberto Valturio", in R. Valturio, *De re militari*, ed. by P. Delbianco, 2 vols., Rimini-Milan, Guaraldi-Y. Press, 2006, vol. II, *Saggi critici*, pp. 69-93
Fritsch A., *Princeps peccans sive tractatus de peccatis principum*, Osterodae, sumptibus B. Fuhrmanni, 1670
From Florence to the Mediterranean and beyond. Essays in Honour of Anthony Molho, ed. by D. Ramada Curto, E.R. Dursteler, J. Kirshner and F. Trivellato, Florence, Olschki, 2009
Fuscaldo G., *La guerra di Ferrara. 1482-1484*, Ferrara, Bresciani, 1925

Gabriel F., "François Ier 'rex christianissimus'. Entre rite et pragmatisme", in *François Ier*, pp. 120-132
Galasso G., *Il Regno di Napoli. Il Mezzogiorno spagnolo. 1494-1622*, Turin, Utet, 2008
Galasso G., *Storia del regno di Napoli*, 6 vols., Turin, Utet, 2006-2011
Gallotta A., Bova G., "Documenti dell'Archivio di Stato di Venezia concernenti il principe ottomano Gem", *Studi magrebini*, 12 (1980), pp. 175-199
García Arenal M., "Mahdī, Murābīt, Sharīf: l'avènement de la dynastie sa'dienne", *Studia Islamica*, 71 (1990), pp. 77-114

García Arenal M., Bunes M.Á. de, *Los españoles y el Norte de África. Siglos XV-XVIII*, Madrid, Mapfre, 1992
Garcia Hernán D., "Consecuencias politico-culturales de la batalla de Lepanto: la literatura española", *Mediterranea*, 23 (2011), pp. 467-500
Gardi A., "Congiure contro i papi in Età moderna", *Roma moderna e contemporanea*, 11 (2003), pp. 29-51
Garin E., *Interpretazioni del Rinascimento*, ed. by M. Ciliberto, 2 vols., Rome, Edizioni di storia e letteratura, 2009
Garnier E., *L'alliance impie. François I*[er] *et Soliman le Magnifique contre Charles Quint (1529-1547)*, Paris, Felin, 2008
Gay and Lesbian Poetry. An Anthology from Sappho to Michelangelo, ed. by J.J. Wilhelm, New York-London, Routledge, 1995
Gennaro P., *Istanbul. L'opera di Sinan*, Milan, CittàStudi, 1992
Gilli P., "Alexandre VI et la France", in *Roma di fronte all'Europa al tempo di Alessandro VI*, ed. by M. Chiabò, 3 vols., Rome, Ministero per i beni e le attività culturali, 2001, vol. I, pp. 59-76
Ginzburg C., *Clues, myths, and the Historical Method*, Baltimore, John Hopkins University Press, 1992
Ginzburg C., *The Judge and the Historian: Marginal Notes on a Late-twentieth-Century Miscarriage of Justice*, London - New York, Verso, 1999
Ginzburg C., "Prefazione" to R. Chartier, *Figure della furfanteria. Marginalità e cultura popolare in Francia tra Cinque e Seicento*, Rome, Istituto della Enciclopedia italiana, 1984, pp. 3-10
Glidden H., "Ces paillards 'Turcqs': Rabelais devant le Levant", in *L'Europa e il Levante nel Cinquecento. Cose turchesche*, ed. by L. Zilli, Padova, Unipress, 2001, pp. 15-24
Gonzaga L., *Lettere*, ed. by R. Bragantini and P. Griguolo, Rovigo, Minelliana, 2009
González Arévalo R., "La guerra di Granada nelle fonti fiorentine", *Archivio storico italiano*, CLXIV (2006), n. 609, pp. 387-418
González Arévalo, "Integración y movilidad social de las naciones italianas en la Corona de Castilla: genoveses, florentinos y venecianos en la Andalucía bajomedieval", in *La mobilità sociale nel Medioevo italiano*, ed. by L. Tanzini and S. Tognetti, Rome, Viella, 2016, pp. 375-401
González Arévalo R., "Italian Renaissance Diplomacy and Commerce with Western Mediterranean Islam: Venice, Florence, and the Nasrid Kingdom of Granada in the Fifteenth Century", *I Tatti. Studies in the Italian Renaissance*, 18 (2015), pp. 215-232
Gorceix S., *Bonneval Pacha, pacha à trois queues. Une vie d'aventure au XVIII*[e] *siècle*, Paris, Plon, 1953
Gorris Camos R., "La stella delle meraviglie: un poète et une étoile, la supernova de 1572", in *Esculape et Dionysos. Mélanges en l'honneur de Jean Céard*, ed. by J. Dupèbe, Genève, Droz, 2008, pp. 543-568
Gorris R., "*'Prudentia perpetuat'*: Vittorio Baldini, editore ferrarese di Francesco Patrizi", in *Francesco Patrizi filosofo platonico nel crepuscolo del Rinascimento*, ed. by P. Castelli, Florence, Olschki, 2002, pp. 219-252
Gounardis P., "L'image de l'autre: le croisés vus par les byzantins", in *Quarta Crociata. Venezia, Bisanzio, Impero Latino*, ed. by G. Ortalli, G. Ravegnani and P. Schreiner, Venice, Istituto veneto di scienze, lettere ed arti, 2006, pp. 81-95
Gouzi Ch., "Louis XIV en Saint Louis: une autre image de la figure royale?", in *Louis XIV: l'image et le mythe*, ed. by M. Da Vinha, A. Maral and N. Milovanovic, Rennes, Presses Universitaires de Rennes, 2014, pp. 57-70

Gregorovius F., *History of the City of Rome in the Middle Ages*, 8 vols., London, George Bell & Sons, 1894-1902, vol. VII/1

Groto L., *Trofeo della vittoria sacra ottenuta dalla christianissima Lega contra turchi nell'anno 1571*, Venetia, Bordogna e Patrigni, [1572]

Guiral–Hadziiossif J., *Valence port méditerranéen au XVe siècle (1410-1525)*, Paris, Publications de la Sorbonne, 1986

Gundersheimer, W., *Ferrara: The Style of a Renaissance Despotism*, Princeton, Princeton University Press, 1973

Gürol Ü., *İtalyan Edebiyatinda Türkler*, Ankara, İmge Yayınları, 1987

Guzzini M., *Boccolino Guzzoni cinquecento anni dopo*, Ancona, Il Lavoro Editoriale, 1995

Hadhri M., *La Méditerranée et le monde arabo-méditerranéen aux portes du XXIe siècle. Choc de cultures ou dialogue de civilisations?*, Tunis, Centre de publication universitaire, 2004

Hampton T., "Turkish Dogs: Rabelais, Erasmus and the Rhetoric of Alterity", *Representations*, 41 (1993), pp. 58-82

Hankins J., "Renaissance Crusaders: Humanist Crusade Literature in the Age of Mehmed II", *Dumbarton Oaks Papers*, 49 (1995), pp. 111-207

Har-El S., *Struggle for Domination in the Middle East. The Ottoman-Mamluk War 1485-91*, Leiden-New York-Köln, Brill, 1995

Heath M.J., *Crusading Commonplaces: La Noue, Lucinge and the Rethoric Against the Turks*, Genève, Droz, 1986

Heers J., *Chute et mort de Constantinople 1205-1453*, Paris, Perrin, 2005

Heers J., *Gênes au XVe siècle. Civilisation méditerranéenne, grand capitalisme et capitalisme populaire*, Paris, Flammarion, 1971

Heidenheimer H., "Die Korrespondenz Sultan Bajazet's II mit Papst Alexander VI.", *Zeitschrift für Kirchengeschichte*, 5 (1882), pp. 511-573

Hélary X., "Le 'dégoût' de la noblesse française à l'égard de la croisade à la fin du XIIIe siècle", in *La noblesse et la croisade à la fin du Moyen Âge*, ed. by M. Nejedly and J. Svàtek, Toulouse, Framespa, 2009, pp. 17-30

Held J.S., "Rubens 'King of Tunis' and Vermeyen's Portrait of Mulay Ahmad", *The Art Quarterly*, 3 (1940), pp. 173-181

Helmrath J., "Pius II und die Türken", in *Europa und die Türken*, pp. 79-137

Hinojosa Montalvo J., "Las relaciones entre Valencia y Granada durante el siglo XV: Balance de una investigación", in *Estudios sobre Málaga*, pp. 84-111

Holban M., "François du Moulin de Rochefort et la querelle de la Madeleine", *Humanisme et Renaissance*, 2 (1935), pp. 26-43, 147-171

Horn H.G., *Jan Cornelisz Vermeyen. Painter of Charles V and His Conquest of Tunis*, Doornspijk, Davaco, 1989

Houben H., "La conquista turca di Otranto: il problema delle fonti salentine", in *La conquista turca*, vol. II, pp. 5-20

Housley N., *Religious warfare in Europe, 1400-1536*, Oxford, Oxford University Press, 2002

Howard D., "Cultural Transfer Between Venice and the Ottomans in the Fifteenth and Sixteenth Centuries", in *Forging European Identities*, ed. by H. Roodenburg, Cambridge, Cambridge University Press, 2007, pp. 138-177

Huntington S.P., *The Clash of Civilizations and the Remaking of World Order*, London, Touchstone Books, 1998

Hyder Patterson P., "Sull'orlo della ragione. I confini del balcanismo nel discorso pubblico sloveno, austriaco e italiano", *Novecento*, 10 (2004), pp. 87-106

Igual L., "Diplomacia y comercio entre Venecia y los reinos hispánico (1450-1520)", in *Italie et Espagne entre Empire, cités et États*, ed. by A. Carette, R.M. Girón-Pascual, R. González Arévalo, C.Terreaux-Scotto, Rome, Viella, 2017, pp. 151-168

Inalcik H., "A Case Study in Renaissance Diplomacy. The Agreement between Innocent VIII and Bâyezîd on Djem Sultan", *Journal of Turkish Studies*, 3 (1979), pp. 209-223

Infessura S., *Diario della città di Roma*, Rome, Forzani, 1890

Inventario delle fonti manoscritte relative all'Africa del Nord esistenti in Italia, vol. 5, *L'Archivio di Stato di Roma*, ed. by C. Lodolini Tupputi, Rome, Herder, 1989

Italien und das Osmanische Reich, ed. by F. Meier, Herne, Schafer Verlag, 2010

Italy and Europe's Eastern Border (1204-1669), ed. by J.M. Damian, M. Popović and A. Simon, Frankfurt am Main, Peter Lang, 2012

Jacquart J., *François Ier*, Paris, Fayard, 1981

Jardine J., Brotton J., *Global Interests: Renaissance Art between East and West*, Ithaca (NY), Cornell University Press, 2000

Jennings R.C., *Christians and Muslims in Ottoman Cyprus and the Mediterranean World. 1571-1640*, New York, New York University Press, 1997

Kahane H., Kahane R., Tietze A., *The Lingua Franca in the Levant. Turkish nautical terms of Italian and Greek origin*, Urbana, University of Illinois Press, 1958

Kaiser W., "Zones de transit. Lieux, temps, modalités du rachat de captifs en Méditerranée", in *Les musulmans dans l'histoire de l'Europe*, ed. by J. Dakhlia, B. Vincent and W. Kaiser, 2 vols., Paris, Albin Michel, 2013, vol. II, pp. 251-272

Kaplan P.H.D., "Black Turks: Venetian Artists and Perceptions of Ottoman Ethnicity", in *The Turk and Islam in the Western Eye, 1450-1750*, ed. by J.C. Harper, Farnham, Ashgate, 2011, pp. 41-66.

Kempers B., "*Sans fiction ne dissimulacion*. The Crowns and Crusaders in the Stanza dell'Incendio", in *Der Medici-Papst Leo X. und Frankreich. Politik, Kultur und Familiengeschäfte in der Europäischen Renaissance*, ed. by G.-R Tewes and M. Rohlmann, Tubingen, Mohr Siebeck, 2002, pp. 373-425

Keriakos S., "Les apparitions de la Vierge en Égypte: un lieu privilégié de la rencontre entre coptes et musulmans?", in *Réligions traversées*, pp. 255-294

Kissling H.J., "Francesco II Gonzaga ed il Sultano Bâyezid II", *Archivio storico italiano*, 125 (1967), pp. 34-68

Kissling H.J., *Sultan Bajezid's 2. Beziehungen zu Markgraf Francesco 2. von Gonzaga*, Munich, Hueber, 1965

Knecht R.J., *Francis I*, Cambridge, Cambridge University Press, 1982

Kumrular Ö., "Ispanyol ve İştalyan Arşiv Kaynaklari ve Kroniklerinin Işiğinda Barbaros'un 1534 Seferi [Italian and Spanish chronicles and archive sources on Barbarossa's campaign of 1534]", in *Türkler ve Deniz*, pp. 187-200

Kurz O., "A Gold Helmet made in Venice for Sultan Suleyman the Magnificent", *Gazette des Beaux Arts*, 74 (1969), pp. 249-258

Labandc-Mailfert Y., *Charles VIII et son milieu (1470-1498). La jeunesse au pouvoir*, Paris, Klincksieck, 1975

[Lando O.], *Due panegirici nuovamente composti, de quali l'uno è in lode della signora marchesana della Padulla et l'altro in comendatione della signora donna Lucretia Gonzaga da Gazuolo*, Vinegia, Giolito de Ferrari, 1552

Lapeyre H., *Charles Quint*, Paris, Presses universitaires de France, 1971

Lavenia V., "Turkophilia and Religion: Machiavelli, Giovio, and the Sixteenth-Century Debate about War", in *Machiavelli, Islam and the East: Reorienting the Foundations of Modern Political Thought*, ed. by L. Biasiori and G. Marcocci, Palgrave McMillan, Basingstoke, 2017, pp. 37-60

Le Fur D., *Charles VIII*, Paris, Perrin, 2006

Le Gall J.-M., *L'honneur perdu de François Ier: Pavie 1525*, Paris, Payot, 2015

Le Gall J.-M., *Un idéal masculin? Barbes et moustaches XVe-XVIIIe siècles*, Paris, Payot, 2011

Le Gall J.-M., *Les guerres d'Italie (1494-1559). Une lecture religieuse*, Genève, Droz, 2017

Le Goff J., *Saint Louis*, Paris, Gallimard, 1996

Le Thiec G., "De Milan à Constantinople: Louis XII et la croisade dans la culture politique du temps (1498-1512)", in *Louis XII en Milanais*, pp. 67-107

Le Thiec G., "Le roi, le pape et l'ôtage. La croisade, entre théocratie pontificale et messianisme royal (1494-1504)", *Revue d'histoire de l'Eglise de France*, 88 (2002), pp. 41-82

Lecoq A.-M., *François Ier imaginaire. Symbolique et politique à l'aube de la Renaissance française*, Paris, Macula, 1987

The Legal Status of ḏimmī-s in the Islamic West (second/eighth-ninth/fifteenth centuries), ed. by M. Fierro and J. Tolan, Turnhout, Brepols, 2013

Lercari A., "Il parentado genovese di Caterina Cybo", in *Caterina Cybo duchessa di Camerino (1501-1557)*, ed. by P. Moriconi, Camerino, La nuova stampa, 2005, pp. 105-183

Lestringant F., *Le livre des îles. Atlas et récits insulaires de la Genèse à Jules Verne*, Genève, Droz, 2002

Lettere degli ambasciatori estensi sulla guerra di Otranto (1480-81). Trascrizioni ottocentesche conservate a Napoli, ed. by H. Houben, Galatina, Congedo, 2013

Letters and Papers Foreign and Domestic of the Reign of Henry VIII, ed. by J.S. Brewer, J. Gairdner and R.H. Brodie, 21 vols., London, H.M. Stationery Office, 1864-1920, vol. II-I

Levi G., "Storia d'Italia e antropologia cattolica", in *From Florence to the Mediterranean*, pp. 545-556

Lévi-Strauss Cl., *Les structures élémentaires de la parenté*, Berlin-New York, Mouton de Gruyter, 2002

Lewis B., *The Muslim Discovery of Europe*, New York, Norton, 1982

Il libro dei vagabondi, ed. by P. Camporesi, Turin, Einaudi, 1973

Lohse R., "L'immagine degli Ottomani nelle commedie e tragedie italiane del Cinquecento", in *Italien und das Osmanische Reich*, pp. 199-216

Loiseau J., "De l'Asie centrale à l'Égypte: le siècle turc", in *Histoire du monde au XVe siècle*, ed. by P. Boucheron, Paris, Fayard, 2009, pp. 33-51

López de Coca Castañer J.E., "Mamelucos, otomanos y caída del reino de Granada", *En la España medieval*, 28 (2005), pp. 229-258

López de Coca Castañer J.E., "Las galeras venecianas de Poniente y Berbería desde la perspectiva española", *Medievalismo. Boletín de la Sociedad Española de Estudios Medievales*, 16 (2006), pp. 113-172

López de Coca Castañer J.E., *El Reino de Granada en la época de los reyes católicos*, 2 vols., Granada, Universidad de Granada, 1989

Lloréns V., "Historia y ficción en el 'Quijote'", *Papeles de son Armadans*, 8 (1963), pp. 235-258

Louis XII en Milanais, ed. by Ph. Contamine and J. Guillaume, Paris, Champion, 2003
Luttrell L., "The Hospitallers of Rhodes Confront the Turks", in *Christians, Jews and Other Worlds. Patterns of Conflict and Accomodation*, ed. by Ph.F. Gallagher, New York-London, University Press of America, 1988, pp. 80-116
Luzzati M., *Una guerra di popolo. Lettere private del tempo dell'assedio di Pisa (1494-1509)*, Pisa, Pacini, 1973

Machiavelli N., *The Mandragola*, in *Five Italian Renaissance Comedies*, ed. by B. Penman, Harmondsworth, Penguin Books, 1978
Machiavelli N., *Opere*, ed. by C. Vivanti, 3 vols., Turin, Einaudi, 1999, vol. II
Maffi D., "'Il problema dell'altro'. La Spagna e l'islam in Africa settentrionale dai Re Cattolici a Carlo V", in *Oriente e Occidente*, pp. 165-176
Mahmoud Helmy N., "Membré, Michele", in *Dizionario Biografico degli Italiani*, Rome, Istituto della Enciclopedia italiana, vol. 73, 2009, pp. 411-413
Malettke K., "Die Vörstosse der Osmanen im 16. Jahrhundert aus Französischer Sicht", in *Europa und die Türken*, pp. 373-394
Mandalà G., "Tra mito e realtà: l'immagine di Roma nella letteratura araba e turca d'età ottomana (secoli XV-XVI)", in *Italien und das Osmanische Reich*, pp. 29-56
"I manoscritti Torrigiani donati al R. Archivio centrale di Stato di Firenze", ed. by C. Guasti, *Archivio storico italiano*, III s., 21 (1875), pp. 189-235
Margolin J.-Cl., "Érasme et la guerre contre les Turcs", *Il Pensiero Politico*, 13 (1980), pp. 3-38
Margolin J.-Cl., "Réflexion sur le commentaire du Père Célestin Pierre Crespet de la lettre du pape Pie II au sultan Mahomet II", in *Chrétiens et musulmans*, pp. 212-239
Maroc médiéval, Un empire de l'Afrique à l'Espagne, ed. by Y. Lintz, C. Déléry and B. Tuil Leonetti, Paris, Hazan, 2014
Martelli M., "Nelle stalle di Lorenzo", *Archivio storico italiano*, 150 (1992), pp. 267-302
Martorelli L., *Memorie historiche dell'antichissima e nobile città d'Osimo*, Venice, Poletti, 1705
Massa G.M. di, *Memorie di Ferrara (1582-1585)*, ed. by M. Provasi, Ferrara, Deputazione provinciale ferrarese di storia patria, 2004
Massimi P., *Les cent élégies. Hecatelegium, Florence 1489*, ed. by J. Desjardins, Grenoble, Éditions littéraires et linguistiques de l'Université de Grenoble, 1986
Massimi P., *Les cent nouvelles élégies. Deuxième Hecatelegium*, ed. by J. Desjardins Daude, Paris, Les belles lettres, 2008
Massimi P. *Hecatelegium*, Florentiae, Miscomini, 1489
Matarrese T., *Parole e forme dei cavalieri boiardeschi*, Novara, Interlinea, 2004
Matschke K-P., *Das Kreuz und der Halbmond. Die Geschichte der Türkenkriege*, Düsseldorf-Zürich, Artemis & Winkler, 2004
Maxim M., "I Principati Romeni e l'Impero Ottomano (1400-1878)", in *Una storia dei Romeni. Studi critici*, ed. by S. Fischer-Galati, D.C. Giurescu and I.-A. Pop, Cluj-Napoca, Fondazione culturale romena-Centro di studi transilvani, 2003, pp. 168-192
McGrath E., "Ludovico il Moro and His Moors", *Journal of the Warburg and Courtauld Institutes*, 65 (2002), pp. 67-94
Medioli Masotti P., "L'Accademia Romana e la congiura del 1468", *Italia medioevale e umanistica*, 25 (1982), pp. 189-204
Meli P., "Firenze di fronte al mondo islamico. Documenti su due ambasciate (1487-1489)", *Annali di storia di Firenze*, 4 (2009), pp. 243-273

Membré M., *Relazione di Persia (1542): ms. inedito dell'Archivio di Stato di Venezia*, ed. by G.R. Cardona, Naples, Istituto universitario orientale, 1969

Menage V.L., "Some Notes on the Devshirme", *Bulletin of the School of Oriental and African Studies*, 29 (1966), pp. 64-78

Mercati A., "Le due lettere di Giorgio da Trebisonda a Maometto II", *Orientalia christiana periodica*, 9 (1943), pp. 65-99

Meschini S., *La Francia nel ducato di Milano. La politica di Luigi XII (1499-1512)*, 2 vols., Milan, FrancoAngeli, 2006

Meschini S., *Uno storico umanista alla corte sforzesca. Biografia di Bernardino Corio*, Milan, Vita e pensiero, 1995

Meserve M., *Empires of Islam in Renaissance Historical Thought*, Cambridge, Harvard University Press, 2008

Messick B., *The Calligraphic State. Textual Domination and History in a Muslim Society*, Berkeley-Los Angeles, University of California Press, 1996

Meyer A., "Spätmittelalterliches Benefizialrecht im Spannungsfeld zwischen päpstlicher Kurie und ordentlicher Kollatur", in *Proceedings of the Eighth International Congress of Medieval Canon Law*, ed. by S. Chodorow, Vatican City State, Vatican Apostolic Library, 1992, pp. 247-262

Mission to the Lord Sophy of Persia (1539-1542), ed. by A.H. Morton, London, School of Oriental and African Studies, 1993

Monfasani J., *George of Trebizond. A Biography and a Study of his Rhetoric and Logic*, Leiden, Brill, 1976

Montanari V., "Momenti di cronaca e storia del XV e XVI secolo nelle pagine inedite di tre notai bolognesi: Niccolò, Eliseo, Andrea Mamellini", *Strenna storica bolognese*, 24 (1974), pp. 165-181

Monter E.W., "Calvinistes en turbans", *Bibliothèque d'Humanisme et Renaissance*, 29 (1967), pp. 443-445

More What If? Eminent Historians Imagine What Might Have Been, ed. by R. Cowley, London, Pan Books, 2003

Morin E., "Penser la Méditerranée et méditerranéiser la pensée", *Confluences Méditerranée*, 28 (2009), pp. 33-47

Mozzarelli C., "Lo Stato gonzaghesco. Mantova dal 1382 al 1707", in *Storia d'Italia*, ed. by G. Galasso, Turin, Utet, vol. XVII, 1979, pp. 359-495

Muir E., *Mad Blood Stirring. Vendetta in Renaissance Italy*, London, The Johns Hopkins University Press, 1998

Najemy J., "Machiavelli Between East and West", in *From Florence to the Mediterranean*, pp. 127-145

Necipoğlu G., *Architecture, Ceremonial and Power: The Topkapı Palace in the Fifteenth and Sixteenth Centuries*, New York-Cambridge (MA)-London, The Architectural History Foundation-MIT Press, 1991

Necipoğlu G., "Süleymân the Magnificent and the Representation of Power", in *Süleymân the Second and His Time*, ed. by H. İnalcik and C. Kafadar, İstanbul, The Isis Press, 1993, pp. 163-187

Necipoğlu-Kafadar G., "Dynastic Imprints on Cityscape. The Collective Message of Imperial Funerary Mosque Complexes in Istanbul", in *Cimetières et traditions funéraires dans le monde islamique*, ed. by J.-L. Bacqué-Grammont and A. Tibet, 2 vols., Ankara, Turk tarih kurumu, 1996, vol. II, pp. 23-36

Nel riscatto di Giuseppe Antonio Benedetto Dotti, Lorenzo Benedetto Pavini e Ugo Forlani ferraresi schiavi in Tunesi di Barberia, Ferrara, Pomatelli, 1726

Nemeth Papo G., Papo A., *Ludovico Gritti. Un principe-mercante del Rinascimento tra Venezia, i Turchi e la Corona d'Ungheria*, Mariano del Friuli, Edizioni della Laguna, 2002

Niccoli O., *Profeti e popolo nell'Italia del Rinascimento*, Rome-Bari, Laterza, 1987

Niccoli O., *Rinascimento anticlericale*, Rome-Bari, Laterza, 2005

Nordman D., *Tempête sur Alger. L'expédition de Charles V en 1541*, Paris, Bouchène, 2011

Norman D., *Islam and the West: The Making of an Image*, Oxford, Oneworld, 1993

Notices et extraits des manuscrits de la Bibliothèque du Roi, 11 vols., Paris, Imprimerie Royale, 1787-1827, vol. II

Nubilonio C., *Cronaca di Vigevano ossia dell'origine e principio di Vigevano*, ed. by C. Negroni, Turin, Paravia, 1892 (Miscellanea di storia italiana, 29)

Nutton V., "The Rise of Medical Humanism: Ferrara 1464-1555", *Renaissance Studies*, 11 (1997), pp. 2-19

Odorici F., "Lettere inedite di Muley-Hassen re di Tunisi a Ferrante Gonzaga 1537-1547", *Atti e memorie delle RR. Deputazioni di storia patria per le provincie modenesi e parmensi*, 3 (1866), pp. 139-219

Oriente e Occidente nel Rinascimento, ed. by L. Secchi Tarugi, Florence, Franco Cesati, 2009

Orlando E., "Venezia e la conquista turca di Otranto", in *La conquista turca*, vol. I, pp. 177-209

Ostrogorsky G., *History of the Byzantine State*, Oxford, Blackwell, 1968

Parenti P. di M., *Storia fiorentina*, ed. by A. Matucci, 2 vols., Florence, Olschki, vol. I, 1994

Paris G., "La 'politique arabe' de la France, un capital symbolique dilapidé", *Le Monde*, 26 febbraio 2011

Pastor L. von, *The History of the Popes, from the Close of the Middle Ages*, 40 vols., St. Louis, Mo., Herder, 1898-1953, vol. V

Pastore A., *Veleno. Credenze, crimini, saperi nell'Italia moderna*, Bologna, Il Mulino, 2010

Patrizi F., *Paralleli militari*, Rome, Zanneti, 1594

Paviot J., "Autour de l'ambassade de d'Aramon: érudits et voyageurs au Levant", in *Voyager à la Renaissance*, ed. by J. Céard and J.-Cl. Margolin, Paris, Éditions Maisonneuve et Larose, 1987, pp. 381-392

Paviot J., *Les Ducs de Bourgogne, la croisade et l'Orient*, Paris, Presses de l'Université de Paris-Sorbonne, 2003

Pedani M.P., *In nome del Gran Signore. Inviati ottomani a Venezia dalla caduta di Costantinopoli alla guerra di Candia*, Venice, Deputazione di storia patria per le Venezie, 1991

Pedani M.P., "I Turchi e il Friuli alla fine del Quattrocento", *Memorie storiche forogiuliesi*, 74 (1994), pp. 203-224

Pedani M.P., *Venezia porta d'Oriente*, Bologna, Il Mulino, 2010

Pedani M.P., "Venezia e l'Impero ottomano: la tentazione dell'*impium foedus*", in *L'Europa e la Serenissima: la svolta del 1509. Nel V centenario della battaglia di Agnadello*, ed. by G. Gullino, Venice, Istituto Veneto di Scienze Lettere ed Arti, 2011, pp. 163-176

Pedani M.P., "Note di storiografia sull'impero ottomano", *Mediterranea*, 12 (2015), 34, pp. 445-458

Pellegrini M., *Ascanio Maria Sforza. La parabola politica di un cardinale-principe del Rinascimento*, Rome, Istituto storico italiano per il Medio Evo, 2002

Pellegrini M., *La crociata nel Rinascimento. Mutazioni di un mito 1400-1600*, Florence, Le Lettere, 2014
Pellegrini M., *Le crociate dopo le crociate: da Nicopoli al Belgrado (1396-1456)*, Bologna, Il Mulino, 2013
Pellegrini M., *Guerra santa contro i Turchi. La crociata impossibile di Carlo V*, Bologna, Il Mulino, 2015
Pellegrini M., *Le guerre d'Italia (1494-1530)*, Bologna, Il Mulino, 2009
Peter J., *Les Barbaresques sous Louis XIV. Le duel entre Alger et la Marine du Roi (1681-1698)*, Paris, Economica, 1997
Pfeffermann H., *Die Zusammenarbeit der Renaissancepäpste mit des Türken*, Winterthur, Mondial, 1946
Piccolomini E.S., *Epistola al Gran Turco*, ed. by A. Baldissera, A. Bresadola and G. Mazzocchi, Como-Pavia, Ibis, 2008
Picotti G.B., "Alessandro VI", in *Dizionario Biografico degli Italiani*, Rome, Istituto della Enciclopedia italiana, vol. II, 1960, pp. 196-205
Picotti G.B., Review to H. Pfeffermann, *Die Zusammenarbeit der Renaissancepäpste mit des Türken*, Winterthur, Mondial, 1946, *Rivista storica italiana*, 63 (1951), pp. 406-410
Piemontese A.-M., "L'ambasciatore di Persia presso Federico da Montefeltro, Ludovico Bononiense O.F.M., e il cardinale Bessarione", in *Miscellanea Bibliothecae Apostolicae Vaticanae*, vol. XI, Vatican City State, 2004, pp. 539-565
Pio II umanista europeo, ed. by L. Secchi Tarugi, Florence, Franco Cesati, 2007
Pirenne H., *Mohammed and Charlemagne*, London, Allen and Unwin, 1939
Piva E., *La guerra di Ferrara del 1482*, Padova, Draghi, 1894
Pop A.-M, Bărdașăn G., "Elemente moștenite sau împrumuturi italiene în lexicul istroromânei?", in *Per Teresa. Obiettivo Romania. Studi e ricerche in ricordo di Teresa Ferro*, ed. by G. Borghello, D. Lombardi and D. Pantaleoni, 2 vols., Udine, Forum, 2009, vol. II, pp. 265-276
Poumarède G., "Justifier l'injustifiable: l'alliance turque au miroir de la Chrétienté (XVIe-XVIIe siècle)", *Revue d'histoire diplomatique*, 110 (1997), pp. 217-246
Poumarède G., "Le patriciat vénitien et la guerre contre les Turcs: débat public, luttes politiques et rivalités institutionnelles à Venise au XVIe siècle", in *La politique par les armes. Conflits internationaux et politisation (XVe-XIXe siècle)*, ed. by L. Bourquin, Ph. Hamon, A. Hugon and Y. Lagadec, Rennes, Presses Universitaires de Rennes, 2013, pp. 25-43
Poumarède G., *Pour en finir avec la croisade. Mythe et réalités de la lutte contre les Turcs aux XVIe et XVIIe siècles*, Paris, Presses universitaires de France, 2004
La première histoire de France en turc ottoman. Chroniques des padichahs de France. 1572, ed. by J.L. Bacqué-Grammont, Paris-Montréal-İstanbul, L'Harmattan, 1997
Preto P., *I servizi segreti di Venezia*, Milan, Il Saggiatore, 1994
Preto P., *Venezia e i turchi*, Florence, Sansoni, 1975
Proceedings of the conference Os territórios de fronteira entre a Cristandade e o Islão. Novas abordagens (forthcoming)
Prodi P., *Il sacramento del potere. Il giuramento politico nella storia costituzionale dell'Occidente*, Bologna, Il Mulino, 1992
Prodi P., *Il sovrano pontefice. Un corpo e due anime: la monarchia papale nella prima età moderna*, Bologna, Il Mulino, 1982
La proposition faicte au pape de par le roy, s.l., s.d.. [1494?]
Prosperi A., *America e Apocalisse e altri saggi*, Pisa-Rome, Istituti editoriali e poligrafici internazionali, 1999

Prosperi A., "*Dominus beneficorum*: il conferimento dei benefici ecclesiastici tra prassi curiale e ragioni politiche negli Stati italiani tra '400 e '500", in *Strutture ecclesiastiche in Italia e in Germania prima della Riforma*, ed. by P. Prodi and P. Johanek, Bologna, Il Mulino, 1984, pp. 51-86

Prosperi A., "Il grano e la zizzania. L'eresia nella cittadella cristiana", in *L'intolleranza. Uguali e diversi nella storia*, ed. by P.C. Bori, Bologna, Il Mulino, 1986, pp. 51-86

Prosperi A., *Il seme dell'intolleranza. Ebrei, eretici, selvaggi. Granada 1492*, Rome-Bari, Laterza, 2011

Pujeau E., "Messer San Marco. Le gonfalonier de la croisade pour Paolo Giovio", *Studi veneziani*, n.s., 60 (2010), pp. 279-324

Pujeau E., *L'Europe et les Turcs. La croisade de l'humaniste Paolo Giovio*, Toulouse, Presses universitaires du Midi, 2015

Quondam A., *La conversazione. Un modello italiano*, Rome, Donzelli, 2007

Rabelais F., "Pantagruel", in F. Rabelais, *Œuvres complètes*, ed. by M. Huchon, Paris, Gallimard, 1994

Raby J., "La Sérénissime et la Sublime Porte: les arts dans l'art diplomatique. 1453-1600", in *Venise et l'Orient*, ed. by S. Carboni, Paris, Gallimard, 2006, pp. 90-119

Raniolo G., "L'eutopia e il fanatismo religioso", in *Il fanatismo. Dalle origini psichiche al sociale*, ed. by F. Spadaro and C. Tabbia, Rome, Armando, 2007, pp. 103-111

Raspadori R., "La Facoltà medica di Ferrara", in *La rinascita del sapere. Libri e maestri dello Studio ferrarese*, ed. by P. Castelli, Venice, Marsilio, 1991, pp. 264-273

Ravegnani R., *Bisanzio e le crociate*, Bologna, Il Mulino, 2011

Regine e sovrane. Il potere, la politica, la vita privata, ed. by G. Motta, Milan, FrancoAngeli, 2002

Reinhard W., "Disciplinamento sociale, confessionalizzazione, modernizzazione", in *Disciplina dell'anima, disciplina del corpo, disciplina della società fra Medioevo ed Età moderna*, ed. by P. Prodi, Bologna, Il Mulino, 1994, pp. 101-123

Reinsch D.R., "Lieber den Turban als was? Bemerkungen zum Diktum des Lukas Notaras", in *Philellen. Studies in honour of Robert Browning*, ed. by C.N. Constantinides, N.M. Panagiotakes, E. Jeffreys and A.D. Angelou, Venice, Istituto ellenico di studi bizantini e postbizantini di Venezia, 1996, pp. 377-389

Relazioni degli ambasciatori veneti al Senato, ed. by E. Alberi, 15 vols., Florence, Società editrice fiorentina, 1839-1863, I s., vol. I

Relazioni di ambasciatori veneti al Senato, ed. by L. Firpo, 13 vols., Turin, Bottega d'Erasmo, 1965-1984, vol. V

Réligions traversées. Lieux saints partagés entre chrétiens, musulmans et juifs en Méditerranée, ed. by D. Albera and M. Couroucli, Arles, Actes Sud, 2009

Renda G., "Les portraits des sultans ottomans et l'Europe de la Renaissance", in *L'empire du sultan: le monde ottoman dans l'art de la Renaissance*, ed. by R. Born, M. Dziewulski and G. Messling, Bruxelles, Bozar Books, 2015, pp. 40-50

Renzulli E., "Loreto, Leo X and the fortification on the Adriatic coast against the Infidel", in Ch. Shaw, *Italy and the European Powers. The Impact of Wars 1500-1530*, Leiden-Boston, Brill, 2006, pp. 57-73

Ricci C., *Il Tempio malatestiano in Rimini*, Milan-Rome, Bestetti and Tuminelli, 1925

Ricci G., "Bâtards princiers entre privilège et révolte. Le fils d'un duc et le fils d'un doge dans l'Italie de la Renaissance", in *Bâtards et bâtardises dans l'Europe médiévale et moderne*, ed. by C. Avignon, Rennes, Presses Universitaires de Rennes, 2016, pp. 289-295.

Ricci G., "Cardinaux de famille et État seigneurial en Italie entre XVe et XVIe siècle: Hippolyte Ier et Louis d'Este", in *Église et État. Évêques et cardinaux princiers et curiaux (XIVe-début XVIe siècle)*, ed. by A. Marchandisse, M. Maillard-Luypaert and B. Schnerb, Turnhout, Brepols, 2017, pp. 227-237.

Ricci G., "Estaba amancebada con el Turco. Venezia contro gli Aragonesi in Italia e in Andalusia", in *La guerra de Granada en su contexto internacional*, ed. by D. Baloup, R. González Arévalo, Toulouse, Meridiennes: presses universitaires du Midi, 2017, pp. 105-121

Ricci G., *I giovani, i morti. Sfide al Rinascimento*, Bologna, Il Mulino, 2007

Ricci G., *Ossessione turca. In una retrovia cristiana dell'Europa moderna*, Bologna, Il Mulino, 2002

Ricci G., "Papa Pio V fra spirito di crociata e politica internazionale", in *San Pio V nella storia*, ed. by C. Bernasconi, Pavia, Ibis, 2012, pp. 13-21

Ricci G., *Il principe e la morte. Corpo, cuore, effigie nel Rinascimento*, Bologna, Il Mulino, 1998

Ricci G., "Profezie e forchette per Mattia Corvino", *Schifanoia*, 24-25 (2003), pp. 179-183

Ricci G., "Ravenna spogliata fra tardo Medioevo e prima Età Moderna", *Quaderni storici*, 71 (1989), pp. 537-561

Ricci G., *I turchi alle porte*, Bologna, Il Mulino, 2008

Ricci G., *Türk Saplantisi. Yeniçağ Avrupa'sinda Korku, Nefret ve Sevgi*, İstanbul, Kitap Yayinevi, 2005

Ricci G., "'Verare la città' (La città e il suo doppio)", in *L'immagine delle città italiane dal XV al XIX secolo*, ed. by C. De Seta, Milan, De Luca, 1998, pp. 67-71

Richer-Rossi F., "Les Espagnols vus par les Vénitiens au milieu du XVIe siècle", in *L'image de l'autre européen*, ed. by J. Dufournet, A.C. Fiorato and A. Redondo, Paris, Presses de la Sorbonne Nouvelle, 1992, pp. 142-143

Ricoeur P., "L'écriture de l'histoire et la représentation du passé", *Annales. Histoires, Sciences Sociales*, 55 (2000), pp. 731-747

Ridolfi R.M., "Gonzaga, Lucrezia", in *Dizionario Biografico degli Italiani*, Rome, Istituto della Enciclopedia italiana, vol. LVII, 2001, pp. 796-797

Rizzi A., *I leoni di San Marco. Il simbolo della Repubblica Veneta nella scultura e nella pittura*, Venice, Arsenale, 2001

Roberts S., "The Lost Map of Matteo de' Pasti: Cartography, Diplomacy, and Espionage in the Renaissance Adriatic", *Journal of Early Modern History*, 20 (2016), pp. 19-38

Robinet A., *G.W. Leibniz. Le meilleur des mondes par la balance de l'Europe*, Paris, Presses Universitaires de France, 1994

Roche D., "Les pouvoirs à cheval (XVIe-XVIIIe siècles)", in *Alberto Tenenti. Scritti in memoria*, ed. by P. Scaramella, Naples, Bibliopolis, 2005, pp. 590-600

Rodríguez Salgado M.J., "¿Carolus Africanus?: el Emperador y el Turco", in *Carlos V*, pp. 487-531

Rodríguez Salgado M.J., *Felipe II, el 'Paladín de la Cristiandad' y la paz con el Turco*, Valladolid, Universidad de Valladolid, 2004

Rodríguez-Salgado M.J., "Terracotta and Iron: Mantuan Politics (ca 1450-ca 1550)", in *La corte di Mantova*, pp. 15-59

Rogers J.M., "Mehmed the Conqueror: Between East and West", in *Bellini and the East*, pp. 80-97

Römer C., "À propos d'une lettre de Soliman le Magnifique à Federico Gonzaga II (1526)", in *Soliman le Magnifique*, pp. 455-463

Ronchey S., *L'enigma di Piero. L'ultimo bizantino e la crociata fantasma nella rivelazione di un grande quadro*, Milan, Rizzoli, 2006
Rosenberg Ch., *The Este Monuments and Urban Development in Renaissance Ferrara*, Cambridge, Cambridge University Press, 1997
Rospocher M., *Il papa guerriero. Giulio II nello spazio pubblico europeo*, Bologna, Il Mulino, 2015
Rothman E.N., "Interpreting Dragomans: Boundaries and Crossing in the Early Modern Mediterranean", *Comparative Studies in Society and History*, 51 (2009), pp. 771-800
Rubello N., "*Una bella et caritativa cosa*. Épisodes de thaumaturgie royale pendant la période des Guerres d'Italie", *Le Moyen Âge*, 120 (2014), pp. 53-77
Ruggiero G., *Machiavelli in Love: Sex, Self, and Society in the Italian Renaissance*, Baltimore, The Johns Hopkins University Press, 2007
Runciman S., *Mistra. Byzantine Capital of the Peloponnese*, London, Thames and Hudson, 1980
Ruzafa García M., "Los mudéjares valencianos y la conquista de Málaga", in *Estudios sobre Málaga*, pp. 401-410
Ryder A., "Ferdinando I (Ferrante) d'Aragona" in *Dizionario Biografico degli Italiani*, Rome, Istituto della Enciclopedia italiana, vol. XLVI,1996, pp. 174-189

Sabatini Scalmati A., "Riflessioni psicoanalitiche sulla guerra e sulle violenze di guerra", *Psicoterapia psicoanalitica*, XIII (2006), 1, pp. 83-98
Sablier E., *Le prisonnier de Bourganeuf. Djem Sultan (1459-1495)*, Paris, Perrin, 2000
Sagundinus N., *Ad serenissimum principem et invictissimum regem Alphonsum [...] oratio*, ed. by C. Caselli, Rome, Istituto storico italiano per il Medio Evo, 2012
Sallmann J.-M., *Géopolitique du XVI*[e] *siècle. 1490-1618*, Paris, Seuil, 2003
Salvador Miguel N., *La conquista de Málaga (1487). Repercusione festivas y literarias en Roma*, Santa Barbara, University of California, 2014
Sanudo M., *I diarii*, ed. by F. Stefani, G. Berchet and N. Barozzi, 58 vols., Venice, Visentini, 1879-1902, vols XL and XLI
Sanudo M., *La spedizione di Carlo VIII in Italia*, ed. by R. Fulin, Venice, Visentini, 1873-1882
Sanudo M., *Le vite dei dogi. 1474-1494*, ed. by A. Caracciolo Aricò, 2 vols., Padova, Antenore, 2001
Il santo patrono e la città. San Benedetto il Moro: culti, devozioni, strategie di età moderna, ed. by G. Fiume, Venice, Marsilio, 2000
Scaraffia L., *Loreto*, Bologna, Il Mulino, 1999
Scaraffia L., *Rinnegati. Per una storia dell'identità occidentale*, Rome-Bari, Laterza, 1993
Schilling H., "The two Papal Souls and the Rise of an Early Modern State System", in *Papato e politica internazionale nella prima età moderna*, ed. by M.A. Visceglia, Rome, Viella, 2013, pp. 103-116
Schmidt H.-G., "Les Suisses en Milanais: coopération et concurrence avec Louis XII", in *Louis XII en Milanais*, pp. 189-225
Schnapp J.E., *Prophéties de fin du monde et peur des Turcs au XV*[e] *siècle*, Paris, Garnier, 2017
Scholem G., *Sabbatai Sevi: The Mystical Messiah*, Princeton, Princeton University Press, 1973
Schwoebel R., *The Shadow of the Crescent: The Renaissance Image of the Turk (1453-1517)*, Nieuwkoop, B. de Graaf, 1967

Secret F., *Les kabbalistes chrétiens de la Renaissance*, Milan, Archè, 2012

Segesvary V., *L'Islam et la Réforme. Étude sur l'attitude des réformateurs zurichois envers l'Islam 1510-1550*, San Francisco, International Scholars publications, 1998

Senatore F., "I diplomatici e gli ambasciatori", in *Viaggiare nel Medioevo*, ed. by S. Gensini, Pisa, Centro di Studi sulla Civiltà del tardo Medioevo, 2000, pp. 267-298

Senatore F., *"Uno mundo de carta". Forme e strutture della diplomazia sforzesca*, Naples, Liguori, 1998

Seneca F., *Venezia e papa Giulio II*, Padua, Liviana, 1962

Serrelli G., "Sardinya Kralliği'nin Savunma Sistemleri ve Terranova'nin Turgut Reis Tarafindan Yağmalanmasi [The systems of defence of the Kingdom of Sardinia and the sack of Terranova by Dragut]", in *Türkler ve Deniz*, pp. 175-185

Settia A.A., *De re militari. Pratica e teoria nella guerra medievale*, Rome, Viella, 2008

Setton K.M., *The Papacy and the Levant (1204-1571)*, 4 vols., Philadelphia, The American Philosophical Society, 1976-1984, vols II-III

Skilliter S.A., "The Hispano-Ottoman Armistice of 1581", in *Iran and Islam. In Memory of the Late Vladimir Minorski*, ed. by C.E. Bosworth, Edinburgh, Edinburgh University Press, 1971, pp. 491-515

Skoufari E., *Cipro veneziana (1473-1571). Istituzioni e culture nel regno della Serenissima*, Rome, Viella, 2011

Slot B.J., *Archipelagus turbatus. Les Cyclades entre colonisation latine et occupation ottomane: c. 1500-1718*, İstanbul, Nederlands historisch-archaeologisch instituut, 1982

Il sogno di Pio II e il viaggio da Roma a Mantova, ed. by A. Calzona, F.P. Fiore, A. Tenenti and C. Vasoli, Florence, Olschki, 2003

Smith L.B., *Treason in Tudor England: Politics and Paranoia*, London-Princeton (N.J.), Princeton University Press,1986

Smith M.H., "Émulation guerrière et stéréotypes nationaux dans les guerres d'Italie", in *Les guerres d'Italie. Histoire, pratiques, représentations*, ed. by D. Boillet and M.F. Pièjus, Paris, Université Paris 3 Sorbonne Nouvelle, 2002, pp. 154-176

Smith, P.J. "'The Captive's Tale': Race, Text, Gender", in *Quixotic Desire: Psychoanalytic Perspectives on Cervantes*, ed. by R.A. El Saffar and D. de Armas Wilson, Ithaca, Cornell UP, 1993, pp. 227-235

Soliman le Magnifique et son temps. Süleimân the Magnificent and his Time, ed. by G. Veinstein, Paris, La Documentation Française, 1992

Soranzo G., "L'arma della disperazione di Ludovico il Moro alla vigilia della sua caduta", *Istituto lombardo di scienze e lettere. Rendiconti. Classe di lettere e scienze morali e storiche*, III s., 88 (1954), pp. 243-260

Soranzo G., "Una missione di Sigismondo Pandolfo Malatesta a Maometto II nel 1461", *La Romagna*, 6 (1909), pp. 43-54

Soranzo G., *Pio II e la politica italiana nella lotta contro i Malatesta (1457-1463)*, Padova, F.lli Drucker, 1911

Sorce F., "Il drago come immagine del nemico turco nella rappresentazione di Età moderna", *Rivista dell'Istituto nazionale di archeologia e storia dell'arte*, 62-63 (2007-2008), pp. 173-198

Sorce F., "Metafore in bianco e nero. Propaganda antiturca nelle stampe di Nicolò Lelli", in *En blanc et noir. Studi in onore di Silvana Macchioni*, ed. by F. Sorce, Rome, Campisano, 2007, pp. 47-60

Spedicato M., "Il riscatto della cristianità offesa. Il culto dei martiri d'Otranto prima e dopo Lepanto", in *La conquista turca*, vol. II, pp. 115-140

Tallon A., "Conflits et médiations dans la politique internationale de la papauté", in *Papato e politica internazionale nella prima età moderna*, ed. by M.A. Visceglia, Rome, Viella, 2013, pp. 117-129

Tateo F., "Crociata e anticrociata nella letteratura umanistica e nella novellistica volgare tra XIII e XIV secolo", in *La conquista turca*, vol. I, pp. 309-317

Tedeschi J., *The Prosecution of Heresy: Collected Studies on the Inquisition in Early Modern Italy*, Binghamton-NewYork, Medieval and Renaissance Texts and Studies, 1991

Teijeiro Fuentes M.A., *Moros y turcos en la narrativa aurea: el tema del cautiverio*, Cáceres, Universidad de Extremadura, 1987

Telò M., *Relations internationales. Une perspective européenne*, Bruxelles, Éditions de l'Université de Bruxelles, 2010

Terzioğlu D., "The Imperial Circumcision Festival of 1582: An Interpretation", *Muqarnas. An Annual on Islamic Art and Architecture*, 12 (1995), pp. 84-100

Thuasne L., *Djem-Sultan, fils de Mohammed II, frère de Bayezid II*, Paris, E. Leroux, 1892

Timpanaro S., *Il lapsus freudiano. Psicanalisi e critica testuale*, Florence, La Nuova Italia, 1974

Tognetti G., "Amaseo, Girolamo", in *Dizionario Biografico degli Italiani*, Rome, Istituto della Enciclopedia italiana, vol. II, 1960, pp. 654-655

Tollet D., "Les Juifs furent-ils, dans la Confédération polono-lituanienne, les agents des Turcs?", in *I Turchi, il Mediterraneo e l'Europa*, ed. by G. Motta, Milan, FrancoAngeli, 1998, pp. 152-168

Tommasino P.M., *L'Alcorano di Macometto. Storia di un libro del Cinquecento europeo*, Bologna, Il Mulino, 2013

Trames de langues: usages et metissages linguistiques dans l'histoire du Maghreb, ed. by J. Dakhlia, Paris-Tunis, Maisonneuve et Larose-IRMC, 2004

Trivellato F., "Renaissance Italy and the Muslim Mediterranean in Recent Historical Work", *The Journal of Modern History*, 82 (2010), 1, pp. 127-155

Tschirgi D., "The Middle East and Religious Fondamentalism as a Source of Identity-Based Conflict", in *International Security Today: Understanding change and debating strategy*, ed. by M. Aydin and K. Ifantis, Ankara, Center for Strategic Research, 2006, pp. 89-115

Turchini A., *Il Tempio malatestiano, Sigismondo Pandolfo Malatesta e Leon Battista Alberti*, Cesena, Il ponte vecchio, 2000

Turkish Miniature Paintings and Manuscripts, ed. by E. Binney, New York, The Metropolitan Museum of Arts, 1973

Türkler ve Deniz [The Turks and the sea], ed. by Ö. Kumrular, İstanbul, Kitap Yayinevi, 2007

Tursun Bey, *La conquista di Costantinopoli*, ed. by J.-L. Bacqué-Grammont and M. Bernardini, Milan, Mondadori, 2007

Unali A., *Ceuta 1415. Alle origini dell'espansione europea in Africa*, Rome, Bulzoni, 2000

Vaglienti F.M., "Galeazzo Maria Sforza", in *Dizionario Biografico degli Italiani*, Rome, Istituto della Enciclopedia italiana, vol. LI, 1998, pp. 398-409

Valensi L., *Venise et la Sublime Porte. La naissance du despote*, Paris, Hachette, 1987

Valensi L., *Ces étrangers familiers: musulmans en Europe (XVIe-XVIIIe siècles)*, Paris, Payot & Rivages, 2012

Valérian D., "La Méditerranée. Rivalités nouvelles dans les marchés de l'Ancien Monde", in *Histoire du monde au XVe siècle*, ed. by P. Boucheron, Paris, Fayard, 2009, pp. 75-91

Varriale G., *Arrivano li Turchi. Guerra navale e spionaggio nel Mediterraneo (1532-1582)*, Novi Ligure, Città del silenzio, 2014
Vatin N., "La conquête de Rhodes", in *Soliman le Magnifique*, pp. 435-454
Vatin N., "Macabre trafic: la destinée post-mortem du prince Djem", in *Mélanges offerts à Louis Bazin*, ed. by J.L. Bacqué-Grammont and R. Dor, Paris, L'Harmattan, 1992, pp. 231-239
Vatin N., "Le siège de Mytilène (1501)", *Turcica*, 21-23 (1991), pp. 437-459
Vatin N., Veinstein G., *Le Sérail ébranlé. Essai sur les morts, dépositions et avènements des sultans ottomans (XIVe-XIXe siècle)*, Paris, Fayard, 2003
Veinstein G., "L'administration ottomane et le problème des interprètes", in *Étude sur les villes du proche Orient (XVIe-XIXe siècle)*, ed. by B. Marino, Damas, Institut français d'Études Arabes de Damas, 2001, pp. 65-79
Veinstein G., "Les capitulations franco-ottomanes de 1536 sont-elles encore controversables?", in *Living in the Ottoman Ecumenical Community. Essays in honour of Suraiya Faroqhi*, ed. by V. Costantini and M. Koller, Leiden-Boston, Brill, 2008, pp. 71-88
Veinstein G., "Retour sur la question de la tolérance ottomane au XVIe siècle", in *Chrétiens et musulmans*, pp. 415-426
Venezia da Stato a Mito, ed. by A. Bettagno, Venice, Marsilio, 1997
Venezia e Istanbul. Incontri, confronti e scambi, ed. by E. Concina, Udine, Forum, 2006
Vergé-Franceschi M., *Toulon. Port-Royal (1481-1789)*, Paris, Tallandier, 2002
Vergé-Franceschi M., Graziani A-M., *La guerre de course en Méditerranée (1515-1830)*, Paris, Presses de l'Universite Paris-Sorbonne, 2000
Vernelli C., "La paura degli 'infedeli'", *Proposte e ricerche*, 22 (1999), n. 43, pp. 171-184
Verrier F., *Les armes de Minerve. L'Humanisme militaire dans l'Italie du XVIe siècle*, Paris, Presses de l'Université de Paris-Sorbonne, 1997
I viaggi in Persia degli ambasciatori veneti Barbaro e Contarini, ed. by L. Lockhart, R. Morozzo della Rocca and M.F. Tiepolo, Rome, Istituto poligrafico dello Stato, 1983
Viallon M.F., *Venise et la Porte ottomane (1453-1566). Un siècle de relations vénéto-ottomanes de la prise de Constantinople à la mort de Soliman*, Paris, Economica, 1995
Viallon-Schoneveld M., "L'epistola latina a Maometto II", in *Pio II umanista*, pp. 165-177
Vianello C.A., "Testimonianze venete su Milano e la Lombardia degli anni 1492-1495", *Archivio storico lombardo*, 4 (1939), pp. 408-423
Viglione M., "La politica antiottomana dei Gonzaga tra spirito di crociata e interessi dinastici: XVI-XVII secolo", *Nuova Rivista Storica*, 100 (2016), pp. 977-998
Virgil, *Aeneid* 2, ed. by N. Horsfall, Leiden-Boston, Brill, 2008
Visceglia M. A., "Napoli e la politica internazionale del papato tra la congiura dei baroni e il regno di Ferdinando il Cattolico", in *El reino de Nápoles y la monarquía de España entre agregación y conquista (1485-1535)*, ed. by G. Galasso and C. Hernando-Sánchez, Madrid, Real Academia de España en Roma, 2004, pp. 453-483
Visceglia M.A., *Riti di corte e simboli della regalità. I regni d'Europa e del Mediterraneo dal Medioevo all'Età moderna*, Rome, Salerno, 2009
Visceglia M.A., "Il viaggio cerimoniale di Carlo V dopo Tunisi", *Dimensioni e problemi della ricerca storica*, 2 (2001), pp. 5-50
Vismara G., *Impium foedus. Le origini della 'Respublica Christiana'*, Milan, Giuffré, 1974
Vocabolario degli Accademici della Crusca, Florence, Nella stamperia dell'Accademia della Crusca, 16913

Ward-Jackson P., *Italian Drawings*, 2 vols., London, Her Majesty's Stationery Office, 1979-1980, vol. I

Weiss R., "The Adventures of a First Edition of Valturio's *De re militari*", in *Studi di bibliografia e di storia in onore di Tammaro de Marinis*, 4 vols., Verona, Stamperia Valdonega, 1964, vol. IV, pp. 297-304

What if? Military Historians Imagine What Might Have Been, ed. by R. Cowley, London, Macmillan, 2001

Wheatcroft A., *The Enemy at the Gate. Habsburgs, Ottomans and the Battle for Europe*, London, Bodley Head, 2008

Yerasimos S., "Les relations franco-ottomanes et la prise de Tripoli en 1551", in *Soliman le Magnifique*, pp. 529-547

Yildirim O., "The Battle of Lepanto and its Impact on Ottoman History and Historiography", in *Mediterraneo in armi (secc. XV-XVIII)*, ed. by R. Cancila, 2 vols., Palermo, Associazione Mediterranea, 2007, vol. II, pp. 533-556

Zachariadou E.A., "Changing Masters in the Aegean", in *The Greek Islands and the Sea*, ed. by J. Chrysostomides, Ch. Dendrinos and J. Harris, Camberley, Porphyrogenitus, 2004, pp. 199-212

Zachariadou E.A., "Τα λόγια κι ο θάνατος του Λουκά Νοταρά", in *Ροδώνια. Τιμή στον Μ.Ι. Μανουσάκα* ['Roseto. In honour of M.I. Manoussakas], Rethimno, University of Crete, 1994, pp. 135-146

Zambotti B., *Diario ferrarese dall'anno 1476 sino al 1504*, ed. by G. Pardi, Bologna, Zanichelli, 1934-1937

Zancarini J.-Cl., "Machiavelli e Guicciardini. Guerra e politica al prisma delle guerre d'Italia", in *Teatri di guerra: rappresentazioni e discorsi tra età moderna ed età contemporanea*, ed. by A. De Benedictis and C. Magoni, Bologna, Bononia University Press, 2010, pp. 61-75

Zapperi R., "Bucciardo, Ambrogio", in *Dizionario Biografico degli Italiani*, Rome, Istituto della Enciclopedia italiana, vol. XIV, 1992, pp. 768-769

Zapperi R., "Bucciardo, Giorgio", in *Dizionario Biografico degli Italiani*, Rome, Istituto della Enciclopedia italiana, vol. XIV, 1972, pp. 769-771

Zapperi R., "Bucciardo, Nicola", in *Dizionario Biografico degli Italiani*, Rome, Istituto della Enciclopedia italiana, vol. XIV, 1972, pp. 771-773

Zemon Davis N., "Cannibalism and Knowledge", *Historein. A Review of the Past and Other Stories*, 2 (2000), pp. 13-30

Zemon Davis N., *The Gift in Sixteenth-Century France*, Oxford, Oxford University Press, 2000

Zolo D., "La questione mediterranea", in *L'alternativa mediterranea*, pp. 13-77

List of illustrations

Index

Printed in Szczecin, Poland
by Booksfactory
May 2018